CW01626486

THE WALNUT TREE

THE WALNUT TREE

WOMEN, VIOLENCE AND THE LAW: A HIDDEN HISTORY

KATE MORGAN

MUDLARK

Mudlark
An imprint of HarperCollins*Publishers*
1 London Bridge Street
London SE1 9GF

www.harpercollins.co.uk

HarperCollins*Publishers*
Macken House, 39/40 Mayor Street Upper
Dublin 1, D01 C9W8, Ireland

First published by Mudlark 2024
This edition published 2025

1 3 5 7 9 10 8 6 4 2

A catalogue record of this book is available from the British Library

ISBN 978-0-00-855961-8

Printed and bound in the UK using 100%
renewable electricity at CPI Group (UK) Ltd

CONTENTS

PART III: IN SICKNESS AND IN HEALTH

PART IV: FOR RICHER, FOR POORER

PART V: 'TIL DEATH US DO PART

AUTHOR'S NOTE

The illustration on the cover of the book is taken from Henry Mayhew's *London Labour and the London Poor*, published in 1851. This was a study of the lives of the working classes of London in the mid-nineteenth century, based on extensive interviews conducted by Mayhew. One of the groups he spoke with were the 'patterers', who scraped a living by selling cheap newssheets and pamphlets on the streets, usually featuring notorious crimes – particularly murders.

In Mayhew's book, one of the graphic illustrations from a patterer's pamphlet was reproduced. It depicted the murder of a young woman named Jael Denny in Essex in 1850. Jael was heavily pregnant when her lover murdered her; she had gone to meet him believing that he wanted to discuss marriage. The illustration appears to be the only image of Jael ever made.

In an interview with Mayhew, the patterer explained that he had nicknamed his new waistcoat 'Jael Denny' as sales of the sheet about her murder had paid for it and, after all, 'a man must show a sense of gratitude in the best way he can'. However, he bemoaned the fact that he had not sold as many as he had expected due to inclement weather impacting on his sales. Nevertheless, the patterer told Mayhew that he generally expected brisk business from grisly reports of the murders of young women; in response, Mayhew observed that 'until the "respectable" press becomes a more healthful public instructor, we have no right to blame the death-hunter who is but an imitator – a follower'.

And indeed what follows here contains some discussion of violence and sexual assault in historical cases. The re-telling of these incidents is based on extensive research into contemporary accounts and sources, but do bear in mind the nature of this content while reading.

PROLOGUE

'A CONSIDERABLY LESS HEINOUS OFFENCE'

At the Manchester Assizes, on Monday, a man named Matthews was brought up for trial on a charge of wife-murder at Bacup. On the night of January 1, when the world was ushering in a 'happy new year' … there were sounds of 'screaming and shrieking' and in the morning it was found that [Ruth Matthews] had bled to death from the kicks which her husband – the brute Matthews – had inflicted upon her. The jury found the prisoner guilty of manslaughter, whereupon [the judge] Mr Commissioner Williams sentenced him to two months' imprisonment!!

Is there no means by which the force of public opinion can be brought to bear upon the conduct of Mr Commissioner Williams, who esteems the crime of wife-murder as being on a level with that of stealing a purse and a considerably less heinous offence than that of 'shop-lifting'?

Women's Gazette and Weekly News,
9 March 1889

On Monday, Mr Bradlaugh [MP for Northampton] called attention in the House of Commons to the sentence passed upon John Matthews of Bacup, who kicked his wife with the result that she bled to death. To Bacup people, and others acquainted with this man's history, two months for such a crime certainly looks, on the face of it, a serious miscarriage of justice and it can hardly be said that the answer given by the Home Secretary to Mr Bradlaugh materially alters the complexity of the matter.

Bacup Times and Rossendale Advertiser,
16 March 1889

* * *

'We are very concerned that some sentences received by men who kill their female partners or ex-partners do not reflect the seriousness of domestic abuse, nor do they reflect the fact that these homicides often follow a period of prolonged abuse ... There is abundant research to demonstrate that many apparently sudden femicides are, in fact the culmination of a hidden history of control and abuse ... The sentence handed down to Anthony Williams was a clear example of this; he was sentenced to just 5 years for manslaughter [of his wife] on the grounds of diminished responsibility, the judge finding, for no apparent reason except that his behaviour was unexpected, that his responsibility was very low.'

Joint letter on domestic homicide from Victims' Commissioner and Domestic Abuse Commissioner to Home Secretary, Lord Chancellor and Attorney General, 5 March 2021

INTRODUCTION

FROM THIS DAY FORWARD

When the Palace of Westminster was rebuilt following a devastating fire in 1834, a series of six large frescos was commissioned to decorate the new chamber of the House of Lords. The paintings comprised three allegorical portraits of the functions of the Lords, namely Justice, Chivalry and Religion. Each allegory in turn was illustrated by a painting of a relevant historical scene. The historical paintings all featured a man as the subject, while each of the allegories was represented by a woman.

In Daniel Maclise's fresco *The Spirit of Justice* a woman stands in the centre of the picture, at the top of a flight of marble stairs. She wears white robes and a navy cape trimmed in gold. Her hair is dark and pulled away from her face. Either side of her stands a winged figure; one a woman with her eyes cast downwards demurely, the other male, holding the hilt of a huge sword and gazing sternly at the figures huddled on the steps below. In front of the angels sit judges, in robes of red and black. Most of the figures sitting on the steps – a knight errant, a mother clutching her small child – look beseechingly at the woman in the robes. But the woman does not meet their gaze and her eyes are drawn upwards towards the heavens. In her hand, she holds a small set of scales.

By the time that the aristocratic Caroline Norton modelled for Maclise's figure of Justice in 1847, she had already endured plenty of her own ordeals at the hands of the law. But in the years that followed, she would become an icon for justice in ways that were more than merely allegorical. Her campaigns for reforms to the laws of England which disadvantaged women at all levels of society contributed to some of the most important legal developments of the Victorian era. She had survived an abusive and unhappy marriage, lost a child and had suffered the public ignominy of an adultery trial, all of which she channelled into her lobbying and writing on the injustices for women arising from the shortcomings of the law as it stood in the middle of the nineteenth century. She made the most of her contacts in government to press her causes and even wrote to Queen Victoria as part of her efforts.

Less than a decade after *The Spirit of Justice* was painted, Caroline published her most influential work. The rather bland title of *English Laws for Women in the Nineteenth Century* belied the fury within. Drawing on her own experiences of marriage, Caroline railed against the lack of financial protection afforded to married women by the law, the inequalities of both gender and class posed by the law of divorce, and the reluctance of the courts to protect women from domestic abuse. All of this she illustrated with accounts of her own experience of violence and financial abuse at the hands of her husband, and the failure of the law to provide relief or protection to her. Her writing in the book covered many of the major legal reforms that would eventually transpire over the rest of the century. But on one point, Caroline was clear: she did not advocate for equality between men and women. Men were, according to her, superior to women by virtue of God's law which no earthly statute could override. What she was arguing for was an acknowledgement that this gave men inherent power over women and that this power came with responsibility to offer protection.

Two decades on from the turn of the twenty-first century we face questions about the status of women under the law, questions that were thought to have been answered a century before. The gender pay gap, no-fault divorce, domestic abuse, policing and fatal violence against women are constants in the headlines. The roots of these contemporary issues – and the law's treatment of them – can be traced back to the time that Caroline Norton was writing, when a succession of campaigns, test cases and individual injustices began to fundamentally re-shape women's status under the law. It is from this point that old certainties began to shift. To understand the law as it is requires an appreciation of what is was – and why.

When Parliament debated the issue of violence against women back in 1853, one MP quoted a popular proverb, as a possible explanation for the public's apparent ambivalence towards stories of domestic abuse and violent assaults against women on the streets:

A woman, a dog and a walnut tree,
The more they are beaten, the better they'll be

The couplet was derived from one of Aesop's fables, concerning a walnut tree which bemoaned the fact that people would beat it to dislodge its fruits. This translated into a folk belief that hitting the tree encouraged it to produce more nuts; the extension of this logic to women and dogs was first recorded proverbially around the seventeenth century in England. So pernicious was the belief that it reflected, it could still be prayed in aid in a parliamentary debate around violence against women two hundred years later. The casual acceptance of this status quo in the adage of the walnut tree was reflected in contemporary laws which most impacted on women; in what a wife was expected to tolerate at the hands of her husband and in the tightly constrained circumstances in which she was permitted to leave a marriage.

Nevertheless, the mid-nineteenth century saw the first significant attempts to redress the balance in favour of women, particularly in cases of domestic abuse and violent crime, through changes to the law and social policy. These changes ran alongside wider debates on women's rights and suffrage, as well as fundamental shifts in the law surrounding marriage and divorce. But Victorian society was stubborn.

Even when legal reform came, the misogynistic attitudes that infected wider society found their way into the courtrooms to influence those tasked with upholding the law, speaking to how the law viewed women both within and without of marriage. This in turn led on to serious consequences in how female victims of violent crime fared from the justice system. As suffrage and women's rights campaigner Matilda Blake wrote in 1892, 'male judges appointed by an exclusively male electorate punish

[male] offenders in a most inadequate way, holding a woman's life at less value than a purse containing a few shillings'.

The Walnut Tree examines the trials, cases and statutes of the latter half of the nineteenth century and the early years of the twentieth, which reveal a hidden history of women, violence and the law. While the suffragists' campaign for equality is the defining story of this era, gathering pace from the 1850s up to its partial success at the end of the First World War, at the same time women were facing other battles in courtrooms up and down the country. Some of these made headlines at the time, but most are now consigned to obscurity. This book explores some of these lesser-known legal milestones and the women behind them, exploring how these compelling stories impacted the law, society and history.

A rise in violent attacks on women, both by partners within the home and by strangers on the streets, had prompted a groundswell of concern for women's safety among the Victorians. At the same time, reforms to the law of marriage opened up the possibility of divorce to more than the privileged few. In theory at least, women were no longer tied to husbands who 'ill-used' them or worse; but the reality was often terrifyingly different.

The period covered by this book was one of great changes in the lives and legal status of women in England. These changes affected women of all classes and backgrounds. When Queen Victoria came to the throne, marriage was still governed by its religious roots and divorce was impossible for all but a tiny elite. In turn, this coloured views of women, sexuality and morality which fed into other areas of the law as well.

This book places the law firmly in the context of its time and wider society, revealing the personal stories of those involved, as well as investigating the broader influences of these stories in culture and the media. How these cases and the women involved were portrayed both in court and in the press helped to shape public perceptions. Some of these women found their way into art and poetry, their grisly fates being memorialised – and monetised – even when their names were forgotten. It is a selection of stories which shine a light on the law's attitudes towards women, intimate relationships and personal violence in a period where these were undergoing fundamental changes that still reverberate today.

The Walnut Tree explores the historical challenges women have faced in securing justice under English law. These have taken place against a backdrop of media and public interest that was as fevered, salacious but sometimes necessary as it is today. From broadsides and penny dreadfuls to tabloid headlines and TV news, the press and media have long had a fascination with violence against women, but more often than not focussing on the perpetrators rather than the victim. As the enduring fascination with Jack the Ripper and others like him shows, we have long been more invested in the killer than those killed.

The following pages explore the law's response to issues including harassment, divorce, domestic violence and women's safety, each explored through the stories of the women whose lives (and sometimes deaths) shine a light on an aspect of the chequered history of the law's attempts to protect them; women whose names are all but forgotten but whose stories, fears and fates still resonate today.

* * *

In her letter to Queen Victoria, Caroline Norton wrote 'from time immemorial, changes in the laws of nations have been brought about by individual examples of oppression. Such examples cannot be unimportant, for they are, and ever will be, the little hinges on which the great doors of justice are made to turn.' The law itself, in black letter statutes or ponderous judgments, only ever tells half of the tale. As Norton recognised, behind these causes and changes sit the real stories of women wronged by the law. It is through their personal histories and experiences that the operation of the law is best understood.

For so long, a woman's legal rights were derived from or denied by the presence of a man, and so the terrifying story of the Clitheroe wife abduction is the starting point to explore the history of the relative positions of husbands and wives within the institution of marriage. From its ancient religious roots, by the nineteenth century the legal concepts that underpinned marriage were beginning to shift. As women asserted financial and physical independence from their spouses, the law had to race to catch up. Yet as late as the last decade of the nineteenth century, a Lancashire husband still considered himself entitled to abduct his wife by force when she tried to get away from him. Most worryingly of all, plenty of people agreed with him. The story of how Emily Jackson's battle to secure her freedom ended up revolutionising the law's treatment of married women is told here alongside those of the other women involved in the other early legal developments in this area. Beginning with the women whose campaigns changed the law on women's rights to own property after marriage, in Part One we will see how these unromantic-sounding issues paved the way to rectifying the power imbalance that was inherent in the law of marriage at this time, with consequences for women up and down the country.

What of the options for wives – or husbands – who wanted to leave a marriage? The law of divorce underwent a radical redrawing over the course of the Georgian and Victorian eras. Like so much of the discourse around marriage explored in Part One, the historical development of divorce was closely tied to the influence of religion on the law and the comparatively recent divergence of the two. While English law had, after a fashion, recognised a concept of divorce since the Reformation, it was only available to a tiny elite. For the vast majority of married couples, there was no escape from an unhappy marriage for much of modern history. Lore stepped in to fill in the gaps in the law, resulting in the popular belief in customs like wife-selling to bring a union to an end – and more disturbing ways of exercising community justice against those who did not cleave to their wedding vows. As the Georgians made way for the Victorians, the scandalous royal divorce trial that had shocked the nation was replaced by proper legal reform. But the double standard inherent in the new law favoured husbands over wives and in part incentivised ill-treatment of women by their spouses. From the trial of the Queen of England to the disturbing cases that determined the level of cruelty that would permit a wife to end a marriage, Part Two looks at the bravery of the women involved in pushing the boundaries of the democratisation of divorce.

When suburban housewife Selina Clarence became ill with gonorrhoea in December 1887, she knew that the only possible source of the infection was her husband Charles. At Selina's insistence, Charles was prosecuted for inflicting grievous bodily harm on her by transmitting the disease. The year before Selina became ill, Parliament had finally repealed the Contagious Diseases Act, which had been on the statute books for over twenty years. Under the act, the Metropolitan Police working in military and naval towns could apprehend any woman suspected of being a prostitute, subject them to a forced medical examination and, if they were found to be infected with venereal disease, incarcerate them in the so-called 'lock wards' of hospitals. Part Three explores the contradictions in the law's treatment of sex and its less savoury consequences, looking at why women could be incarcerated to prevent the spread of disease, but men who knowingly transmitted it to their partners faced no sanction. It examines the dark and compelling stories of the women kept in the lock hospitals, their mistreatment at the hands of the Met and the campaign to abolish the law that kept them there. Almost by accident, Charles Clarence's acquittal created one of the most dangerous and destructive legal myth of modern times – that it was impossible for a husband to rape his wife. This damaging precedent was applied by the English courts repeatedly for a century after the case and was only formally overturned at the end of the twentieth century.

Part Four investigates two shocking murder cases from the first decade of the twentieth century which hold a mirror up to contemporary attitudes to violent crime, class and women.

While we try to reassure ourselves that our attitudes have matured, there are uncanny echoes of the coverage of these cases in contemporary accounts of violent crime and homicide involving female victims. The fevered fascination with grisly murders of women ran in parallel to the quieter campaign to get women into the courtroom as lawyers and jurors, not simply victims or witnesses. The lives of Phyllis Dimmock and Ruth Hadley were eclipsed by their deaths, until it became expedient to employ the narrative of their lives to absolve their murderers. This called into question who was really on trial in these cases – the women who died or the men who killed them? And how does the cultural capital ascribed to the glamorisation of the murder of women obscure the failings in the justice system? How far did the presentation of victims in court influence the outcome of the trials of their killers? Most importantly, did the exclusion of women from the lawyers' benches and the jury box of a courtroom mean that female victims of crime faced injustice?

On a March morning in 1896, Laura Glendell sat down in the front parlour of her terraced home in Windsor and composed a letter. Her neat, slanting handwriting belied the desperation of her missive. Her soldier husband from whom she was estranged had come to the house the day before and assaulted her. She was writing to his commanding officer to implore him to keep him in the barracks and away from her. Laura's plight typified that of many women in the second half of the nineteenth century. While changes in the law had made divorce more accessible, and offered some means of escape from domestic violence – at least in theory – the reality was very different. New laws meant that women suffering violence at the hands of their husbands could obtain protection from the courts. But as the contemporary publication *The Women's Suffrage Journal* documented, it remained the case that 'wives under bodily fear suffer not merely through the inadequacy of the existing law for their protection but from the apparent unwillingness of magistrates to extend to them such protection as it allows'. As far back as the 1850s, Parliament had brought in the Aggravated Assaults Act. This landmark legislation was the first time that English law had recognised a specific offence of assaults on women and the law was strengthened throughout the latter half of the nineteenth century. The stories of some of the women who inspired the lawmakers to act and bring in the Aggravated Assaults legislation in the 1850s are explored in Part Five, which looks at the law's often muted response (or tacit acceptance) of domestic violence in the recent past. And when such violence reaches its inevitable conclusion and a woman is killed, how does the law treat this crime?

At first glance, Emily Jackson did not appear to be a typical icon of women's rights. Neither did Selina Clarence nor Laura Glendell. Weaved into their stories are those of the women at the forefront of the organised campaigns, of which these legal cases represented the sharp end. Josephine Butler spearheaded the push to repeal the Contagious Diseases Acts, which in turn helped to set up some of the machinery for the suffrage campaigns that blossomed a generation later. Female writers like Florence Fenwick Miller and Matilda Blake used their platforms to raise the issue of violence against women in the press, which the ordinary women who were most often affected lacked. And Caroline Norton's own experience of divorce and exploitation by her husband led her to champion the cause of married women and the inequalities meted out to them by the English legal system of her time.

These famous campaigns – and campaigners – form a backdrop to the narrative that unfolds. But it is the stories of ordinary women that most exemplify and best illustrate the prejudices and failings of the law, as well as the impact of the remarkable campaigns for its reform and improvement. Wherever possible, I have told the stories of these 'little hinges' through the voices of the women themselves. Some, like Emily Jackson, published detailed accounts of their experiences for all to read; but this is not the case for many of the women who feature in the following pages. Some are conspicuous by their absence during the trials of their murderers, where they are seen only through the eyes of others, notably those who are trying to excuse their own conduct towards them. Others leave even fewer traces, appearing only on records 'which are heavily mediated by the authorities that produced them. Most of all, these women only appear to us in times of duress: after an arrest, within a prison, as a victim of an attack.' Accounts of incidents and crimes are based on written records and direct speech is taken from witness statements, quotations or transcripts of testimony, with just the barest touch of imagination to fill in any blanks.

The context of these stories is a conception of relationships and gender that we struggle to recognise today. Until recently, the law countenanced no other tie than marriage between a man and a woman. While clearly of its time, it is worth remembering how far this one principle shaped so much of the law and social policy in this era, with consequences for everyone, regardless of marital or social status. The myth of a wife as a husband's chattel translated into legal reality in the laws around property ownership which restricted a woman's independence after her marriage. Once the law on married women's property ownership had been reformed, the whole legal basis of marriage underwent review and reform, finally leading to the liberalisation of divorce.

The threshold for cruelty suffered by wives set by the divorce court spoke to society's tolerance of violence against women both in the domestic and public spheres. But contemporary attitudes to female sexuality meant that the dice were heavily loaded against wives in the new divorce court of the latter half of the nineteenth century. These double standards, particularly around sexual behaviour and perceived morality, created other legal dangers for women. The atmosphere of official and public condemnation of sex work was translated into the laws surrounding it, which were targeted at those who sold, rather than bought, sex. It was only in this climate that the contagious diseases legislation could have come about, where the divergence was writ even larger. All of this contributes to a public atmosphere in which violence against women, committed by partners in the home or strangers in the street, was at best tolerated and at worst tacitly encouraged by the law itself.

In the end, the most dangerous legal fiction is the idea that the law applies equally to all. From time immemorial sufficient wealth, power or connections have allowed people to exploit the vagaries in the enforcement or the application of the law, or eased the bending of the rules in their favour. But what of the times when inequality is written into the black letter of the law itself? The stories in this book are all tied by this theme, of laws which expressly allow for people to be treated differently on account of who they are. Discrimination by the law itself, simply on account of some inalienable fact of someone's identity, is something that we would hope we are now more alive to than at any other point in our history. But as we will see, some of these historical issues created damaging legal precedents that persisted well into living memory.

The thread that runs through this book is the law itself. There are countless lenses through which the stories and issues covered within could be viewed: criminological, political, sociological, psychological, to name a few. But it is the law that fascinates and is often overlooked in other analyses. It is the law that proscribes and prescribes our behaviours. It is the law that both reflects and directs public opinion and attitudes. As a tool of historical study, it tells us most about what – and who – we have collectively believed to be wrong and worthy of punishment at any given moment. Conversely, it tells of society's power structures through those who seek – and perhaps fail to find – its protection. All of this is best explained, and understood, through the microcosms of the 'little hinges', the women on whom so much turned during the second half of the nineteenth century. This builds into a picture of the legal history behind some of the most important laws and protections that we take for granted today.

PART I

TO HAVE AND TO HOLD

CHAPTER ONE

'YOU SHALL HAVE THE BODY'

The small carriage clattered around the corner into Blackburn's Rover Street at quite a lick. The horses, dripping with sweat and mud, were pulled up to an abrupt halt outside one of the redbrick villas, as the residents of the street peeped out from behind their drapes. As the horses steamed and pawed, three men jumped down from the carriage. They were smartly dressed in the suits of gentlemen, but the face of one was streaked with blood dripping from a cut above his eye. The neighbours watched on as a lady was pulled down the steps of the carriage and was ushered, almost dragged, down the garden path to the house. The door closed firmly behind the odd party and almost simultaneously the window blinds were drawn down. There was a thudding from behind the front door, as if it was being barricaded shut from within.

The residents of Rover Street had barely had time to digest this interruption into the usual calm of their Sunday afternoon when an even more startling arrival burst into the street. Another small carriage, this time accompanied by a gang of curious onlookers running alongside it, turned into the street and raced up to the house in question. Its occupants, an elderly man and a younger one, both of staid and sedate appearance, clambered out of the carriage and marched up to the door of the house, as the neighbours once again watched on with interest. They banged on the front door and loudly demanded entry. Suddenly a first-floor window was thrown open and the bloodied man stuck his head out and began to remonstrate with the visitors. The gentlemen at the door threatened to break it down if he did not open up; he shouted down that he would resist them with all force necessary and pulled down the sash window with a bang. More people began to gather in the narrow street, drawn by the noise. At first it was just near neighbours, unable to contain their curiosity at the spectacle and wanting to get a better look. But, as whispers began to spread around the area of the strange siege of the house, their numbers were swelled by those looking for some entertainment on a Sunday afternoon. Occasionally, the spectators glimpsed the figure of a woman at the upstairs window, whistling and murmuring when they did so. The two men paced in the street outside the house, looking up at the window and staring hard at the front door. They were joined by a couple of friends, and periodically retreated to their carriage to talk away from the ears of the now fairly boisterous crowd. After an hour or so, they left.

By late afternoon, news of the goings-on in Rover Street had reached the ears of the local press, and a couple of reporters had arrived on the scene. As they mingled with the crowd and asked their questions, a picture began to emerge. The house, called West View, belonged to the man with blood on his face;

his name was Edmund Jackson, a middle-aged gentleman of independent means and no apparent occupation. The woman whose fleeting appearances at the window so excited the crowd was his wife, Emily. The couple were estranged and Emily had refused to leave her home in Clitheroe to live with Edmund. Earlier that day, he had taken matters into his own hands and abducted her as she left the morning service at St Mary's Church in Clitheroe. Emily had not gone without a fight, as evidenced by the cut on Edmund's face. The two men who had followed Jackson to the house were Emily's brother-in-law and nephew, who had been in hot pursuit of the carriage all the way from Clitheroe. They had now gone to implore the Blackburn police to take action to secure her release.

Armed with these bare facts, one enterprising reporter prevailed upon a neighbour to let him use their telephone to speak to Edmund and get his side of the story. The conversation was brief but unambiguous: 'Mr Jackson asserted that, having both right and law on his side, he should continue in the course he had decided to follow. If necessary, he could hold out against his enemies for a month, for he had ample means to provision the "citadel" ... No opportunity was afforded of learning the view of the imprisoned lady.'

As the night drew in, the crowd assumed something of a carnival atmosphere, heckling and jeering at each twitch of the curtains inside West View. Fearing that the throng could turn ugly, the police despatched constables to the scene to keep order. But that was as far as they would go as the chief constable was unconvinced that anything illegal had taken place outside the church that morning. He did, however, agree to issue a warrant for the arrest of Jackson and his friends, for assaulting Emily's sister Mrs Baldwin during the struggle outside the church.

The siege of Rover Street continued for another two days, 'the gallant trio within the fortress keeping a constant watch upon their foes in the street'. The provisions that Edmund had spoken of to the reporter were delivered by a parade of tradesmen, whose goods were winched up to a first-floor window in a basket, much to the amusement of the onlookers. One shop delivered a large box of cigars, another groceries and wine. The afternoon of the second day was briefly enlivened by the appearance of a friend of Jackson's, who had managed to sneak into the house during a lull in the crowd. When he came to leave and found the house once again surrounded, he took inspiration from the deliverymen, and was lowered down to the garden on a rope from a bedroom window 'heartily cheered by the spectators who, almost without exception, favour Mr Jackson'.

The next day, the chief constable received a surprising telegram. Signed by Emily Jackson, it stated that she was content to remain at West View with her husband and did not wish any charges to be brought against him for her abduction. At the same time, Edmund's friends advised the police that he would surrender himself the following day, to answer the charge of assaulting Mrs Baldwin at the church. Deprived of their entertainment, the remaining spectators drifted away. The siege of Rover Street had ended; but the drama of the Clitheroe Wife-Abduction was not over yet.

* * *

The abduction of Emily Jackson would be as shocking if it took place today as it was when it occurred in 1891. The events outside the church on that Sunday morning made it a cause célèbre at the time, but it is the legal battle that ensued, with its disturbing commentary on the rights of one person over the freedom, body and life of another – on account only of the fact that he was married to her – that has secured its immortality. The story of the Jacksons might have remained a local scandal, of interest only in the drawing rooms of Clitheroe and the saloon bars of Blackburn. But Emily Jackson was about to become an unlikely pioneer for women's rights in a case that would redefine the concept of marriage and a woman's place within it, for a generation. Her ordeal at the hands of her husband, and the seeming unwillingness of the law to free her from it, would become one of the most important legal milestones for married women in the modern era.

Behind the melodramatic gloss of the reports of her abduction lies a disturbing case study of the inequalities that lay at the heart of the law's conception of marriage in the late nineteenth century. Her ordeal came at the end of fifty years of apparent progress in the legal position of married women. Reforms had finally allowed wives to own property after marriage and the long-held belief that a wife became the chattel of her husband should have been confined to legal history by the 1890s. But Emily Jackson's story brought this debate back into the public consciousness. What powers did a husband have over a wife – and what rights did a wife have against a husband? Behind whom would the law throw its weight? To understand why Emily's relations towards her husband were so controversial, and why Edmund's treatment of his wife was not immediately condemned, we must look back at the position of wives and husbands in English law, which had undergone something of a revolution over the second half of the nineteenth century.

The relationship between the law and marriage is a long and complex one. As will be seen, for much of its history the institution of marriage was as much a holy one as a legal one, and the indissolubility of the marital state lay at the heart of this. While divorce crept into the law in the wake of the Reformation, for centuries it remained available only to the higher echelons of society. For most people who found themselves trapped in unhappy marriages, there was no legal way out.

The permanence – or inescapability – of marriage was also reinforced in other ways. The law in effect treated married couples as bound to remain together except in very narrow circumstances. A breach of this duty was enforced through the courts through a procedure called restitution of conjugal rights. This was an archaic element of the law of matrimony, originating in the ecclesiastical courts which governed the legalities of marriage for many centuries. Desertion was not then a ground for divorce, and so the remedy of restitution of conjugal rights was intended to bring an absent spouse to heel. For many years, failure to comply with an order was punishable by excommunication, but as the church's influence over the judicial system began to wane from the early nineteenth century, a more secular approach was needed. In 1813, the sentence of excommunication was replaced by a custodial one.

A spouse who had been abandoned could use this process to force an errant partner to return to the marital home under order of the court.

All in all, as English law stood up to the middle of the nineteenth century, marriage was not something to be entered into lightly, as the options for leaving it were so limited. That unwilling husbands and wives could be made to resume unhappy marital relations against their own will seems unthinkable to us now. But this was all grounded in more disturbing legal concepts underpinning marriage itself. It is trite to say that wives surrendered their own identity upon marriage, but that does not make it any less true. And while, in theory at least, this should have all changed by 1891, Emily Jackson's ordeal revealed that the reforms to the law had only achieved so much. While things had progressed during the latter half of the nineteenth century, less than a decade before Emily's abduction writer and barrister Thomas Barrett-Lennard had suggested – apparently without irony – that 'married women have occupied a position in law analogous to that occupied by infants and lunatics'.

So behind the story of one middle-aged woman from the provincial northwest of England actually lies a half century of controversy and reform that should have revolutionised the legal position of married women. The truth was more nuanced and this wider history of women's rights against their husbands is, as Caroline Norton recognised, best told through the personal stories and experiences of those who lived it. Let us therefore return to Clitheroe and the very beginnings of what the newspapers christened the 'Lancashire Romance'.

* * *

Emily Hall was a woman of independent means, from one of Clitheroe's most prominent families. She was the youngest of three girls. Her father Henry had practised as a solicitor in the town for almost fifty years, before his death in 1875 which had left his widow and daughters comfortably off. In her early thirties, Emily had embarked on a romance with another local solicitor. Her family, for reasons unrecorded, had objected to the match and Emily broke it off. Her suitor never recovered from his heartbreak and when he died a few years later left all of his money to Emily. The Halls' reaction to her previous affair deterred Emily from any further attachments. That was until 1881, when she made the acquaintance of Edmund Jackson at a country picnic. Edmund was in his forties, around the same age as Emily, from a naval family and living with his sister in Blackburn. He had served in foreign armies, apparently fighting in the New Zealand army's 'irregulars'. He was also rumoured to have fought in the American Civil War. Over the next few years, the couple maintained a cordial but respectful friendship. The rural Lancashire social circle was not large, and they regularly met at balls and parties. After a while, Edmund began to visit Emily at the home she shared with her unmarried sister Esther at Shaw Bridge, on the edge of the town. Another sister, Betsy, lived with her husband, local solicitor Hartley Baldwin, in one of Clitheroe's finest houses, next to the church at the top of the town.

Edmund proposed marriage several times, but Emily always refused him; Edmund believed that her family and friends would not allow it. But when he asked again, late in October of 1887, she accepted. The couple were married at Saint Paul's Church in Blackburn, in front of a handful of the groom's friends, just a week after their engagement. Emily's family knew nothing of the wedding. After the short service, the newlyweds took tea with Edmund's elderly sister before making the journey to the bride's family home at Clitheroe. There they broke the news of their marriage to Emily's bewildered mother and sisters, before Edmund left his new wife to return home to Blackburn. At no point on their strange, sad wedding day had the couple been alone together. Two days after the wedding, Emily signed over her annual income of £600 to her new husband; at the same time Edmund was boarding a ship bound for New Zealand with his friend, a young man named Dixon Robinson.

He intended to buy land and set up a homestead for the couple, but shortly after his departure Emily had a change of heart, on account of her health. When she wrote to Edmund to ask him to return to England so that they could live together by the sea at Southport, his reply shocked her. Her husband said that he would only return to live with Emily on condition that she signed over all of her wealth and assets to him. His curt letter closed with a demand that his wife also arrange to pay his (and his friend's) fare back to England. Emily's family's misgivings about the marriage had all been vindicated; Edmund had revealed himself to be that feared bogeyman of all wealthy Victorian spinsters – the fortune hunter.

When Edmund did finally return to England in the summer of 1888, he bombarded Emily with letters, by turns wheedling and threatening, but she refused to meet him. One evening he turned up at the house at Shaw Bridge. Emily remained out of sight upstairs, while her husband loudly demanded to see her. When Esther asked him to leave, he squared up to her, growled that she was 'a lying bitch and a prostitute' before stalking out of the front door. Shortly afterwards, Emily agreed to meet Edmund, if only to refute his accusation that she was being held captive by her family. They journeyed separately to London, to a hotel in Charing Cross, where they dissected their marriage over tea and cake; but the conversation soon descended into accusation and recrimination. Emily claimed Edmund had deceived her as to his financial position and had only married her for her money. Edmund continued his attacks on her family, in particular her sister Esther, saying that everyone in Clitheroe thought she was of low morals. They parted in acrimony and a reconciliation was not to be. For the next two years, Emily heard very little from her husband, bar the occasional furious letter. She lived a respectable life in Clitheroe, busy with church and the other genteel business with which middle-class ladies filled their days. The observant among the townsfolk noticed that Mrs Jackson was always accompanied by her sister or another relative around the town; she never left the house on her own.

After his return from New Zealand and the failed attempts at a reunion, Edmund commenced proceedings for a decree for restitution of conjugal rights against Emily, which she steadfastly ignored. She did not respond to any letters or court papers regarding the case. The court granted Edmund the decree in her absence, the effect of which was to order Emily to return to

Edmund. In continuing to refuse to reconcile with her husband, Emily was now breaking the law – even if only in a symbolic way. She could not be sent to jail, as the punishment had been abolished a couple of years earlier.* But it remained the case that the marriage tie could still be affirmed in court, even if that were contrary to the express wish of one spouse against another.

With a decree that was in effect unenforceable without the sanction of imprisonment, Edmund was left to fume from his home in Blackburn while his wife lived with her spinster sister just ten miles up the road in Clitheroe. His pleas, threats and even legal action had not induced her to return to him. His friends, mostly younger men, kept him entertained. It was observed by the local press that, 'Mr Jackson is as to his spirit and feeling, a big boy. His hair is greying and he is nearing the fifties, yet boys are his companions; he entertains them, they are at home with him, he is at home with them.' If the reporters were hinting at something else, they left it unsaid. But not even the best efforts of his friends could take Edmund's mind of his troubles, and the humiliation at the hands of his wife still rankled. He had been cast out and aside, denounced as a gold digger and condemned by his wife to the life of a bachelor, while still married.

By the early part of 1891, he had brooded on the situation long enough. The court may no longer be empowered to punish his wife for deserting him, so he must take matters into his own hands. As Edmund saw it, if his wife refused to 'resume

* This change itself came about as a result of another controversial case, which we will explore further in Chapter Two.

marital relations' with him voluntarily then she must be compelled to do so by force. If the law could no longer imprison her, then he would do it himself.

For three consecutive Sundays, he had travelled to Clitheroe with a couple of friends and driven up to the church gates in time for the end of morning service. But on each occasion, Emily was either not present at the church or left in the company of male relatives, and Edmund had no desire to become embroiled in a fight with them in the churchyard. Each time he retreated, and plotted to return the following week.

When he arrived in Clitheroe on Sunday, 8 March, he went first to the Baldwins' house, just a few steps down the hill from the church. When Hartley Baldwin answered the door, Edmund demanded to speak to Emily. Baldwin refused, and Edmund stalked off towards the church with the solicitor's insults ringing in his ears – 'You scoundrel! You swindler! You hanger on a woman's nose!'

Emily and her sister Betsy were in fact in church that morning, oblivious to the altercation taking place just next door. When they left the service, the walk down the churchyard path afforded fine views over the rooftops of the town, towards its castle and out to the hills beyond. Daffodils bloomed around the church and the golden clockface glinted in the spring sunshine. But Emily's attention was caught by a small carriage with two horses, drawn up close to the lych-gate.

As they walked down towards the gate, the sisters both became vaguely aware of a man walking closely behind them. Another man stepped out of the carriage and stood watching intently as they walked along the path. He was smartly dressed in a suit but his face was almost entirely covered by a woollen scarf. Just his eyes, disconcertingly familiar, were visible to Emily as she approached. A second too late, she realised that something was wrong. The man pulled down the scarf and she saw that it was Edmund.

Emily was just a few steps from the carriage when she felt a sharp jolt in her back. The man behind her shoved her forwards, as Edmund grabbed her arms, pulling her roughly towards him.

'Emily!' he shouted, 'I want you to go home with me.'

'I will not go, I will not go!' she cried in return.

There was shouting and cursing, drowning out the sound of the church bells. Emily screamed as she was dragged by her husband backwards into the open door of the carriage. Edmund stumbled over the top step of the carriage and fell back into it, pulling Emily down with him, her legs sticking out of the open door. Betsy screamed in protest as she was thrown to the ground in the melee, while the rest of the departing churchgoers looked on in stunned silence. No one stepped forward to challenge the men. Weeping, Betsy scrambled to her feet just in time to see the carriage carrying her sister drive away at speed down the hill.

For the good people of Clitheroe ambling through the town that Sunday morning, all was calm in the spring sunshine. Suddenly there was a clattering, as the carriage, pulled by two horses, raced down Church Brow from St Mary's. People crossing the high street stepped swiftly back as the carriage rumbled past. The driver was whipping the horses to drive them up the incline towards the castle, and a man was sitting on the high seat at the back of the carriage, looking over his shoulder back towards the church. Even the clattering of the horses' hooves on the cobbled street could not drown out the sounds of an argument coming from inside the carriage. It was impossible to make out what they were saying, but two voices – one male, one female – could be heard, raised in passionate and excited tones. The curtains of the carriage windows were not closed and Edmund Jackson could be seen, standing inside the carriage and looking down at his wife prostrate on the floor. His arms were flailing, and he appeared convulsed with anger.

The onlookers watched as the carriage reached the castle grounds and rounded the corner of the street, dropping down another hill and gaining pace. It thundered to the bottom, past Holmes Mill and out towards the edge of the town, heading south towards the road for Blackburn. The shouts and the clatter died away as the carriage sped on, and the town was quiet once more.

According to Emily's later account of her ordeal, when they arrived at the house in Blackburn, she was ushered into the downstairs parlour where Edmund's sister Miss Jackson was waiting. The elderly lady watched on as Edmund unleashed a tirade of abuse at his estranged wife, making 'foul and abominable insinuations' about her and her family. He ripped off Emily's bonnet from her head and flung it into the fireplace, before pushing her back onto the sofa. If she moved from there, he threatened, he would wring her neck. With that, he stormed out of the room and Emily began to cry.

Later that evening, at Edmund's invitation, the superintendent of the Blackburn police visited the house and spoke to Emily. Tearfully she recounted the story of her abduction and implored him to help her. Superintendent Lewis listened to her story before explaining with a sigh that it was not for the police to intervene in matters between a husband and wife. With that, he stood up to leave. Edmund showed him out of the house with a smile and the two men shook hands on the doorstep. Emily slumped back in her chair in despair. A couple of days later the chief constable received the telegram, purportedly from Emily, saying that she was happy to remain with her husband. At around the same time, Edmund returned in triumph from an appearance at Clitheroe Magistrates' Court: the assault charge against him had been dropped and he had been greeted outside the court by a cheering crowd. To the outside world at least, he was a hero; an ordinary husband who had reasserted his legal and personal supremacy over his wife.

For the next week, Emily was kept as a prisoner in the house which was guarded by several burly acquaintances of Edmund's. She was mostly confined to a bedroom overlooking the street and no one was allowed into the house, not even a doctor. Afraid that any food prepared for her would be drugged – or poisoned – she ate very little for the first few days. During the day, she would read or was sometimes allowed out of her room to play the piano, watched over by Edmund's elderly sister and his friends, who remained in the house day and night. She was still bruised and sore from the altercation at the church. She also had a jarred neck, caused when Edmund had torn her bonnet from her head when they arrived at the house. The evenings were the worst; he would come to her room and sit next to her on the bed. Why did they not, he wheedled, agree to settle down together? The first step, he murmured, would be to consummate the marriage. He kissed and stroked Emily, who sat frozen. When she refused to kiss him back, he strode out of the room. But he would keep returning. So afraid was Emily of these advances that for the first four nights she did not undress or get into bed, but sat up all night in a chair, dreading Edmund's return.

Emily's sister Esther came to Rover Street every day. She managed to get into a house on the opposite side of the street from West View and signalled to Emily in sign language whenever she appeared at the window. When Edmund saw what was happening, he dragged Emily away and drew the curtains. But unbeknownst to her, Emily's frantic family had swung into action. Her brother-in-law, Mr Baldwin, was a prominent lawyer in Clitheroe. Wracking his brains, the only legal recourse that Baldwin could think of was the arcane process of *habeas corpus*. This has long been a bastion of the law against false imprisonment. The literal translation of the phrase is 'you shall have the body'. Where a court suspects someone is being unlawfully detained, it can order the person holding them to bring the prisoner to court, in order for a judge to determine if the imprisonment is legal. Although Edmund was bullish about his actions – and the police apparently disinterested – Baldwin felt sure that a court would take a different view; if he could only get Emily out of the house and in front of one.

CHAPTER TWO

FEMMES SOLES

Pressed later on when she had first had doubts about her marriage, Emily Jackson would recall that it was shortly after her husband of only a few weeks had arrived in New Zealand. When she made it clear to Edmund that she did not wish to join him there, something in him seemed to snap. He claimed that he did not have enough money to get home and pushed her to pay the return fare for both himself and his friend Dixon Robinson. After all, he said, 'Dick is so good.' When Emily refused to pay, Edmund responded viciously; he said he would never live with her unless he had control of all of her money.

Just how much money Emily had may not have been clear to her husband. Some later reports put her personal fortune at £47,000, worth almost £4 million in modern money. For her part, Emily maintained that the stories of her personal wealth were greatly exaggerated. However, she had already gifted Edmund her annual income of £600, equivalent to £50,000 today. For a man without any other apparent means of support, she must have been an enticing prospect. And it wasn't just her husband who was taking a keen interest in Emily's finances. Her new sister-in-law, Edmund's unmarried older sister, was not backward in coming forward either. In one of her letters to Edmund in New Zealand, Emily complained:

> *Miss Jackson keeps annoying me by writing about nothing but money that I have been compelled to let her know that I intend to be the sole master of my money and interfered with by nobody. I now plainly see why you have married me, and am very sorry I was blind enough before not to find out.*

But perhaps when viewed in the context of their times, the attitude of the Jackson siblings was not so surprising. The latter half of the nineteenth century was a turning point for the rights of married women, an issue which polarised public and official opinion. For centuries, in the eyes of the law women had been viewed financially and physically as an extension of a husband's property, losing all rights to their own money and assets upon marriage.

The 'Clitheroe Wife-Abduction' is a deeply dark story concealed beneath a thin veneer of Victorian middle-class propriety. It illustrates how the law's treatment of marriage – and a woman's place within it – acquiesced to and even encouraged cruelty and violence. The unromantic history of this aspect of the law reveals the extent to which, only a little over a century ago, a wife's rights, liberties and even safety remained contingent on the whims of her husband. And the reaction of the public – from the jeering crowds gathered outside the house, to the cheers of support when a charge of assault against Edmund was dropped by the local magistrates – reveals much about Victorian society's attitudes to men, women, wives and husbands, as well.

The financial motivations for Edmund Jackson's actions were self-evident. If he had married his wealthy wife a few years earlier, he would have taken control of her fortune as of right. Nevertheless, he still considered himself entitled to take physical control of Emily when she refused to meekly assent to his wishes. So the timing of the affair influenced its notoriety. It came at the end of a half century hailed as a period of great progress for the rights of married women. But the actions of Mr Jackson and the law's apparent support for them brought that progress to a juddering halt.

Financial independence, even for wealthy women, more or less dissolved as soon as they made their wedding vows. Single women and widows were known, in legal terms, as '*femmes soles*', able to hold property and money, and enter into contracts in their own right. Upon marriage, women became '*femmes coverts*', under the 'coverture' of their husbands and no longer able to exercise any separate legal personality. A wife's assets became her husband's as soon as they married.

Historically, the law had treated marriage as an almost spiritual contract, a sacrament that only God could put asunder 'to the extent of considering it in each case as an act highly spiritual, consecrated by divine authority and as such indissoluble by human power for any cause whatsoever'. Spiritually, financially and legally, husband and wife were in effect treated as one person, 'but that person was not a combination of the two, but was represented by the husband alone'. It was ever thus; but by the beginning of the nineteenth century, dissatisfaction with the status quo had begun to grow. The rich, as in so many areas of life, were largely able to get around the problem. Wealthy families with eligible daughters would tie up inheritances in trusts, often known as marriage settlements, to ring-fence family money when a daughter married. While the wife received the benefit of the money held in the trust, it was controlled by the trustees appointed to manage it on her behalf, and all access was through them. As the money was subject to a trust, rather than owned outright by a wife, it could not legally pass to her husband.

For poorer women or even those of comfortable but modest means, a settlement was not practicable. And it was not only a woman's inherited money that passed to her husband on marriage. Any earnings, income, investments or other property that she had acquired were lost as well. In effect, married women were the only group in society prevented from exercising any property rights whatsoever, save for 'infants and lunatics'. The right of a husband to take even the wages earned by a woman's own work or skills was long the most controversial aspect of the law. But from the early nineteenth century, the law faced a series of challenges, initially from women testing the law on their own account at court and then from a widespread and concerted lobby for change.

For some women, marrying a feckless husband could risk her own personal and professional ruin. Mrs Julia Glover was the grande dame of the Covent Garden stage in the early part of the nineteenth century. She was born Julia Betterton in

Ireland in 1782 into an acting family. She made her stage debut at the age of just five years old and as a teenager was the toast of the season in Bath. She gave her first professional performance in London in 1797. Three years later, aged just eighteen, she married Samuel Glover and 'sealed for herself a series of miseries almost unparalleled'. Glover had apparently agreed to pay Julia's father a thousand pounds for her hand; the bridegroom welched on the deal but Julia's father still forced her to go through with the marriage. The Glovers settled in London and had eight children, four of whom survived into adulthood. Over the early years of the nineteenth century, Julia steadily built a solid career on the stage. By 1810, she was playing to packed crowds at the Drury Lane Theatre in Covent Garden. She had a good line in 'the vivacious matrons, the buxom widows and spirited women of quality'. She made the role of Mrs Malaprop in Sheridan's *The Rivals* her own and also played Mrs Candour in the playwright's *The School for Scandal*, to great acclaim.

But behind the scenes, Julia's professional success was bankrolling the shiftless Samuel, who maintained several mistresses on his wife's earnings from the theatre. When she discovered his infidelity and threw him out of their home, Samuel took off abroad for several weeks. Upon his return, he demanded that the theatre pay his wife's wages over to him, but they refused, arguing that their agreement was with Julia herself. He sued the theatre for a hundred guineas, representing Julia's wages of ten guineas a week for a ten-week run. During this time, she had performed as Margaret of Anjou in an adaptation of Shakespeare's *Henry VI* and Lady Racket in Hannah Cowley's play *The Belle's Stratagem*. The Drury Lane Theatre Company stood by its star performer. In court, it accused Samuel of having 'the meanness and the want of manhood to wish to deprive his wife of the fruits of her labour, which were intended for the support of herself and her children – to which Mr Glover has not contributed one farthing for years'. It would never have engaged Julia to perform on its stage if it had known she was to be deprived of her earnings from it.

However, even the theatre had to concede that, legally if not morally, Samuel was entitled to make his claim. The jury was sympathetic. While Samuel won his case, they awarded him damages of only a farthing. The theatre sought to appeal the award at another court hearing, challenging the point of principle of the law that a husband was entitled to any and all of his wife's property and income. Mulling over the case, one of the judges slyly pointed out that even women who had established their own career were still subject to the doctrine of coverture and 'unluckily there is in the English law no such thing as a "femme sole" by custom of the theatre'. Death itself was no escape, as another judge reminisced fondly about an old case where a widowed wife was ordered to pay her later earnings to her husband's executors rather than keep them for herself.

From these remarks, the theatre and Julia quickly gathered that the case was not going as they would have hoped. Before the appeal court could reach a decision on Julia's earnings, the parties agreed to negotiate and the later fate of Mrs Glover's earnings is not recorded. Her professional career continued to flourish for many years; she died in 1850, a few days after giving her swansong performance as Mrs Malaprop.

* * *

Julia Glover's own views on her pernicious financial position were either never sought or not recorded. While she found her voice on stage, in accounts of the legal case she is silent, as the theatre made a stand on her behalf. Although the public – and some of the judiciary – may have been on Julia Glover's side, the law was clear. As a married woman she had no right to hold or even earn money on her own account. By law if not by justice, it belonged to her husband. But resistance would grow over the next few decades.

In the years following the case, as a concerted campaign for women's rights began to emerge in the early Victorian era, a few figureheads stepped forward to take up the fights for women's property rights. One of the most famous was Caroline Norton, the society beauty, writer and spirited political campaigner who was chosen to represent the figure of *Justice* on the walls of the chamber of the House of Lords. It was Caroline's troubled personal history and her determination to channel this into change for all women that made her the perfect model for the allegorical painting. Caroline was born in 1808 into the Sheridan family; her grandfather was the playwright Richard who had written some of Julia Glover's most memorable roles. At the age of nineteen, Caroline married MP George Norton. But George's early infatuation with his wife soon turned sour. Within weeks of their honeymoon, he began abusing and assaulting Caroline. There were horrific tales of how he had beaten and burned her with a hot kettle. In an argument when she was pregnant with the youngest of her three sons, Norton threatened to throw her down the stairs of their home at Storey's Gate, Westminster. Worse still were the rumours that Caroline had suffered a miscarriage when Norton hit her during a later pregnancy.

Unsurprisingly, the Nortons grew increasingly estranged and by the 1830s George was spending very little time with his family. In spite of her private struggles, in public Caroline remained the consummate society hostess and she had some influential friends. Chief among these was Lord Melbourne, the home secretary and, from 1835, prime minister. George Norton had no hesitation in exploiting his wife's connections for his own benefit, relying on her to secure him positions, including as a magistrate. But when the close friendship between the middle-aged premier and the lady of fashion twenty years his junior became a source of gossip around Westminster, wider London society and the scandal sheets, George was sufficiently humiliated to take action. Firstly, he took the couple's sons away from Caroline and refused to let her see them. Then he decided to sue Melbourne for 'criminal conversation' with his wife.

'Crim con', as it was often abbreviated, was an action for damages for adultery, in which a cuckolded husband could pursue his wife's lover for interference with 'his legal property in human form'. It was the ultimate embodiment of the law's treatment of a married woman as her husband's chattel. Just as if Melbourne had crashed Norton's carriage or injured his horse, he was entitled to be compensated for the 'damage' the premier had caused to his property by fraternising with his wife. Caroline herself was not party to or even in attendance at the court proceedings, but she was effectively on trial as much, if not more so, than Melbourne. At the trial, there were scurrilous stories of maids catching the PM and Mrs Norton mid-embrace and heavy reliance on their frequent and affectionate letters to each other. But the court was not convinced and Norton lost his claim. Melbourne and, more importantly, Caroline had been exonerated, but she later felt that 'it had never seemed fair ... that Melbourne, her co-defendant in the case in truth if not in law, had emerged smoothly from the process, the favourite of the Queen, while she suffered ignominy'.

But the spectacle of the court case and her husband's treatment of her had ignited something in Caroline. She had written professionally for almost all of her adult life. Her first volume of poetry was published when she was just seventeen, and she had continued to turn out a steady stream of novels, poems and articles. She now turned her pen towards campaigning against the injustices she, and countless other married women, had suffered under the law. She began to publish campaigning pamphlets and lobby her contacts in Parliament to advance the cause of women's rights through changes to the law.

Caroline's interests were necessarily informed by her personal experiences but they chimed with a growing push for reform in various areas of the law. Her own relationship had shown her the worst aspects of marriage and the vulnerabilities of women within it, both physically and financially. 'There was a feeling that if a married woman was her husband's property – "she does not exist", in Caroline Norton's words – then a man had a right to treat his own property as he wished.' As a writer, she boasted that she could earn more in a month than her husband brought home in a year; but that it was immaterial, as George automatically owned the copyright to all of her works. She would later observe that his 'dependence upon my literary efforts for all extra resources runs as a matter of course through all the letters I received from him during our union. The names of my publishers occur as if they were Mr Norton's bankers.' But her literary fame helped to draw attention to her cause, which she championed on behalf of women up and down the country. She had the profile, political connections and lived experience to lend some real weight to the issue.

In 1854, Caroline published a treatise on women's rights (or lack thereof) under English law. Encompassing inequalities in divorce, property ownership, child custody and many other issues, *English Laws for Women in the Nineteenth Century* may not have been Caroline's most commercially successful work but it was certainly her most influential. Changes to the law around divorce were being debated in the House of Commons at the time and so the question of married women's property rights and lack of legal personality was on everyone's lips. For Caroline, the question was an extremely pertinent one. Her mother had died a couple of years before and so, as well as benefiting from her writing earnings, George had also received his wife's inheritance. She even wrote to Queen Victoria to press the case for reform: 'I deny that this is my personal cause; it is the cause of all the women of England ... Meanwhile my husband has ... the copyright of my works. Let him claim the copyright of THIS!'

Over the next decade, Caroline continued to lend her voice to the campaigns for changes in the law, until ill-health slowed down her work. She was eventually widowed in 1875; despite the breakdown of the relationship the Nortons had never divorced. Two years later, at the age of sixty-seven and in poor health, Caroline married her long-time friend Sir William Stirling-Maxwell. It took until the end of her life, but Caroline did at last find matrimonial happiness, though sadly the couple had just three months of married life together before Caroline died in June 1877.

* * *

Caroline did see one significant change to the law to the benefit of women come into law during her lifetime, although it came too late to alleviate her dispute with her first husband. There had been several false starts in attempts to change the law around married women's property rights during the middle of the nineteenth century. But in 1870, a new Married Women's Property Bill was brought forward and managed to make more progress through Parliament than previous attempts. The idea of reforming the law to allow women to hold property and assets independently from their husbands was not without controversy. In the House of Lords, one peer decried it as 'an entire subversion of the system of domestic rule which had prevailed in this country for more than a thousand years'; while several MPs claimed it would undermine the entire basis of marriage, bring discord and distress to countless families up and down the land, and foment social rebellion. One Commons wag was moved to poetry at the bill's second reading: 'But oh! Ye lords of ladies intellectual, inform us truly, have they not henpecked you all?'

While upper-class women were able to protect themselves and their inherited fortunes, the inequity of the law was felt most keenly by middle-, and in particular, working-class women. The MPs in favour of changing the law estimated that, out of around 3 million married women in England at the time, 800,000 of those were employed in some form or another. In effect, all of them found their wages liable to be 'confiscated' by their husbands. Another example cited was that of female authors like Caroline Norton. While women writers of the era used pen-names for various reasons, one member of the House of Lords quoted the injustice of the efforts of 'literary ladies' being exploited by their husbands. He knew of one writer who was forced to keep moving publishers and changing her pseudonym to keep the royalties from her books out of the hands of her husband.

There was considerable support for the bill in industrial towns and cities, where the issue had been a political and moral quandary for many years. Back in the 1840s, a group of artisans from the mill town of Rochdale had set up the world's first co-operative society. The model for all future co-ops, the 'Rochdale Pioneers' started something of a social revolution in more ways than one. Members would purchase shares in the co-op, which initially sold a small selection of consumables in its first shop; and from the profits of the shop would receive a dividend (or 'divi'). The Rochdale Co-Op allowed married women to purchase its shares and, most importantly, it would refuse to pay over their divis to their husbands. It struck an early blow for women's property rights, and this cause was championed 'in most of the manufacturing districts, especially in the North of England [where] there [were] abundant instances in which poor and industrious women, who had exerted themselves to maintain their families ... after working very hardly for very small wages – had been exposed to the evil of having their small earnings pounced upon ... by intemperate, idle or dissolute husbands'. The Liberal MP for Sheffield, Anthony Mundella, also owned a hosiery factory in Nottingham, which employed 2000 women; he was vocal in his support for the bill and recounted the stories of some of his female employees who were trapped in abusive marriages with no means to leave and support themselves. A petition in support of the change to the law was signed by 5000 people in Manchester.

Finally, in 1870, and despite the opposition in the House of Lords, the Married Women's Property Act became law. Under the act, women were entitled to keep their own income, earned through 'employment, occupation, trade, literary, artistic or scientific skill'. Initially it was income only that was kept from the husband's grasp, with a woman's heritable property (and likely the bulk of a fortune) still passing to a spouse on marriage, save for a small amount of just £200. Further legislation in 1882 brought all of a wife's property, including inherited money, within the law's protection.

* * *

So if Edmund Jackson really was a fortune hunter, he was a decade or so too late. But perhaps his plan was more subtle than that. The Married Women's Property Act 1870 was a legal landmark but, even as women secured more financial freedom within marriage, they remained bound in other ways. The law continued to allow husbands like Jackson to use the courts to compel wives to return to a marriage from which they had tried to escape. The foundation for Jackson's subsequent actions was the decree for restitution of conjugal rights that he had obtained against Emily a few years before the abduction.

The remedy of restitution was available to both husbands and wives, but tended to be used by each in different ways. For men, it was mostly employed as it was originally intended, to enforce their wife's marital obligations, whether she wanted to or not. For wives, a suit was usually more tactical, to secure an offer of maintenance or other support from an absent husband. But in the early 1880s, one woman took a markedly different tack.

Georgina Weldon and her husband William had married in 1860. He was an army colonel and she was an enthusiastic, if mostly amateur, soprano and musician. They lived at Tavistock House in Bloomsbury, the former home of Charles Dickens. From the house, Georgina set up a school for musically gifted orphans, while William spent much of his time with his mistress and their young son. In 1875, the marriage finally broke down and William then signed the lease of Tavistock House over to his wife, together with a financial settlement of £1,000 per year. When he tired of making these payments after a few years, things deteriorated further. Georgina had always had what might be termed unconventional interests, and William decided to use these against her. Citing her enthusiasm for spiritualism, he attempted to have her committed to a lunatic asylum. He persuaded two doctors to certify that his estranged wife was indeed insane, but when they arrived to take Georgina to the institution she managed to evade them.

The colonel's plan may have failed, but the battle of the Weldons then took another extraordinary turn. After several years' estrangement, Georgina brought a claim for restitution of conjugal relations against her husband. She was already financially provided for, so this was no ploy to secure money; her case would test the equity of the application of the law between husbands and wives, and leave it radically altered. One newspaper commented: 'That famous lady, Mrs Weldon, has the credit of bringing the question [of conjugal relations] to trial under new conditions. Her husband ... has no valid reason for leaving her. Her moral character is irreproachable and eccentricity is not a crime.' In retaliation, William alleged that Georgina had been unfaithful with no less than three men. This so outraged her (it seems impossible that she did not know of his own domestic arrangements outside of the marriage) that she insisted that the court ask her about the allegations, so that she could deny them under oath. The allegation of infidelity was, said Mrs Weldon, 'an infamous lie'. She then went on to name the three men who were alleged to be her lovers, much to the chagrin of the judge who had her ushered from the witness stand immediately. While he was content for Mrs Weldon's reputation to be impugned in open court, it would not do to have her alleged paramours so maligned. However, he could find no grounds on which to refuse the decree for restitution of conjugal rights, and reluctantly ordered William Weldon to return to his wife.

If Georgina thought that a decree would bring about an improvement in the relationship, she was sadly mistaken. William steadfastly refused to return to Tavistock House and believed that his wife should be satisfied with his financial provision. But she was not. Over the next three years, Georgina continued to pursue her husband through the courts. When he did not resume marital relations, she applied for an order for his imprisonment for breach of the order and – albeit reluctantly – the courts granted it. But Colonel Weldon refused to surrender and the authorities clearly balked at taking action to apprehend him. He launched a series of appeals, no doubt intended to frustrate his wife as much as the legal process. But behind the scenes, there were deep misgivings that the law had been turned against husbands in this way. And so, while the Weldons' case was rumbling through the courts, the law was quietly changed to abolish the custodial sentence for a breach of such an order. By the time the case reached the Court of Appeal in 1885, Colonel Weldon's lawyers were able to argue, with only a hint of smugness, that the question of imprisonment was now academic as the law had been changed the year before. So ended the unhappy saga of the Weldons' marriage.

Georgina Weldon was almost as well known for her litigious habits as for her singing. At the same time as she was pursuing the matrimonial case through the courts, she was also engaged in a series of suits against those who had been involved in her attempted committal a few years before, all of which she won. She never used lawyers and represented herself robustly at each of her court appearances. In the same week that her case against William finally concluded, she had been in court a few days before in a libel trial against a Paris magazine, which she also won. But she was not always so lucky: in the years after her case against her husband, she was imprisoned twice after being convicted of criminal libel in two separate cases. She died in much reduced circumstances in Brighton in 1914.

While Georgina Weldon's antics at court often made good newspaper copy and turned her into something of a celebrity litigant, her action against the colonel left a lasting legal legacy for women. There was no doubt that the abolition of the custodial sentence in restitution cases was a direct result of her pursuing the imprisonment of her husband through the courts. A law that had hung over many women was swiftly changed when it appeared unduly prejudicial to one man. It meant that women who had left a marriage, for whatever reason, need not fear being compelled to return under pain of imprisonment. And it would have a direct bearing on the outcome of the Jackson case.

On the face of it, the spinsterly wife from Clitheroe, the society confidante of a prime minister and the eccentric Bloomsbury matron had little in common. But in directly challenging the laws that disadvantaged them in their own marriage they raised the issues in the public consciousness and paved the way for support for reform. The battles that Caroline Norton and Georgina Weldon had fought, for equality of property rights and conjugal obligations, appeared to have been won. But as Emily Jackson was to discover, the war itself continued.

CHAPTER THREE
ABSOLUTE DOMINION

The first skirmish in the battle for Emily Jackson's freedom took place just a week after her capture outside St Mary's in Clitheroe. For the intervening days, she had been held at her husband Edmund's family home in Rover Street in Blackburn, in dark parody of marital cohabitation. A judge in the Royal Courts of Justice in London was to decide whether to issue the writ of *habeas corpus* that her family was seeking. If the writ was granted, then her husband would have to bring Emily from Blackburn to London, so that the court could judge whether her captivity was lawful. And if it was found not to be, then she must be immediately released. The court hearing pitched Jackson and his associates against Emily's relatives, including her lawyer brother-in-law Mr Baldwin. She, of course, remained under guard at Rover Street. Presiding over the hearing was Mr Justice Cave, Sir Lewis to his friends. Cave was a large man, his jowls partly hidden by bushy whiskers, and he surveyed his courtroom through small round spectacles. He was 'burly in person and bluff in manner and looked, as he was, the very incarnation of sound common sense'.

The court hearing was fractious and belligerent, with both sides hurling accusations at the others; the Baldwins claimed Jackson had been violent and cruel to Emily, while Jackson's lawyers insinuated that the family's main concern was to maintain their own influence over his wife – and her money.

The question of whether a husband's imprisonment of his own wife was lawful was not an entirely novel issue for the Victorian courts. Jackson's lawyers relied heavily on a contentious case from earlier in the nineteenth century as justification for his actions. In 1840, a Mr Alexander Cochrane had pursued an almost identical course to Edmund Jackson when his wife had left their apartments near Regent Street and fled to France to live with her mother. The Cochranes had been married for three years and had two children, but the relationship had soured. Incensed at reports that his wife was attending masked balls and parties in Paris, to all appearances a single woman, Cochrane made a claim for restitution of conjugal rights in London. However, while she remained abroad, he had no means of enforcing this. Her sojourn in Paris kept her well away from the jurisdiction of the English courts. But eventually, by fair means or foul, he managed to induce his estranged wife to return to England and visit their home. She was told that he would be away on business during her visit. When Mrs Cochrane arrived, she was ambushed by her husband and prevented from leaving. Proceedings for a writ of *habeas corpus* to secure her freedom soon followed.

At court, as in the Jackson case, the question was a seemingly straightforward one – in English law, does a husband have the right to confine his own wife and restrain her from her liberty? And in the Cochrane case, the answer given by the court was equally blunt – yes. The judge observed that 'there can be no doubt of the general dominion which the law of England attributes to the husband over the wife'. In fact, the remedy to the situation was almost entirely in Mrs Cochrane's hands as she could at once render her own imprisonment unnecessary by 'cheerfully and frankly performing the contract into which she has entered'. Her custody was not therefore unlawful. In the aftermath of the hearing, Mr Cochrane wrote to a newspaper to defend his actions even further:

> *Permit me, Sir, to add that I did not lock the door of my apartments until my wife was told to make her escape, and even after this, I took her into the Parks and offered to take her to the different places of amusement.*

The Cochrane case was controversial at the time and relied heavily on an interpretation of the law of marriage that was starting to fall out of fashion even then. London newspaper *The Statesman* editorialised that the decision was

> *a monstrous hardship. Yet the judge went out of his way to eulogise the English law of indissoluble marriage; forgetting, however, to say that no such obstacle stands in the way of the rich and the vicious. This is too commonly the one-sided way in which our legal luminaries look at the law.*

When the same issue came back to the courts in the Jacksons' case, fifty years after the saga of the Cochranes, it would perhaps have been expected that attitudes towards marriage and the 'dominion' of a husband over a wife might have moved on. But perhaps it could be deduced from Mr Justice Cave's demeanour that he was not a natural defender of women's rights. He was most experienced in the mercantile courts, adjudicating on the ownership of ships' cargoes and the like; and he seemed determined to apply the same unromantic approach to the question of Emily Jackson's custody. He cut short her lawyers when he tired of their argument and from the off seemed most receptive to the forthright advocacy of Edmund's counsel. By the time he came to deliver his judgment, it was something of a foregone conclusion.

'The husband has a decree of restitution of conjugal rights,' Cave intoned, 'and if his wife refused to obey the order of the court, the husband was justified in using reasonable force to enforce his rights.' There was, he said, nothing cruel, improper or illegal in Edmund's behaviour, in fact he reserved his strongest criticism for Emily's sisters for interfering in the couple's relationship and then for protesting at her seizure. The writ was refused. As *The Globe* newspaper put it, 'the medieval style in which Mr Jackson of Clitheroe carried off his wife from her family circle and stood a regular siege, as if his house were a feudal castle [is now] appropriately accompanied by what a number of people will hold to be an equally antiquated law'.

Seen in the light of the changes to the law related to married women and their property in the preceding decades, the decision of Judge Cave was particularly surprising and it drew fire from many quarters. Methodists condemned it as an 'odious and abominable relic of the despotism of the past'. Suffrage groups seized on the irony that what the law gave with one hand, it took with the other; just twenty years after the Married Women's Property Act, Emily Jackson was still treated as her husband's chattel, under his complete control as effectively ordered by the court.

But before the ink was dry on the front pages decrying the decision, the case took another twist. Emily's lawyers went straight to the Court of Appeal to challenge Cave's ruling – and this time, they had some success. On the morning of 17 March, Emily's sister Esther Hall was keeping her vigil outside West View when her nephew, Master Baldwin, arrived waving a telegram in the air. The Court of Appeal had agreed to hear the case, and so Edmund Jackson was required to bring his wife to London under order of the court. When he read the telegram, Jackson flew into a rage. The house shook as he slammed doors and threw crockery. So afraid was Emily that she suffered palpitations, the strain of her ordeal telling on her even as it seemed to be coming to an end. Later that day, the Jacksons together with Edmund's friends (and Emily's captors) boarded the London train. They stayed the night at Edmund's father's house in Harrington Gardens, a handsome square of imposing redbrick houses in Kensington. Emily could scarcely allow herself to hope that it might be her last night under her husband's custody.

The next morning, Emily dressed carefully for her day in court. She wore a dark silk dress underneath a sealskin jacket with a high, stiff collar and topped off her outfit with a bonnet to match her dress. As she walked into the court building, in the Royal Courts of Justice on the Strand, Emily was accompanied by Edmund and his friends. But she was heartened to see the groups of women, some in pairs and others in larger throngs, standing on the pavement outside the court building. A number of reporters also filed into court, eager to see the next act in the drama of the Clitheroe Wife-Abduction.

The Court of Appeal had before them an affidavit from Edmund, in which he strove to justify his actions. He related the saga of the marriage, the abortive move to New Zealand and Emily's continued resistance to his efforts to resume conjugal relations.

> *I, therefore, on the 8th March instant, took my said wife and have since detained her in my house, using no more force or constraint than was necessary to take her or to prevent her from returning to her said relations. She has had perfect liberty in and the full run of the house, short of leaving it. Such restraint I submit that I could lawfully use in order to have an opportunity of regaining the affection of my wife which had become alienated from me, and which it was impossible that I could do when she was under the influence of her said relations.*

But Emily had been prevented from speaking to her lawyers while being held at West View, so the court had no statement from her to rebut her husband's rather blasé account of her abduction and captivity. They were reluctant to rely on

Edmund's statements, although they stopped short of calling him a liar. The panel of appeal judges who were hearing the case therefore invited her into their chambers to discuss the situation away from the ears of her husband and his lawyers. This was the first time that Emily had been able to speak for herself about the situation since she had been taken.

After hearing Emily's account and returning to open court, the judges mulled over the finer points of Judge Cave's controversial ruling, picking apart some of its absurdities. To laughter from the ladies in the public gallery, the Lord Chancellor pointed out that earlier cases like Cochrane's had suggested that 'a husband may beat his wife, but not in a violent and a cruel manner'. But the judges became serious when delivering their judgment. The arguments put forward by Edmund Jackson were 'tainted with the false notion that a husband in law had absolute dominion over his wife ... There was no law to support the absurd theory that a wife was a slave – the abject slave – the absolute property, the chattel of a husband.' And if the power of the court to imprison a wife for refusing to submit to an order for conjugal rights had been removed, then a husband certainly did not have the right to do so himself. Emily Jackson's imprisonment was unlawful; the writ was granted and Edmund was ordered to release her immediately. Such was the throng of onlookers gathered at the front of the court that Emily and her family had to be smuggled out of the judges' entrance at the rear of the Royal Courts building. Emily Jackson was a free woman at last and the English law of matrimony had once again undergone a small but significant shift in favour of women.

* * *

The aftermath of the court hearings was almost as dramatic as the abduction itself. If Emily expected to return to Clitheroe in triumph, she was sadly mistaken. When she arrived back in the town a couple of days after the Court of Appeal hearing, she was greeted from the train by a mob of people, none too friendly. By the evening of that day, a rumour had spread that an effigy of the unfortunate Mrs Jackson was to be burned in the Market Place, and a crowd of hundreds began to gather, ready for some Saturday evening entertainment. While they waited for the effigy to appear, they sang several choruses of 'For he's a jolly good fellow', in support of Edmund who had retreated back to Blackburn to lick his wounds. Soon the crowd became restless and swarmed up the hill, past St Mary's and to the Baldwins' house, where they shouted and jeered, throwing stones at the windows of the imposing property. When they grew tired of this, they moved as one down through the town to the house at Shaw Bridge where Emily's sister Esther Hall lived. Three windows were smashed before the police managed to break up the crowd.

This kind of community demonstration of displeasure was sometimes known as 'rough music', an organised display of popular disapproval towards an individual that sometimes tipped over into vigilantism. As far as the townspeople of Clitheroe were concerned, the London courts had not delivered justice in the Jackson case and so they had to deliver it themselves. The mob took Sunday off but on Monday evening resumed their protests. An even larger crowd gathered this time, filling the Market Place and spreading up the hill towards the church. A crude likeness of Emily had been constructed and was waiting around the corner, to be brought into the square and set alight. More police were sent to the scene this time and the crowd thought better of bringing the effigy out. But it took the constables until gone midnight, and the threat of reading the Riot Act, to get the mob to disperse.

Over the next few days the excitement in the town died away and Emily Jackson was able to resume something of a normal life, away from her husband. But the couple's battle continued in the public eye. Both published their own accounts of the case, with – as might be expected – wildly different viewpoints. Emily gave a lengthy interview to *The Times* which published her story in a serial form, entitled 'Mrs Jackson's Vindication' – a rival newspaper dismissed it as a 'tedious tale of the crooked course of middle-aged matrimony'. In retaliation, Edmund found a sympathetic publisher and brought out a pamphlet on the case, waggishly titled 'The True Story of the Clitheroe Wife-Abduction; or Why I ran away with my wife'. He claimed that many people had contacted him after the Court of Appeal hearing to offer their support and urge him to appeal the case further to the House of Lords – although he ultimately decided against this. Some had even encouraged him to stand for Parliament, running on a promise to alter the law that had so unjustly deprived him of his wife's society and personage. Soon, one correspondent complained, men would have to organise themselves, in a similar manner to women's campaigners. Perhaps Edmund could found and chair a 'Husbands' Rights Protection Association', another suggested.

As for the mob rule that had overtaken Clitheroe since Emily's return, Edmund could not bring himself to condemn it and supposed that a hundred years ago things might have been taken even further. Mrs Jackson should count herself lucky that the locals had not resurrected the old northern custom of 'riding the stang', a form of community justice that saw wrongdoers carried through the streets in a basket or on a frame, while an accompanying crowd heckled and threw rubbish and anything else that came to hand at them. 'In all parts of the world there is an unwritten as well as a written law, of which the former is a rough-and-ready outcome of the sentiments of the common people, and the latter the deliberate calm expression of constituted authority.'

But even though the Court of Appeal's decision was surely the 'expression of constituted authority' on the case, not everyone was prepared to treat it as such. A few weeks after the judgment, magistrates in Watford heard the case of the unhappy Mr and Mrs Hughes, which had remarkable similarities to the Jackson story. Mrs Hughes had left her marriage to live with her mother, and when her husband discovered this, he had threatened both women with violence. Dismissing all charges against Mr Hughes, the magistrates announced that they would not follow the Court of Appeal's rationale and in their view, 'a husband had a perfect right to demand his wife at all times'. There were also local rumours that a Clitheroe man had attempted to kidnap his wife in a repeat of the Jackson scandal, but he did not garner the same level of attention, and the story never moved beyond that of town gossip.

Nevertheless, the case remained a sensation across the country for weeks afterwards. The Cambridge Union Society devoted a debate to the motion 'that this House commends the conduct of Mr Jackson in the Clitheroe case and regrets the influence which the judgment of the Court of Appeal will have on English social life'.* Sketches about the Jacksons' troubled marriage began to appear on music hall stages and at theatrical revues up and down the country. The Theatre Royal in Blackburn was getting ready to stage a four-act play about the case, with the names and details only lightly fictionalised, when it was pulled at the eleventh hour because the Lord Chamberlain's office refused to issue a licence for the performance.

Gradually, the furore died away and the key players eventually resumed their lives of provincial anonymity. Emily Jackson continued her quiet life in Clitheroe, living again with her sister Esther in the house in Shaw Bridge. She did nothing further to attract the kind of attention that she had received in 1891. Just seven years after her abduction, she underwent a minor procedure on her foot to remove a corn. But she contracted blood poisoning from the surgery, which in turn led to heart failure and she died a few days later, aged just fifty-four. Her funeral took place at a church in a village just outside Clitheroe and, in accordance with her wishes for a death as quiet as the last years of her life, was as simple as possible.

Emily's will, changed just a year after her doomed marriage, contained some bequests to servants, her nephews and her brother-in-law Hartley Baldwin, who had helped her in the

* The motion was carried by 82 votes to 37.

battle with Edmund years before. The rest of her estate of £7600 – worth around £600,000 in modern money – was left to her sisters Betsy and Esther. She left her husband nothing. But Edmund, as he had once predicted in his published account of the case, went on to live a long life and survived his estranged wife by a quarter of a century. He died in 1924, aged eighty-five.

* * *

It is hard not to conclude that if Emily Jackson had been younger and the setting for her ordeal more glamorous than Blackburn, she might not have received the same level of opprobrium in the aftermath of her case. As it was, her understated role in striking a blow for women's rights was largely overlooked; but not by everyone. Suffrage groups throughout the country championed her bravery in taking her husband to court and believed that the case had given hope to many women trapped in similar situations. In the aftermath of the case, the Women's Franchise League wrote to Emily to express their support and admiration: 'By your quiet determination and unflinching courage you have struck a splendid blow for freedom, and rendered inestimable service to your countrywomen. For this many thank you openly, thousands in whispers, whilst tens of thousands thank you in their hearts who do not dare speak with their lips.'

Far from being simply a tale of middle-aged marital disharmony in provincial Lancashire, the Jackson case can actually be seen as a treatise on the law's historical treatment of women, taken to its logical conclusion. Treated as a chattel of a husband for so long and bereft of any legal identity once married, it is little wonder that Edmund Jackson saw nothing wrong in carrying away his wife when she showed herself to have a mind of her own. When a married woman could not own property and was in essence the property of her husband, then how can he be constrained in how he treats his own possession? Although attitudes – and the law – had begun to change from the mid-nineteenth century, the reaction to the story showed that public support for this was far from universal. While the Married Women's Property Act of 1870 was primarily concerned with financial matters, the debates around it revealed much about how women were viewed in Victorian society and the extent to which their financial and physical security were linked. As campaigners pointed out, women themselves had no voice in these arguments.

It took the escalation of the case to one of the highest courts in the country to secure Emily Jackson's freedom from imprisonment by her own husband. The legal arguments in the case went to the heart of women's rights both inside and outside of marriage, and had ramifications far beyond Clitheroe. It was a shift, albeit a tentative one, in how the courts approached the power imbalance between husband and wife; and it highlighted the contradictions that still remained in the law around marriage. The case would go down in legal history as a battle for women's rights which 'began with an unhappy and abusive marriage. It ended as a landmark for all married women and authority for the – now perhaps obvious – proposition that a man cannot abduct and detain a woman simply because she is married to him.'

But while the Jackson case was a legal milestone, correcting the power imbalance that up until then had been inherent, if unspoken, in the law's view of marriage, it highlighted other equally fundamental problems with the institution itself. It is not recorded whether Emily and Edmund Jackson saw each other again before her early death just a few years after the court case. Given their history, it seems unlikely. But they did remain married – the grant of probate of Emily's will noted that she was the wife of Edmund Jackson, although he was not appointed to administer her estate. So why did the Jacksons remain bound to one another in matrimony for so many years after their relationship had broken down in the most spectacular way? In truth, they had no option. Much of the reaction to the case in the press centred on how it had highlighted the absurdities of divorce law in Britain. The indissoluble bond of marriage that Mr Justice Cave was so keen to uphold meant that in the nineteenth century the circumstances in which an unhappily married couple could end their union were extremely limited. Adultery was the sole legal ground to obtain a divorce at the time. Whatever the state of their relationship, neither of the Jacksons had been unfaithful to the other, either before or after their estrangement.

Supporters of Edmund bemoaned the fact that, his wife having left him, he now had no power to compel her to return to him; the power of the court to order restitution of conjugal rights had been rendered toothless by the Court of Appeal's decision. But neither could he move on with his life, by divorcing and marrying someone else. He was trapped in a marriage but at the same time forced to live as a bachelor by a wife who refused to honour her wedding vows. Women were now apparently free to leave a marriage whenever they liked but, provided that they had not been unfaithful, their husband was powerless to seek either a reconciliation or a renunciation.

The controversial question of what circumstances were sufficiently serious to bring about an end to the sacred bond of marriage had troubled Britain throughout the nineteenth century. The chequered legal history of divorce – in particular the difficulties that women faced in obtaining one, even into modern times – is a story of one law for the rich, another for the poor, but also of the same law operating in very different ways for husbands and wives.

PART II

FOR BETTER, FOR WORSE

CHAPTER FOUR

LOT 29

The marketplace at Belper was bustling on a sunny morning in 1873. Farmers had chained up their cows to the railings outside the pubs that lined the steep square, high on the hill-side at the top of the Derbyshire town. Among the stalls, one man stood in front of a rather forlorn pile of belongings: a couple of chairs, some clothing and shoes, plates and cutlery. He called for offers on the items, which were the only known property of a local man who had fled the town for America, to escape his creditors. The man on the market was one of those owed money, and had cleared out the possessions from the debtor's cottage to try and recoup some of his money. A few people picked over the items, which were for the most part shabby and worn.

Then the market man bellowed across the square, 'Bring out Lot 29!' From the door of a pub down one of the narrow jitties that ran off the marketplace into the town below, another man emerged. He was holding a length of rope, the end of which was attached to a halter, such as might be placed on horses or cows to lead them to market. But the halter was around the waist of a young woman, who followed the man out of the shadows of the alley and into the marketplace. He proceeded to lead her on a slow procession over the cobbles and round the square, so that the people gathered there could get a good look. The other man stayed in the middle of the marketplace, calling out for bidders on the lot. She was the debtor's wife, left abandoned when he had skipped the town, and she was now offered for sale to discharge his indebtedness. She would make a fine wife, the man shouted. But the townsfolk of Belper were unmoved, and Lot 29 was not sold.

The Belper wife-sale of 1873 may well have been apocryphal; the reports of it all come several years after the alleged event and contain scant details of those involved. Neither the unfortunate wife nor the fugitive husband is even given a name. Nevertheless, the story is one of many that can be found in the news sheets of the late eighteenth and early nineteenth centuries, speaking to a rich tradition of 'wife-selling' in England's country towns and villages. While many stories have the whiff of folklore about them, there are some cases that were recorded in a more formal manner. In 1828, Charles and Mary Skinner together with a man named John Savage were indicted in Kent upon a charge that they did

> *unlawfully and immorally, amongst themselves, conspire, combine, confederate and agree together to bring into contempt the holy estate of matrimony, and the duties enjoined thereby, and to corrupt the morals of His Majesty's liege subjects, and to encourage a state of adultery, wickedness and debauchery.*

The accusation against them was that Charles had agreed to sell Mary to John Savage, the deal being done in the George and Dragon pub in the village of Tonbridge. The price agreed? A shilling and a pot of beer. All three were sent to prison for one month.

The local pub seems to have been a popular venue for wife-sales: an Axbridge man named Vowles sold his wife in the village hostelry for 5 shillings and a gallon of beer in the 1840s. In 1887, the Monmouthshire magistrates charged Evans Morgan for bigamy when his second wife discovered that his first was still alive. Evans's defence was that he had sold the first Mrs Morgan four years earlier for half a crown and a jar of ale, so considered himself free to marry again. The observance of certain formalities was believed to lend a legal gloss to the proceedings by many. When George Hitchinson sold his wife Elizabeth to Thomas Snape, in the market at Walsall in the Black Country in 1837, Snape and Elizabeth had in fact been living together for several years already. George believed he had complied with the necessary customs to make the sale valid, 'because he had brought her through a turnpike gate in a halter and had publicly sold her in the market before witnesses'.

Even as late as the end of the nineteenth century, cases were still being reported in a tone of moral panic in some newspapers. Following reports of a spate of sales in Sheffield and the towns surrounding the Peak District, the *Sheffield Evening Telegraph* noted that the practice had been thought to have died out, having been 'outrageously common among the humbler classes of the English people' during the Georgian era. Another press report, written in 1876 in the *Western Morning News*, suggested that the custom had emerged at the end of the Napoleonic Wars when many soldiers returned home to find that their wives had remarried, after hearing erroneous reports that they had been killed in action. It was believed that the practice of 'wife-selling' was adopted to regularise these new marriages after the fact. Such was the popular myth of the custom that Thomas Hardy included it in his novel *The Mayor of Casterbridge*, published in 1886. The story opens with the sale of Susan Henchard by her husband Michael, in a tent at a village fair in Wessex. The purchaser is a mysterious sailor, who buys Susan from Michael for five guineas.

The sales of husbands are a little harder to find, but there is a tantalising report from 1888 that indicates that they did indeed take place. According to the *York Herald*, an unnamed man left his wife in England to travel to Australia to make his fortune. While there, he met another woman who wished to marry him, and so she wrote to his wife back in England to negotiate a sale. The wife agreed a price of twenty pounds, a little over £1,500 in modern money. But the Australian bride drove a hard bargain: she had knocked the English wife down from a hundred pounds. The later fate of the couple was not recorded.

And so had Edmund Jackson belonged to what one newspaper termed 'the lower orders', he might have been able to avoid the quandary posed by the court's ruling on the abduction of his wife, and simply put her up for sale in Clitheroe marketplace. Instead, he was left with a marriage in name only that he was not able to terminate by divorce. The complex history of the legalities surrounding the end of a marriage is one reason why the habit of wife-selling may have in fact been more widespread than even the scandalised press reports of the late nineteenth century would have us believe.

The sale of a wife, on the open market or before the patrons of a hostelry, is the ultimate embodiment of the proprietary nature of marriage throughout most of the nineteenth century. The same logic that prevented a married woman from holding her own property conceptualised a wife as the chattel of a husband and therefore as eligible for sale as any of his other possessions. There was a vogue for tales of wife-selling that preoccupied the chattering classes of the late Victorian era, who seemed keen to dismiss the practice as the rustic custom of rude mechanicals. The smell of mown hay and foaming ale permeates the scene of the sale of Susan Henchard in *The Mayor of Casterbridge*; and there does seem to be a clear class divide in the reporting of stories in the press. Most take place in working-class areas, in the marketplaces of mill towns like Belper or the inns of poor rural villages up and down the country. In her treatise, Caroline Norton pitied the 'poorer classes' for their ignorance of the law and belief in the legitimacy of crude customs like wife-selling; but she did concede that it was no wonder given the complexities and inequities of the law of divorce in the nineteenth century. Why did people in these areas resort to selling their spouses like prize cattle? Or, if it was indeed more apocryphal than true, why did the Victorians so eagerly believe that they did? Like many urban legends, the stories of wife-selling speak to a wider truth about the difficulties in dissolving unhappy marriages for the vast majority of society for a long stretch of our history.

Tracing the law back to the saga of Henry VIII, Catherine of Aragon and the King's subsequent break from Rome, Caroline Norton had noted that 'out of that mass of sin, misery, struggle and lawless confusion, sprang the germ of our English form of divorce'. The legend of Henry's marital troubles has gone down in legal history as Caroline observed. But historian Antonia Fraser noted that, even before Henry, the English nobility had become relatively adept at 'the repudiation of a wife'. Catholicism held that marriage was a sacrament between husband and wife, indissoluble under – almost – any circumstances. The common, but unofficial, way of getting round this was to argue that the marriage itself had been invalid from the outset. As Fraser put it, in the absence of the death of an inconvenient spouse, efforts would turn to 'discover[ing] some flaw in the original marriage contract. Some awkward affinity,* some hitherto unsuspected precontract, some incorrectly framed dispensation sufficed to end the unwelcome union.'

This same method was employed by Henry VIII when he tired of Catherine of Aragon and their son-less marriage in the 1520s. Before becoming Henry's queen, the teenage Catherine had first been married to his brother Arthur, who died aged just 15. Henry had subsequently married Catherine in 1509. Almost two decades later, he decided that the act of marrying his brother's widow had in fact contravened the laws of reli-

* Meaning here a familial relationship between the spouses.

gion, as proven by the fact that God had not blessed the King with a son. He sought confirmation from Rome that this was the case, meaning that his marriage to Catherine would be invalid and he would be free to marry Anne Boleyn. The infamous wrangling over the royal marriage lasted several years and led ultimately to Henry's break from Rome when he was not granted the declarations he sought. In 1533, Archbishop Thomas Cranmer pronounced that the marriage between Henry and Catherine was not – and had never been – valid under canon law. By this time, Henry had already married Anne and their daughter Elizabeth would be born a couple of months later. Pope Clement VII's later ruling in favour of Catherine (who maintained that she was the true wife of the King) became moot when Henry enacted the Acts of Supremacy and of Succession. These laws made the King head of the new Church of England and confirmed the place of his children with Anne in the line of Tudor succession.

Henry's second divorce, from Anne of Cleves in 1540, was far more straightforward. This was due in no small part to Anne's willingness to acquiesce to the demands of her husband of barely six months. Of course by this time Henry had no need to seek papal approval. A panel of clergy declared the marriage void on the grounds of non-consummation and also duress on the part of Thomas Cromwell, who had brokered the wedding before falling from Henry's favour. Henry was once again free to re-marry, this time to Catherine Howard. A further change in the law was passed at this time, decreeing that a consummated marriage would always take precedence over an earlier unconsummated attachment. This ensured that there could be no doubt that the King's enthusiastically consummated marriage to Catherine was lawful, as opposed to his earlier – and strictly platonic – union with Anne.

'Divorced, beheaded, died, divorced, beheaded, survived' goes the rhyme that commemorates all six of Henry's unfortunate wives, but it is not strictly correct. The King's separations from his first and third spouses were not divorces in the modern sense of the word or the law. They were in reality annulments, voiding the first wedding in order to validate the next. The sacrament of marriage did not need to be dissolved if it was found to have never actually been entered into in the first place. His divorces from Catherine of Aragon and Anne of Cleves did not represent a termination of the marriages but rather a legal fiction that they had never in fact taken place. But as the law inched closer to recognising the concept of divorce, it would remain fit only for a King for a long time to come.

Nevertheless, in the wake of the Reformation, English law began to make glacial progress in moving away from the Roman Catholic conception of marriage as an indissoluble sacrament. Shortly after Henry's break from Rome, a committee of sixteen lawyers and sixteen clerics was established to inquire into those areas of the law that fell under the jurisdiction of the Church and how they might be adapted for the new religious landscape. The committee proposed a remarkably liberal reinterpretation of the legal concept of divorce, which the Church had hitherto only contemplated as a theoretical possibility in cases of adultery. The committee recommended that divorce be granted in much wider circumstance, such as desertion or cruelty.

These proposals were not brought into the law, but they did encourage an increasing awareness of divorce as at least a possibility. In the seventeenth century, a handful of lords and nobles brought forward claims for marital separation in the church courts, and from the early eighteenth century, there was a gradual move towards secularisation of divorce, albeit one of limited effect. While Henry VIII had opened the door to divorce, the English judiciary and legislature were in no rush to go through with it. There were philosophical questions around what the term even meant, as the ecclesiastical courts recognised two categories of separation. *Divorce a mensa et thoro* (literally 'from bed and board') was more commonly granted, and was in effect a judicial separation, releasing spouses from their matrimonial obligations, including co-habitation. But crucially it did not dissolve the marriage tie and leave the spouses free to get married to other people. In order to re-marry, a *divorce a vinculo matrimonii* ('from the bonds of marriage') was required; and the religious courts were very reluctant to grant these.

But from the eighteenth century onwards, the number of divorces granted in England grew steadily, albeit from a tiny base, as the law became increasingly willing to recognise the concept. The lesser category of *divorce a mensa et thoro*, akin to a judicially ordered separation, was granted in a wider range of circumstances than a full *divorce a vinculo matrimonii*, which was only permitted when adultery was proven. At the same time, the courts were also acknowledging the idea of ill-treatment as a ground to permit couples to separate from each other. A succession of bleak trials weighed the level of abuse that was determined to be sufficient to release a spouse from their marital obligations. Husbands and wives could petition for a separation on the basis of the other's cruelty, but it was most commonly wives that sought divorces on this basis. When statutory reform to divorce was made in the Victorian era, the historic concept of spousal cruelty as a ground for separation was carried through into the new law; but it was expressly applied to wives only this time. Women seeking a full divorce had to prove both their husband's adultery and an additional aggravating factor, one of which was cruelty. The application of this aspect of the new divorce law would therefore have a significant impact on the position of women trapped in abusive marriages and how far the law would assist them in escaping. As late as the very close of the nineteenth century, the law of divorce was still heavily weighted in favour of husbands against wives. This was not limited by class.

In the aftermath of George Norton's action for crim con, for instance, Caroline sought advice from lawyers on whether her husband's treatment of her entitled her to divorce him. She listed the instances of violence, abuse and his false accusations of her infidelity with Melbourne. But her lawyers were adamant. Cruelty alone was not sufficient to fully dissolve the marriage and, in any case, Caroline's own conduct would be taken into account by the court. While she had left the marital home for periods of time, she had returned. In the court's eyes, this suggested that she had forgiven or even condoned George's assaults and so would nullify any case for a separation based on cruelty.

So the law as it stood in the middle of the nineteenth century left many wives in an invidious position. In effect, they were barred from seeking a full divorce by the arcane and expensive process that, as we shall see, required multiple court judgments and a ruling from the House of Lords. A husband's abuse might give them a right to a separation, but this was very much a question of fact and degree. If a wife fled the marriage, then she risked being ordered to return under a decree for restitution of conjugal rights. But if she stayed with a violent spouse, she risked a court concluding that she had acquiesced to or even forgiven her treatment.

The roots of the nineteenth-century law of cruelty lay in the 1790 case of *Evans v. Evans*, an unusually full and detailed consideration of a miserable Georgian marriage and what went on within it. Evans was working for the governor-general of Calcutta* when Miss Webb visited the city to stay with friends. They were introduced by friends and after a brief courtship married in 1778. In the early 1780s, Mrs Evans returned to live in England for a few years, ostensibly for health reasons. Her husband remained in India, where she rejoined him in 1785. Two years after that, they embarked together on the six-month voyage to return to England together, this time for good.

It was on the passage from India that things began to go wrong between the couple. Mrs Evans had remained in a delicate state of health throughout her married life and the long sea trip did not agree with her. She was accompanied by a

* Now Kolkata.

friend named Mrs Hartle who was to observe the discord between the couple at first hand. Mr Evans refused to open the windows and doors of their cabins to allow fresh air in. One afternoon, as her husband sat reading with his legs propped up on a table in an attitude of relaxation, Mrs Evans herself got up and strode to the door to open it. Without saying a word, her husband threw down his book, jumped to his feet and 'with savage fierceness, seized her by both her arms, and, in great rage, with his utmost force and violence, threw her down three times ... and thereby very much hurt and bruised her, put her to great pain and anguish, and increased her illness'. Shortly afterwards, while she was still suffering from the effects of this attack, he again threw her across the cabin while she was trying to get into bed. He left her lying on the floor and returned to his adjacent cabin, shouting oaths and abuse at her through the thin wooden partition between the cabins.

By the time the voyage ended, Mrs Evans had discovered that she was pregnant. Upon their arrival in England, they took a house in Bond Street, where Evans's behaviour towards his wife deteriorated even further. In January 1788, the climax of his alleged cruelty to his wife occurred. She went into labour seven months into her pregnancy. He claimed to friends that it was brought on by a fall when they were on their way to a ball; she later attributed it to the stress of living with her husband and his abuse towards her. Mrs Evans's friend, who was with her at the time, claimed that Evans refused to call a doctor for her until it was almost too late and throughout her ordeal showed a callous disregard for the lives of both his wife and child.*

Throughout their time in Bond Street, the marriage remained abusive. The most disturbing account of Evans's violence towards his wife was recounted in graphic detail by the judge at the later divorce trial. As the couple lay in bed one night, Mr Evans started to quarrel and shout at this wife, and then

> *with great force and violence seized her, and dragged her to every part of the bed; beat her head against each of the bed-posts, and twisted, distorted, forced her limbs to so violent a degree, that he brought her feet close up to her mouth; in which condition she swooned away; and in that helpless state, after giving her several dreadful blows and kicks, which caused the blood to issue from her mouth and other parts of her body, he turned her out of bed naked on the floor.*

When Mrs Evans's maids, alerted by the commotion in the bedroom, came to her aid, she was barely conscious.

There were other accounts of violence, including one apparently witnessed by several friends, when Mr Evans knocked his wife to the floor during a card party at their new home in Conduit Street. Various members of their respective families counselled them to separate but Mrs Evans steadfastly refused to leave her husband. But shortly before Christmas of 1788,

* The fate of the baby is unclear. Some accounts describe Mrs Evans giving birth prematurely, others refer to her suffering a 'miscarriage'.

Evans left the couple's home insisting that he would not return. He took their eldest daughter with him and wrote to his wife shortly afterwards, offering to give her a settlement of £500 per year. Rejecting this, Mrs Evans sought a formal divorce and, with it, a hopefully higher amount of maintenance from her husband.

The job of the court in the case was to decide firstly if Mrs Evans's allegations of violence from her husband were true and, if they were, assess whether this behaviour was sufficient to entitle her to divorce him. The judgment delivered by Sir William Scott in the case was an uncompromising one. He rejected almost all of Mrs Evans's allegations, including those supported by the eyewitness testimony of her friends and servants. He questioned why, after witnessing the assault on board the ship from India, Mrs Hartle had failed to immediately seek assistance from the ship's crew. The attack in the bedroom in Conduit Street could, concluded the judge, have actually been a fall or even an invention by Mrs Evans. The entire story of cruelty was, in the judge's final analysis

> *an history very heavy and formidable in its commencement, whilst it rests in mere allegation; but which grows weaker and more insignificant every step as it advances towards proof … I therefore full exculpate [Mr Evans] from that charge of unmanly cruelty, which is founded upon these facts; and I do very sincerely regret that, under any advice, this poor lady should have preferred so black an accusation against her husband, and one so totally destitute of all reasonable colour.*

The judge's assessment of the sad story of the Evans's marriage and his broad statements around the reluctance of the law to intervene in the marriage bond other than in the gravest of circumstances would colour the attitude of the courts towards wives, divorce and cruelty for several generations to come. The high threshold set by the case, particularly that a wife must be able to demonstrate beyond all doubt her own physical peril if she remained in the marriage, not only influenced the law of divorce but also contemporary attitudes to domestic violence, setting a baseline of mistreatment that women should expect within an abusive marriage. This in turn bled into further laws around assault and violence that, as we shall see, disproportionately affected women.

CHAPTER FIVE

PAINS AND PENALTIES

Although the law grudgingly granted divorces in the centuries after the Reformation, it made the process highly convoluted and accessible to very few. Men seeking to end a marriage – and it was virtually exclusively husbands at this time – were required to obtain orders confirming that adultery had occurred from both the common law and ecclesiastical courts in order to initiate a separation. Following this a divorce could only be granted by the House of Lords through the enactment of an individual Act of Parliament. Every divorce in the country therefore required its own piece of legislation, placing it beyond the reach and means of all but the highest echelons of society.

The ability of ordinary citizens to avail themselves of this process in order to terminate their marriages was of course extremely limited. But over the course of the 1700s and early 1800s the practice grew steadily. From just five divorces being recorded prior to the accession of the Hanoverians, a total of ninety divorces were recorded over the thirty years between 1800 and 1830. It can be difficult to pin down figures for divorces as the quoted numbers vary according to the sources quoting them. But it is a safe assumption that the number of divorces remained in the low three figures for the entire country over this period.

The most notorious – although ultimately unsuccessful – of these 'divorce acts' related to another royal scandal, this time one concerning the marriage of the future King George IV and his wife, Princess Caroline of Brunswick. Like her predecessor Catherine of Aragon, Caroline was to find herself at the centre of a legal battle over her marriage and her royal status, all at the instigation of her husband. The royal couple had married in 1795 and their daughter Charlotte was born the following January. By 1797, they had separated and had remained estranged for several years. But a decade before his wedding to Caroline, George had already been through a secret wedding ceremony with the widowed Maria Fitzherbert, several years his senior. Without his father's consent, the authorities deemed to the marriage to be invalid and saw no bar to his subsequent wedding to Caroline.

When George ascended the throne in 1820 Caroline swiftly made plans to return from her exile in Europe, planning to take her place as Queen beside her estranged husband. But George had other ideas. He demanded that the cabinet allow him to divorce Caroline. In February of 1820, Henry Banks MP observed:

> *His present Majesty ... is most firmly bent on a divorce from his odious and infamous consort. This ... is natural enough for him to wish, but as those who must carry his project into effect very naturally cast about and calculate their means,*

his Ministers report to him unanimously that it is not feasible, and neither can nor ought to be attempted.

In early June of 1820, Caroline landed once again on English soil; *The Times* compared her arrival to that of William the Conqueror. It was said that Londoners placed lighted candles in their windows to illuminate their houses in support of the returning Queen Consort. It was said that when her barge sailed down the Thames 200,000 people crammed onto Blackfriars Bridge to cheer her. But behind the scenes, the new King was continuing his machinations to end the marriage. He threatened to dismiss the entire government and appoint a new one more sympathetic to his marital woes. In the summer of 1820, the cabinet finally caved and brought forward:

*An Act to deprive Her Majesty Caroline Amelia Elizabeth of the Title, Prerogatives, Rights, Privileges and Exemptions of Queen Consort of this Realm; and to dissolve the Marriage between His Majesty and the said Caroline Amelia Elizabeth.**

The only possible ground on which George could be granted a divorce was Caroline's infidelity. The parliamentary debates of the act were to become in effect a trial of Caroline, of her character, her conduct and her relationships since she had left England. For her part, the Queen Consort vehemently denied the allegations against her, aside from admitting in an arch reference to George's own chequered romantic history that 'it

* Often known by its shorter title 'The Pains and Penalties Bill 1820'.

is true she did commit adultery once, but it was with the Husband of Mrs Fitzherbert'.

To determine whether the bill should be passed, the Lords had to establish the truth of the allegations contained within it. Witnesses were brought from all over Europe to testify in front of a committee of Lords gathered to debate and test the accusations set forth in George's bill. Caroline attended each day of the debate with her lawyers, and passed the time by playing backgammon as she listened to the lurid stories presented against her. She had spent the years following her separation from George on a grand tour of Europe, travelling extensively over sea and land. She had sailed around the Mediterranean and visited the grandest palaces of Italy and Central Europe. The allegations made against her by her husband centred on her relationship with her Italian servant, Bartolomeo Pergami, who had accompanied her on many of her travels, during which the 'most unbecoming and degrading intimacy' had allegedly developed between them.

A succession of servants, innkeepers and other witnesses were brought halfway across Europe to give evidence of their observations of Caroline and Pergami on their travels around the continent over several years. Some of their testimony was more compromising than completely damning. Paolo Raggazoni, a stonemason at the Villa d'Este – Caroline's home on the banks of Lake Como – told of seeing the couple in a grotto in the grounds of the Villa. He watched Caroline and Pergami inspecting statues of Adam and Eve, before they both peeped under the carvings' fig leaves and giggled. Another servant reported an evening where Bartolomeo dressed in a

Turkish costume for the Queen's amusement. His outfit included a roll of wadding pushed down the front of his trousers, which 'he took ... in his hand and made gesticulations', much to Caroline's delight.

But, salacious as this innuendo was, it was not sufficient to prove adultery on Caroline's part. For that, the government needed even more lurid eyewitness accounts. They summoned Pietro Cuchi, owner of Le Burgo Grande Inn in Trieste, where Caroline and her party had stayed briefly in 1816. The curious Cuchi had peeped through the keyhole into Caroline's suite one morning and claimed to have seen Pergami leaving the Queen's bedroom. He also reported that two chamber pots had been used in Caroline's bedroom, while Pergami's bed did not appear to have been slept in. A maid at the Post Inn in the German town of Karlsruhe blushingly testified to finding certain stains on the bedsheets in Pergami's room. Giuseppe Restelli, the stable master at Villa d'Este, gave an even more damning statement to Parliament in his testimony. He said that he had caught Caroline with her hand in Pergami's 'small-clothes' during a carriage ride.

But the MPs and Lords did remain cognisant of the public support for Caroline which continued to grow as the 'trial' progressed, stoked by the fortitude with which the Queen bore the indignities of the evidence given against her. George himself was not universally liked and there was public discontent at his treatment of his wife and his hypocrisy in seeking the divorce, given his own relationship with Mrs Fitzherbert. 'On every count – deception, betrayal, abandonment, rejection and hatred – Caroline was a wronged woman whose plight sounded a chord of alarm and concern in the breast of every wife in the Kingdom.' With each reading, the bill's majority reduced and eventually, in November of 1820, the government withdrew it entirely. George would not be given his divorce. On hearing of this, it was said that audiences in the theatres of Covent Garden burst into cries of 'God Save the Queen'. On 29 November, a service of thanksgiving for Caroline was held at St Paul's Cathedral and it was said that the streets were lined with cheering crowds who had turned out to see her de facto coronation. But when George's actual coronation – which had to be postponed by a year while the trial of his wife was ongoing – took place at Westminster Abbey, things had changed. Caroline was officially barred from attending and what followed was something of a pathetic sight:

> *The spectacle of the Queen, refused admittance to the abbey, running from one door to another in a vain attempt to gain entrance, aroused the derision, rather than the sympathy of the crowd which only seven months before had hailed her triumph over the King.*

She was taken ill the following day and less than a month after her humiliation on the steps of Westminster Abbey, Queen Caroline died aged just fifty-three. Some historians have suggested that it was the ordeal at her husband's coronation that killed her. Nevertheless, she died still George's wife and Queen of England. Death had done what the English law could not, and granted the King his final separation from his wife.

* * *

George and Caroline were not representative of the average married couple experiencing nuptial disharmony in the early nineteenth century. But the story of their battles and the ultimately unsuccessful lengths George went to in order to dissolve their union illustrates the law's fundamental problems with the concept of divorce at that time. Caroline had no standing to bring the marriage to an end herself, and even the King himself was unable to terminate his marriage if his government did not support him. It would take another three decades before the law finally began to address these difficulties.

When George's niece Victoria came to the throne in 1837, calls for reform were growing. By the middle of the nineteenth century, various committees and commissions had been appointed by the government to examine the issue of divorce in English law. While it had been possible – in theory – to divorce in England since the mid-sixteenth century, the reality was very different for most of the population. Caroline Norton had attacked the hypocrisy inherent in the law of divorce as it stood three hundred years after Henry VIII had secured his divorce from Catherine of Aragon:

> *It [marriage] is besides – practically – a sacrament for the poor and a civil contract for the rich: as the rich break it by application to Parliament; and the poor are frequently put on trial for bigamy from not being able to go through that expensive form. It is – practically – a sacrament for the wife, and a civil contract for the husband; the husband can break*

it almost as a matter of course, on proof of the wife's infidelity; the wife, though nominally able to apply for a divorce, seldom or ever obtains one: I believe there are but three cases of record in the House of Lords, of marriages broken on the wife's petition.

Two bills had been put before Parliament proposing an overhaul of the law during this period, but had not been passed. Finally, in 1857, the Divorce and Matrimonial Causes Bill managed to make further progress through both the House of Commons and House of Lords, and was finally passed. England had its first secular law of divorce.

The Divorce and Matrimonial Causes Act was a milestone in many ways. It marked a philosophical shift in the perception of marriage, by society, the state and the church. Marriage itself was moving from a religious conception of a sacred sacrament between a couple dissolvable only by God to something more akin to a contract. This view posited a wedding as a transaction between a couple, with rights and obligations on both sides. If those terms were not upheld, by one party or both, then the law would now step in to terminate the matrimonial contract as it would any other commercial agreement. This change was fundamental and a long time coming, but the legislation itself did not necessarily go as far as first appeared.

The act created a new Court of Divorce and Matrimonial Causes in London which would take over conduct of marital disputes from the church courts and would have ultimate jurisdiction over all divorce cases. It was England's first secular divorce court and nullified the need to seek parliamentary approval for individual divorces. But how easy was it to obtain a separation from the new court? The fundamental legal basis for divorce remained in line with its biblical roots; adultery was the only ground on which a spouse could petition for divorce. But while a wife's adultery gave a husband an absolute right to a divorce, a wife's ability to seek a separation was qualified. Wives were required to prove an additional element of fault on the part of a husband in order to be granted a divorce. The infidelity itself must have been accompanied by an aggravating factor, such as bigamy, desertion or, most notoriously, cruelty.

When introducing the legislation, the Lord Chancellor acknowledged the prima facia hypocrisy in making such a distinction between spouses, but explained it away thus:

> *If adultery on the part of the husband is to entitle him to a divorce, inasmuch as the husband – which may be bad morality but it is the fact – suffers little on that account in the opinion of the world at large – for it is notorious that, while the wife who also commits adultery loses her station in society, the same punishment is not awarded to the husband who is guilty of the same crime – he may, without any great sacrifice, on his own part, but merely by being a little profligate, and multiplying his acts of adultery, be able to effect his object.*

In other words, men were more likely to stray and making a divorce too easy for a cheated wife to obtain might encourage husbands to do so repeatedly, in the hope that it would bring about an end to the marriage with little inconvenience to them. But in practice, this codified a sexual and moral double standard that had long lurked in the background of debates around marriage and women's role within it. Sexual infidelity by a wife was sufficiently fatal to the marriage tie on its own, whereas a straying husband must be guilty of something more. This was often explained as the 'difference between a lapse and a fall'.

Indeed, a close reading of the House of Lords debates on the divorce legislation reveals the faux naivety of the government's position. There was serious consideration given to an amendment which would have barred a woman found to have committed adultery from re-marrying after divorce – with no like prohibition for husbands. In support of this, the Bishop of Oxford commented that allowing a woman to re-marry in such circumstances would mean 'she would suffer no loss of caste whatever. The law would leave no check whatever upon the woman and the most unbridled licentiousness would prevail among the lower classes.' Such an allowance would, railed the Bishop, put the law of England on a direct collision course with the law of Christ. And the cleric was not saying anything revolutionary.

In a conversation with his friend and biographer James Boswell back in 1779, Dr Samuel Johnson had summed up the prevailing attitudes that were still informing the law almost a century later. Boswell, himself no paragon of marital virtue, had put the issue of adultery within marriage to Johnson and was rewarded with the anticipated bon mots, which were still being quoted in the parliamentary debates around the Matrimonial Causes Act in the middle of the nineteenth century:

> *I mentioned to him a dispute between a friend of mine and his lady, concerning conjugal infidelity, which my friend had maintained was by no means so bad in the husband as in the wife. JOHNSON: 'Your friend was in the right, Sir. Between a man and his Maker it is a different question: but between a man and his wife, a husband's infidelity is nothing. They are connected by children, by fortune, by serious considerations of community. Wise married women don't trouble themselves about infidelity in their husbands.' BOSWELL: 'To be sure there is a great difference between the offence of infidelity in a man and that of this wife.' JOHNSON: 'The difference is boundless. The man imposes no bastards upon his wife.'*

This double standard pervaded the legislation in other forms as well, even procedural. In a divorce suit brought by a husband, the act required the naming of co-respondents – those with whom the wife was alleged to have committed adultery. This was so that the husband could recover financial damages from those named, for interference with his marital property. In effect, this aspect of the legislation preserved the action of 'criminal conversation' that had dogged Caroline Norton and Lord Melbourne in the 1830s. There was no like requirement for a wife's divorce petition to name those with whom her husband had been unfaithful, again reflecting the Johnsonian view of men merely lapsing, while women irredeemably fell.

The fact that sales of wives were occurring – or at least were being reported – well after the Divorce and Matrimonial Causes Act had been passed in the 1850s illustrates the difficulties that huge sections of society still faced in accessing divorce, even after an apparently momentous change in the law. In practical terms, it was still only available to those who could afford both the legal fees and the travel to London to visit the only court in the country with jurisdiction to hear the cases. Even for those who could pay, the new laws ensured that divorces were granted only in very limited circumstances.

The religious origins of the legalities of marriage and divorce cast a long shadow over English law that has barely begun to lift even now. The belief in the legitimacy of wife-selling in the eighteenth and nineteenth centuries, provided that certain rituals were followed, has an almost ecclesiastical feel to it. Indeed this blend of law and lore seems unique in how it attached itself to the governance of relationships and sexual behaviour. The biblical roots of adultery as the supreme sin of a wife was of course reinforced by the law itself, even as it made apparent progress in the second half of the nineteenth century. There remained a communal – and community – interest in the most intimate of relationships. The people of Clitheroe took to the streets in their hundreds to demonstrate against Emily Jackson when she returned to the town after the outcome of the court case arising from her abduction. This 'rough music' was a form of community justice, condemning her for her unwifely conduct even after the court had sided with her and ordered her husband to release her. It had a long ancestry in the towns and villages of Britain which even the rapid urbanisation of the Victorian era had not entirely eradicated.

Furthermore, a woman's inconstancy was still viewed in almost biblical terms, even as the law began to shift. As late as 1852, villagers in the small parish of Amroth in the far west of Wales took matters into their own hands when a local governess was caught in an affair with her employer. She was strapped to a wooden ladder and carried around the village by a gang of masked men, to the hoots and jeers of an assembled crowd. This custom of '*y ceffyl pren*' ('the wooden horse') was an ancient form of community justice that illuminated the prevailing attitudes.

In making the concept of cruelty central to a wife's right to obtain a divorce, the act was similarly codifying another long-standing legal tradition. The lesser category of *divorce a mensa et thoro* did not cleave so heavily to the biblical teachings on adultery, and separations were ordered on other grounds. In these cases a husband's behaviour towards his wife was a recurring theme and while it was not considered sufficient to dissolve their union altogether, it could be adequate reason to absolve her of the rest of the duties inherent in a marriage. The ecclesiastical courts had previously granted these divorces where a wife could establish a case of ill-treatment by her husband. How would the question of determining the level of cruelty sufficient to fully dissolve a marriage be approached by the courts now that a secular law of divorce had been created?

CHAPTER SIX

SAEVITIA

The photographer made a few adjustments to the hanging draped across the back of his little studio, painted to look like a wooded glade. A shaggy green carpet, roughed up and shaken out, represented the heathland grass. Happy with his *mise en scène*, he inspected his camera plates and wiped the lens. Just then, the studio door opened and his subjects came in. Two men and a woman, all rather theatrically attired. The photography session had been booked to take publicity pictures for a new production of *The Runaway Girl*, a musical comedy that was touring provincial theatres under the watchful eye of West End impresario George Edwardes.

The taller of the young men was dressed as an Englishman at leisure, in a double-breasted suit and with a boater perched on his head. The other was shorter, dressed in breeches that were just a little too wide, tucked into tall leather boots. He wore a rounded jockey's cap and an oversized jacket. The third member of the trio was a dark-eyed young woman, dressed in a romantic version of a peasant's costume. She wore a white blouse with a smock front, tucked into an impossibly tight black girdle. Her skirt was long and patterned with colourful stripes and her dark hair was crowned with a rustic headdress. The three actors struck their poses: the gentleman upright, the jockey with a hapless expression, the peasant girl winsome. They held them stiffly for the slow seconds after the camera's flash while the plate was exposed. At the signal from the photographer, they relaxed in giggling exhalation.

The photographs were splashed across the papers as the cast headed out on tour to packed theatres in Plymouth, Birmingham and Blackpool in the spring of 1901. It was the peasant girl that the audience were most eager to see and she was credited in the play's programme under her full title of Mabel, Countess Russell. Mabel was accompanied on the tour by her mother Lady Scott, who seemed to have no misgivings about putting her daughter on the stage. When local press came to interview the countess in her hotel rooms up and down the country, Lady Scott was always present, interjecting to answer questions put to her daughter when she felt it necessary.

In an interview with a London journalist, the countess explained why she had taken up a theatrical career:

> *I want to start life afresh … I desire nothing more than that all the past and its bickerings may be clean forgotten by the world. I have no wish to fight for my rights against my husband. I don't want to say anything at all about past things. I bear my husband no ill will for all that has gone; I hope he bears me none … As I want to be independent, I must maintain myself, and to do this I am going on the stage.*

The 'bickerings' with her husband to which Mabel had referred were part of the reason that George Edwardes had hired her to perform in the first place. For the Russells had been involved in one of the most high-profile divorce cases of the day. Her marital breakdown had made Mabel notorious; and in order to support herself and her mother, she had no alternative but to cash in on her fleeting celebrity and accept Edwardes' offer to join his touring company. He knew that the countess's appearance in his shows would draw a curious crowd wherever they played. But Mabel's new career was more than just a means of securing her financial position. It was an attempt to draw a line under a difficult period for both her and her mother.

Mabel's disastrous marriage had ended in a scandalous legal battle that had gone on for several years. It had outraged polite society, exposed her to opprobrium and financial jeopardy; she had been stalked by a serial killer and her patrician mother had found herself standing in the dock of the Old Bailey facing criminal charges. Mabel herself had ended up at the heart of a complex legal saga, a microcosmic study of the complexities and contradictions that had plagued the law of divorce until remarkably recent times. Around the blushing countess swirled a maelstrom of double standards and shifting precedents that illustrate the law's own complex relationship with matrimonial separation. In pursuing her suits against her estranged husband for such a long time, her story became something of an allegory for the protracted and complex history of the law of divorce itself.

Mabel Edith Russell, née Scott, had married John, Earl Russell in 1890. The Earl was a couple of years older than

Mabel, a 'tall, stout, fair-haired, fresh-coloured, spectacled young peer'. The Russells were a noble but not especially wealthy dynasty. When John had been sent down from Oxford, he had established his own electrical engineering business. His interests were perhaps a little more eccentric than the average aristocrat: he was fascinated by the new technology of the railways and campaigned for passengers' rights against the railway companies. He had also been a practising Buddhist while at Oxford; his younger brother Bertrand was of an even more philosophical bent.

The couple made their home on Eaton Square in the heart of Belgravia. But behind the closed doors of the Russells' white stucco townhouse, all was not well. When the new Countess Russell was taken ill on their honeymoon on the south coast, her husband refused to curtail their plans and insisted upon her leaving her sick bed and driving around the highways and byways with him at speed in their carriage. Back home, his behaviour towards her grew increasingly unsympathetic. In general conversation he was abrupt or simply downright rude towards her. He would insist on Mabel carrying out pointless, demoralising tasks, seemingly for his own entertainment; he would make her stand next to his desk and watch while he spent hours writing up his business accounts and, on one occasion, sent her into the house's wine cellar to count the bottles. Despite the several servants in the couple's employ, he insisted that she 'perform a distasteful duty in connection with the outhouses every morning'.

Lord Russell's belligerence was not confined to his wife.

It seemed also that he was in the habit of using cruelty to the cats kept in the house. He would drag them about by strings fastened around their necks. He threw one of them up against the ceiling a number of times until the poor beast was half killed. When [Lady Russell] remonstrated, he told her it was necessary to 'lick the cat into shape' and that he would do the same thing to her and lick her into shape too.

Within weeks of their wedding, the relationship had deteriorated beyond redemption. Earl Russell's insults towards his wife had taken a darker turn. In one row, he called her a 'beastly barren woman ... [and said] he would like to see her carried out in her coffin from his door'. Another argument in April of 1890 turned violent when he threw Lady Russell to the floor. He then went hunting round the house for his pistol, shouting that he would shoot either her or himself, he didn't much care which.

Lady Scott was a frequent visitor to her daughter and son-in-law. She was protective of Mabel, who had always been known as 'Baby' in the family. To one friend, the Earl 'complained bitterly of suffering from too much mother-in-law'. But Mabel had her own misgivings about her husband's associates as well. She was unhappy at his close relationship with his friend Herbert Roberts. Russell and Roberts had known each other for several years and Roberts was a junior mathematics master at Bath College. Roberts was a regular houseguest at Eaton Square and Mabel was unhappy at her exclusion from her husband's company when he was staying.

Her husband frequently left the marital bed to sit with Roberts in his bedroom, talking until the early hours of the morning. Mabel's suspicions were aroused.

By June, after less than six months of marriage, she left Eaton Square for the last time and returned to live with her mother at Walton. The couple remained estranged for over a year until late 1891, when the countess decided to take steps to end the marriage formally. She would have had no way of knowing at the time, but she was about to embark on a process that would drag her name and her marriage through the courts and the papers for years to come.

In early December, the case came on for hearing at the Divorce and Matrimonial Causes Court within the Royal Courts of Justice building on the Strand. Divorce cases were heard before a jury at that time and Countess Russell tearfully related her tale of marital woe from the witness box. The allegations of her husband's physical abuse and even death threats did not excite much reaction from the impassive jurors, but it was when the lawyers probed her insinuations about her husband and Herbert Roberts that their ears really pricked up. After Mabel had tiptoed around the precise nature of her complaint about their friendship for some time, the barrister became exasperated. 'Do you wish to make a charge against Mr Roberts?' he pressed. The countess looked down and replied, 'I do not wish to make a charge unless I am driven to it.' She paused and looked up with a steady gaze across the court at her husband. 'Still, I know my own mind on the subject.' The barrister asked again if she wished to make any specific allegation against her husband's close friend. After a pause of some moments, during which there was a pin-drop silence in the courtroom, Mabel answered in the affirmative. The hush of the court was replaced by politely appalled gasps and mutterings. This time, she did not meet her husband's eyes, now blazing, across the well of the court.

Earl Russell had every reason to be furious at his wife's statement to the court. The implication, while unspoken, was clear; hence the gasps of shock from those watching the proceedings in the courtroom. The suggestion that there was more to his relationship with Roberts exposed both men to considerable legal peril. Just six years earlier, Parliament had passed the Criminal Law Amendment Act. This legislation was sub-titled 'an Act to make further provision for the Protection of Women and Girls' and most of its clauses were aimed at preventing the sexual exploitation of young women. The new law included offences of unlawful carnal knowledge of girls between the ages of thirteen and sixteen, effectively raising the age of consent from the former to the latter. It also strengthened the laws against prostitution, criminalising the procurement of women into sex work and imposing harsh sentences on those who allowed their premises to be used for immoral purposes.

But hidden among the clauses relating to brothel-keeping, the age of consent and other sexual offences, was the notorious section eleven. Also known as the 'Labouchere Amendment', after the MP who introduced it into the draft legislation at the eleventh hour, it has gone down in legal history as the statutory provision that criminalised male homosexuality.* Section eleven of the act made it an offence for 'any male person who, in public or in private, [to] commit or [be] party to the commission of, or procure or attempt to procure the commission by any male person of any act of gross indecency with another male person'. The actual behaviour prohibited under the law was left undefined. What amounted to 'gross indecency' was therefore subject to wide interpretation. Unlike much of the criminal legislation around sex up to that point, which concentrated on activities in the public sphere, section eleven extended the law's reach into private spaces.

It is one of legal history's great ironies that a piece of legislation intended to protect women and girls from sexual exploitation is now most remembered – and reviled – for its treatment of men. And while a detailed discussion of this troubling area of the law is beyond the scope of this book, it illustrates the instinctive reaction to any sexual behaviour falling outside of the strict Victorian moral code. As we shall see, most often the burden of these laws fell on women; but men were not entirely immune from the worst effects of the moral panics and reform campaigns that dominated and influenced so much of the law at this time.

So Mabel's accusation against Roberts, made in open court, exposed both the mathematics master and Earl Russell to potential criminal investigation and charges. The young peer

* Henry Labouchere MP (1831–1912) proposed the new clause late into the night during a parliamentary debate and it survived when the bill was subsequently made law.

must have breathed a sigh of relief when the trial judge skated over the comments in his summing up of the case the jury. The countess' allegations against her husband, explained the judge, would certainly amount to marital cruelty such as to entitle her to a separation, but were subject to one important caveat. The jury must be persuaded that they were substantially true and not motivated by malice or embellished by hysteria.

After deliberating for just under an hour, the jurors returned to the courtroom with their decision. They rejected Mabel's allegations and acquitted John of all of the accusations of cruelty. Her petition for a separation was accordingly dismissed. The earl's friends and family who had gathered in the courtroom to support him cheered heartily and some of them reached over the benches to clap him on the back. As he walked out of the court building, passing under its Gothic entrance arch, he was astonished to see a crowd, numbering a couple of hundred people at least, gathered within the black railings that separated the court buildings from the pavement of the Strand. As he stepped into the low winter sunshine, the assembled throng burst into cheers and applause. A few people pushed forward to shake the earl's hand as he made his way towards a waiting cab.

In the aftermath of the hearing, the gossip pages of the newspapers speculated on the estranged couple's future. The earl of course had his business interests to occupy him; one paper suggested that the countess might retreat to Europe with her mother until things had died down, noting that 'this, of course, will only be a matter of months. Society forgives good-looking people very quickly.' But in the following summer, she would return to court in the most remarkable of circumstances.

In the spring of 1892, the countess received a rather strange letter. The writer accused her of attempting to poison Earl Russell in order to rid herself of him by different means following the failure of her divorce suit. The letter concluded with a threat to expose her attempt at murder to the public. At around the same time, her coachman also received a letter in the same hand making an even more disturbing allegation. This letter did not refer to Mabel but instead accused Earl Russell of the murder of a young woman named Ellen Donworth, who had been found dead in Lambeth a few months earlier. The earl had, said the letter, poisoned Ellen with strychnine. Both of the letters were signed Dr Thomas Neill. The identity of Neill and the source of his allegations against both the earl and countess were a mystery to them both. But all was revealed a few months later, when Mabel was called to give evidence at the coroner's inquest into the death of another young woman named Matilda Clover, who had also died from strychnine poisoning in Lambeth. The man accused of Matilda's murder was none other than Dr Thomas Neill, also known as Dr Thomas Neill Cream.

A Scot by birth, Cream had emigrated to Canada in his youth where he had studied medicine. Shortly after his marriage there, he had returned to Scotland to set up practice in Edinburgh, and thence to Chicago, from where he had returned just a matter of weeks before the poisoning deaths began in 1891. Rumours of the suspicious deaths suffered by several of his patients had dogged Cream throughout his medical career. His Canadian wife Flora had died after consuming some medicine that he had given her and, while he was working in Edinburgh, a female patient of his was found dead from a chloroform overdose; her body had been dumped behind a shed in the garden of the building in which he had his consulting rooms. In Chicago, he had abandoned all pretence of being a respectable doctor and had been working as an abortionist. He was acquitted of the murder of one young woman who had been found dead after visiting Cream for a procedure. But things finally caught up with him in 1881, when he was arrested for the murder of Daniel Stott. Cream was having an affair with Stott's wife Julia and persuaded her to administer some medication to her husband. When Stott subsequently developed symptoms of strychnine poisoning and died, Cream was accused and then convicted of his murder. He served just ten years in jail in Illinois and immediately upon his release in 1891 had come to London, going by the name of Dr Neill. Shortly after, the strychnine deaths in Lambeth had begun.

Dressed all in black and perturbed at having to sit in the waiting room with the disreputable denizens of the coroner's court, the countess's appearance added a dash of glamour to a case that the press had already christened 'the Lambeth poisonings'. She brusquely confirmed that she had received the letter from the doctor, condescended to deny his allegation that she had poisoned her husband and then demanded reimbursement of her train fare for attending the court. Why Cream had chosen to latch on to the Russells was never explained; their divorce case was featuring prominently in the national press around the time that he arrived in England and perhaps he hoped to muddy the waters by sending the press on a wild goose chase. But whatever his thinking, it was to no avail. He was tried and convicted of the murder of Matilda Clover and was hanged in November of 1892. The press interest in the Russells and their marriage, briefly revived by their cameo appearances in the Cream case, once again subsided.

For the next couple of years, the Russells remained estranged and apparently oblivious of each other. But in 1894, Mabel decided to re-litigate the issues in their marriage once again; which is when things became even more complicated. Like Edmund Jackson had done a couple of years earlier, as a precursor to his abduction of his wife, she commenced proceedings against her husband for restitution of conjugal rights, claiming that Earl Russell should be compelled to return to the marriage so that they could live as husband and wife. For his part, the earl believed that the new suit was nothing more than a ruse to pressure him into paying off his wife in order to avoid more negative publicity and salacious gossip. So he hatched a plan of his own. He brought a counter-suit against Mabel, claiming for a judicial separation on the grounds of *her* cruelty. The basis of his claim was her previous allegations, made at the first trial back in 1891. His wife's false accusation of his own cruelty and, more importantly, her outrageous allegation about his relationship with Herbert Roberts, were – in and of themselves – a form of cruelty towards him which should entitle him to a dissolution of the marriage.

* * *

The difficulties in dissolving a marriage, notwithstanding the progress that had been made in the nineteenth century to reform the law, meant that the case would rumble on for several years, through courts of appeal and of public opinion, both titillating and scandalising the social elite. The fact that the unhappy saga of the Russells' divorce lasted so much longer than the marriage that they were attempting to leave sums up many of the controversies around the law of divorce that dogged the government and the legal system through much of the nineteenth century.

But even following statutory reform, the law itself remained wedded to the intrinsic form of misfeasance at the heart of the necessity to end a marriage. Even now, the concept of a 'no fault' divorce attracts accolades and approbation in almost equal measure. Although on the face of it, the new legislation of 1857 made divorce much more accessible, in reality there were still significant disparities between the wealthy and the less well-off. The new divorce court established by the act was situated in London and was the only one in the country. Those without the means to travel to the capital to plead their cases before the matrimonial judges had no other way to avail themselves of the new law. This is evident from the case records of the latter half of the nineteenth century, from which it is clear that the overwhelming majority of parties in divorce cases were from the upper middle class and above. The aristocracy were habitual customers of the new court.

In the century or so between the divorce proceedings of the Evanses and the Russells, Parliament had apparently revolutionised the law of divorce. But the provisions of the

Matrimonial Causes Act expressly preserved the concept of cruelty by husbands towards wives as an essential requirement for a woman to obtain a divorce. Often referred to by the Latin term *saevitia*, meaning cruelty, the cases involving allegations of marital cruelty are some of the most controversial in this field of the law and, as we have seen, the debate about the type, nature and extent of behaviour that constituted it was still raging at the end of the nineteenth century. How to define the conduct that would amount to so-called 'legal cruelty' and – just as importantly – adjudge the extent of this conduct required to justify ending a marriage would preoccupy the new Divorce and Matrimonial Court for the remainder of a century.

A husband's adultery alone was insufficient; it must be combined with some form of mistreatment towards his wife. The court's decision in the Evans case therefore remained an important benchmark for judges to measure the level of cruelty they would deem sufficient to satisfy the threshold to secure a separation. The convoluted Russell saga – which had progressed all the way to the House of Lords, then the highest court in the land – gave an opportunity for the courts to reassess the concept of cruelty ready for the twentieth century.

By the time that the case reached the Law Lords, it was in fact Earl Russell that was seeking to rely on his wife's conduct as grounds for a separation, an unusual development in a divorce case at the time. Cruelty had long been seen as something inflicted by husbands upon their wives, rather than the other way around. The behaviour that he relied upon was so specific that it was unlikely to create any sort of precedent. It was her veiled accusation, made against him in her original petition to the court and almost dragged out of her by the questioning of the barrister, that he was engaged in a relationship with Herbert Roberts. This statement was damaging to both his reputation and freedom, carrying with it the risk of criminal investigation and even imprisonment. For his wife to make such an allegation and, crucially, doing so knowing it to be false, was an act of unspeakable cruelty to her husband. Countess Russell now found herself on the other side of the cruelty argument; from being told that her husband's abuse and violence towards her were insufficient to end their marriage, she was now compelled to defend herself against the same charge.

Among the complications of the Russells' suits, counter-suits and myriad accusations against each other, the key legal question that the House of Lords had to answer was the level of mistreatment that would entitle one spouse to a divorce from the other. Lord Herschell, one of the panel of judges convened to consider the case, observed that 'it is beyond controversy that it is not every act of cruelty in the ordinary and popular sense of the word which amounted to "*saevitia*", entitling the party aggrieved to a divorce'. As a result, the law reports and textbooks introduced the concept of 'legal' or 'matrimonial' cruelty, to signify the law's recognition only of behaviour which went above that understood to be cruel in a common or garden sense. There had long been a hesitation to set down a prescriptive definition of this legal cruelty, partly in recognition that it was subjective, at least to a certain extent. What may be considered intolerably cruel in one couple's marriage may not even raise an eyebrow in another. As a result, the law books of the time contained bleak checklists of the types of behaviours that the courts had deemed to be sufficiently cruel to permit a wife to divorce her husband in individual cases. These ranged from public insults to sexual abuse and assault.

The final decision of the House of Lords in the Russell divorce suit was to set down as near to a definitive statement of the meaning of matrimonial cruelty as the law was prepared to make at the time. It was decided that, without listing any specific behaviour, an allegation of legal cruelty would only be upheld if it carried with it a clear and unambiguous threat to a spouse's physical health. Behaviour would only be classed as cruel if it resulted in direct physical harm or the reasonable apprehension of it. A minority of the Law Lords favoured a different test, one which considered whether or not the conduct had made the continuance of married life an impossibility. But they were overruled in favour of the emphasis on the threat to life and limb. The concept of cruelty recognised by the law was mired in sex prejudice. Its reliance on physical mistreatment or violence was an inherently gendered one; it seemed highly unlikely that a husband would be able to satisfy a court that he was in reasonable apprehension of physical danger from his wife. But of course the concept was largely only relevant to wives in any case, for it was they who were required to prove the additional element of cruelty as an aggravating factor to adultery in a divorce suit. The test set down in the Russell case raised an already unequal threshold even higher for married women.

The House of Lord's judgment was equally momentous for the individuals involved in the case. It left the Russells still joined in holy matrimony and the coda to the case was as dramatic as anything that had gone before it. As the Russells' lawyers were arguing their respective cases in one of the earlier hearings of their divorce case at the Royal Courts of Justice, just up the road at the Old Bailey another sensational court case was underway. The playwright Oscar Wilde was taking to the witness stand to give evidence in his libel case against the Marquess of Queensberry. The charge of criminal libel against Queensberry was based on his comment, inscribed on a calling card left at Wilde's club, that Wilde was a 'posing Sodomite'. In such a climate, Earl Russell and Herbert Roberts themselves were reluctant to let the Countess's allegation go unchallenged. She had already been ordered to pay Herbert Roberts damages for libel in the civil courts and, as the divorce case rumbled towards its belated conclusion, her mother Lady Scott was also being called to account for the allegations. Earl Russell, perhaps inspired by Oscar Wilde's ultimately misguided attempt to vindicate himself of a similar accusation through the courts, had commenced a private prosecution for criminal libel against his estranged mother-in-law.

Lady Scott's troubles began when she was arrested late one evening at a London hotel and brought to the police station to be charged with libelling Earl Russell by her repetition and promulgation of her daughter's accusations against him. Lady Scott had been assiduous in supporting her daughter's case against her husband but had taken it a little too far. She had tracked down former servants of the earl and asked them to write down accounts of his friendships that they had observed dating back several years. She had also been in contact with sympathetic reporters, who had run slyly prurient articles in their coverage of the original divorce hearing. One Fleet Street wag had noted that it was of course possible that Russell and Roberts had been sitting up into the small hours doing mathematical equations in the latter's bedroom, but it seemed unlikely. From the peer's perspective, it was dangerous to let such allegations pass unchallenged. And he ultimately fared better in the courts than Wilde did. Lady Scott was convicted of libel and sentenced to several months in prison, the judge noting that she should be confined in conditions befitting someone of her status.

By 1900, Earl Russell was in a new relationship with Mollie Somerville, a prominent suffragist and radical campaigner; but he remained married to Mabel. Russell and Mollie travelled to the US, where he obtained a divorce order from a court in Nevada, purportedly ending his first marriage. The next day, he married Mollie. This was all little more than a stunt, for the earl knew full well that his 'Nevada divorce' would not be valid in England. But on his return, his wedding to Mollie gave Mabel enough evidence to sue for divorce on the basis of his adultery, aggravated by bigamy. The London divorce court finally granted a *decree nisi* to Mabel Russell in March of 1901 and Earl Russell went on to regularise his relationship with Mollie with a second wedding in England. But this did not satisfy the authorities and a couple of months later the 'wicked earl' was arrested for bigamy. As a sitting peer, he was able to opt to be tried in the House of Lords, who convicted him and sentenced him to three months in prison. From his cell in Holloway, Russell wrote extensively on the subject of marriage and divorce; in the years following his release, he proposed several bills in the Lords containing reforms to the law. All were rejected. His second marriage to Mollie ended in a similar round of litigation to his first; his third, to novelist Elizabeth von Arnim, lasted only a matter of months.

His first former wife's subsequent relationships were similarly colourful. In 1902, Mabel made the acquaintance of Prince Arthobold Stuart de Modena at Henley Regatta. The prince told the countess – and the ever-present Lady Scott – that he was a member of the Austrian royal family and was living in England while completing his military education at Sandhurst. A short while later, Mabel and her prince were married at Portsmouth. But by the spring of 1903, her new husband had been unmasked as plain William Brown, a footman from Sussex. The marriage ended in divorce the following year. Mabel continued to perform on the stage, including at the Tivoli Music Hall on the Strand. But her health steadily worsened. In the summer of 1908, she was treated for consumption at a sanatorium, but her fragile constitution was not able to fight off the disease. She died, aged only thirty-six, in the early hours of a September morning with Lady Scott at her bedside.

* * *

The Russell divorce case became an infamous legal quagmire, sucking its participants down into a morass of accusations, rebuttals, petitions and counter-suits that would drag on for many years. As a tale it is a cautionary one, about the confusing state of matrimonial law and the ordeals it inflicted on those involved in divorce cases, almost half a century after it had undergone the most radical reforms in history. After generations of muddling along between religious doctrine translated into ecclesiastical law, English law had finally recognised a secular concept of divorce in the middle of the nineteenth century. The passage of the Matrimonial Causes Act in 1857 was hailed, sometimes for good and sometimes for ill, as a huge legal milestone. This was particularly the case for women who, save for some infamous and pioneering exceptions, had little ability to dissolve marriages regardless of circumstances. Divorce, such as it was until the Victorian era, was almost exclusively the preserve of one party to a marriage.

The enactment of the Matrimonial Causes Act in 1857 was not the end of the arguments around divorce in English law; if anything it was the beginning. As other aspects of the law remained in flux throughout the second half of the Victorian era, so did the law of matrimony ebb and flow. Legal academic Anne Sumner Holmes saw the issue of divorce as part of the wider web of laws affecting women in the late nineteenth and into the twentieth century. The hypocrisy around male and female sexual morality which was embodied by the divorce statute would go on to find other, even more disturbing, outlets via the legal system during this time as well. As we shall see in Part Three, it would form the basis of controversial legislation that would directly discriminate between male and female sexuality in a way that would revolt society for several decades. It is unlikely that the Contagious Diseases Acts, which required women to undergo forced medical examination and treatment for venereal disease while leaving men unmolested, would have enjoyed the support that they did without the legal background of the double standard of the divorce law. But changes for women in other areas of the law would undermine the status quo. Once the Married Women's Property Acts came into law in the 1870s and 1880s, 'a married woman's ability to own property weakened the image of a wife as either a chattel of her husband or a mere bearer of his heirs'. The shift in a woman's position within marriage would necessarily call into question the compatibility of this with the contemporary law of divorce.

The 1909 Royal Commission on divorce recommended the equalisation of the law, so that the requirement for wives to prove an additional element of fault beyond adultery would be abolished. But this recommendation was not finally implemented until the early 1920s, when a new Matrimonial Causes Act was passed. Matrimonial cruelty as a prerequisite for a wife to secure a divorce from a husband was eradicated from the law, and adultery, on the part of either spouse, was the only legal ground for termination of a marriage by the court. Of course, by that time the Parliament debating the law contained female MPs and was elected by a partly female electorate.

The Russell case, like many other society divorce suits of its time and beyond, may seem to be the frivolous dramatics of the idle rich. But it was an important measure of the inequalities in the law of divorce and it would impact on countless women for decades to come. It set a high threshold for legal cruelty, requiring a wife to be in fear for her physical safety before the law would countenance a divorce. This contrasted with the apparent willingness of the lower courts to entertain Lord Russell's argument that words and accusations could be sufficiently cruel on the part of his wife to allow him a separation from her. The concept of cruelty set down in the case would remain an unequal one for another thirty years, until further reform of the law occurred. Alongside this ran a hypocrisy around sex and sexuality which spread into other areas of the law that disproportionately targeted women over men.

PART III

IN SICKNESS AND IN HEALTH

CHAPTER SEVEN

THE EXAMINATION PLACE

Elizabeth Burley quickened her step down Dover's Snargate Street. She half-turned to look over her shoulder; the two men were still there, about twenty yards back along the street. Panicked, she began to run. Up ahead, she saw a group of young boys across her path, laughing and jeering as she came towards them. With her head down, she managed to push her way through them. One of the men pursuing her stopped to remonstrate with the gang but, as she turned down a narrow lane off the main street, she saw that the other was still coming, running now to keep up with her.

She turned again, deeper into the warren of alleys that edged the Granville dock, the masts of the tall ships at anchor there just visible between some of the buildings. Stopping to catch her breath in a narrow court of houses, Elizabeth saw the man coming towards her down a passage between the buildings. He slowed a little, sensing that he had her cornered in a dead end. As he drew closer, she cast about for an escape. 'Come with me,' he shouted as he came into the court. 'You must come to the examination place.' In terror, Elizabeth saw the other man turning into the alley as well. 'I won't, I won't!' she cried, backing into a corner of the yard. As the man reached towards her, she glimpsed daylight and a fluttering sail down the side of the buildings. She dived down the gap and ran, her chest pounding. The dark alley suddenly opened up onto the expanse of the dock, but she could sense the men close behind her. Looking neither right nor left, she was aware only of the open space ahead of her. Elizabeth threw herself under the heavy chain fence at the edge of harbour and plunged into the oily water of the dock.

Her thick skirt billowed and she could feel the weight of it dragging her further below the water. The shock of the cold drove the breath from her chest, but she pushed up and broke the surface, gasping for air. She could see the dockworkers and the stevedores gathered on the edge of the basin, shouting in alarm. Someone threw a rope to her and she grabbed on to it. There was a splash in the water near to her and a young man swam over to her. He caught her under the arms and held her up above the surface of the water. He told her a boat was on its way to rescue her. As Elizabeth looked up at the worried faces peering down at her from the harbour wall, she realised that her pursuers had melted away into the crowd.

A few months after her desperate dive into the waters of the harbour at Dover, Elizabeth Burley's story was told to a government select committee hearing; because the men who had chased her through the streets and into the dock were Metropolitan Police officers working in the town under the ordinances of the Contagious Diseases Act. This was one of the most controversial laws of the nineteenth century, and the lobbying to repeal it became a touchstone issue for many of the most prominent women's campaigners of the era. The act itself reveals as much about contemporary attitudes to sex, morality, gender inequality and class prejudice as it does about the social evils of the disease that it was intended to address. All of these are epitomised in the stories of the ordinary women whose refusal to go quietly was as powerful a campaigning force as the middle-class ladies who organised in support of their cause.

The Contagious Diseases Act – or rather Acts – were a series of statutes enacted between 1864 and 1869 which were intended to control the spread of venereal infection among men serving in the army and navy in garrison towns in the south of England. But it was not the soldiers or sailors themselves who were the subject of the legislation. The first act was passed in 1864, with little fanfare or even debate. It almost snuck onto the statute books; but as the legislation was expanded and extended over the coming years, an organised resistance movement formed in opposition. The story of the acts, of the parallel campaigns to extend and abolish them, and the tales of the women subjected to them all provide a compelling history of inequality before the law.

The acts empowered the police to apprehend any woman that they suspected of being a 'common prostitute' within a certain radius of specific towns, and require them to report for a medical examination to ascertain whether they were suffering from venereal disease, primarily syphilis. If a woman was found to be infected, she would then be taken to a 'lock hospital' for compulsory treatment. While convicted of no crime, she would be forbidden from leaving the hospital until cured. Detention of up to one year was permitted under the act. The locks – either standalone institutions or wards within larger hospitals – were the successor to leper hospitals, as venereal infection replaced leprosy as the 'dreaded social contagion' of the nineteenth century. The term 'lock' was applied to the hospitals not because they were used for incarceration, but from the French word *loques*, an informal term for the rags or bandages applied to patients in leprosy treatment. The name had endured and there was a grim irony in it being applied to the hospitals which had become facilities of detention under the new legislation.

The Contagious Diseases Act applied to thirteen military towns, all concentrated in the south of England, as well as two areas in Ireland. The towns subjected to the legislation were Aldershot, Canterbury, Chatham, Colchester, Dover, Maidstone, Plymouth, Portsmouth, Shorncliffe, Southampton, Winchester, Windsor and Woolwich, as well as the Curragh in County Kildare and Queenstown* in County Cork. Driven by a fear that venereal disease was incapacitating Her Majesty's troops, attention was turned to the women that were associated with the garrisons. Further acts were passed in 1866 and 1869, extending the radius of application of the legislation from five to fifteen miles around the subjected towns and, more grimly, requiring sex workers to attend periodic medical examinations.

The acts were part of a trend towards using the law as a tool of public health, which gathered pace from the

* Now Cobh.

mid-nineteenth century onwards. Swathes of legislation were introduced to regulate many issues, most often in response to epidemics of disease that flourished in the squalid living conditions of newly urbanised areas that were filled to capacity. From the 1840s onwards, there were a series of Public Health Acts, which introduced municipal health boards, medical officers and mandated provision of clean drinking water supplies and sewerage systems in towns, to tackle the cholera outbreaks that were occurring with increasing frequency in poor areas. As medical science progressed and developed inoculation as a more effective measure against disease, particularly smallpox, the Vaccination Act mandated vaccination of young children and imposed penalties on parents who refused to comply. In 1851 the Common Lodging Houses Act was passed to improve conditions for residents of the cramped shared housing that often provided a bed for the night for those on the brink of destitution.

But the Contagious Diseases Acts were a little different. The other public health statutes brought in at this time promised a clear health benefit for large portions of society whereas the original aim of the CDAs was to prevent disease among the military only. Any health benefits for the women concerned were of secondary interest. None of the other public health laws introduced during this period applied to a single group in the same way as the apprehension and inspection measures applied to women only under the acts. None of them relied so heavily on the discretion of the authorities to determine to whom and when they should be applied. In short, 'the acts represented a "high water mark" of an officially sanctioned double standard of sexual morality, one that upheld different standards of chastity for men and women and carefully tried to demarcate pure women from the impure'. The legislation entered the law less than a decade after the Matrimonial Causes Act, which itself contained the same double standard, in holding a wife's adultery to be more serious than a husband's in the context of separation.

In the beginning, the acts themselves attracted fairly little public outcry. The first, in 1864, was brought in with little fanfare – and even less debate. It is important to remember that the area of the country covered by the statute was very selective and there was a clear north–south divide; none of the towns or 'districts' subjected to the legislation lay north of London. Large swathes of England were barely aware that they had been introduced. But within a couple of years, as the acts themselves were renewed and extended, they attracted more attention and a movement began to grow to campaign for the extension of the regime to other parts of the country and to apply it to the civilian population in addition to the military. In light of this, a House of Lords select committee inquired into the matter in 1867–8, following receipt of petitions from other towns and cities in the country seeking the perceived benefits of the legislation. In places including Newcastle, Exeter, Bath and Liverpool, there was apparently a groundswell of support for adopting the measures. In Liverpool, which was a maritime city even if not a naval one, there was a belief that merchant seamen were contracting disease at an alarming rate and risked spreading it into the general population.

The select committee heard evidence from doctors, public health officials, the police and the Admiralty. Almost without exception, those testifying expressed strident support for the legislation and its extension. Only one doctor hesitantly expressed scepticism about the extent of the spread of syphilis claimed by those in favour of extending the act; and he was swiftly shouted down by the calling of other medical witnesses to counter his suggestion.

To modern eyes, emerging blinking from a pandemic historic in its scale and impact upon all of our lives, some of the proposals put forward to the Committee are eerily familiar. Walter Vesey, an official from the War Office, proposed a new system

> *very much the same as that adopted in reference to the contagious diseases for animals; when a district is declared to be infected, then the Privy Council might upon notice … intimate that the Act would be applied to that particular place.*

The comparison with diseased livestock may have been an unfortunate choice of words, but it was at one with the attitudes of other witnesses towards the women subjected to the measures of the legislation. Berkeley Hill, a lock hospital surgeon and Secretary to the Society for the Extension of the Contagious Diseases Acts, was asked his opinion on the morality of knowingly spreading infection:

> [COMMITTEE] *'You do not think that the feeling exists among [women] that they have no right to infect men if they have the means of being cured?'*
>
> [HILL] *'I am certain that there is no feeling of that kind. They always consider that it is everybody's business to take care of themselves, and they would not have any scruple about infecting men as far as that went.'*

Metropolitan Police Assistant Commissioner William Harris went further in proposing a solution to the supposed root of the problem. He suggested to the committee that the acts should be extended to make the transmission of disease by a woman to a man a criminal offence, in addition to requiring all 'registered' prostitutes to carry a card confirming the date of their last medical inspection, which should be carried out every seven to ten days. This venereal 'passport' would be presentable to any police officer upon request. When asked how the police would be able to identify those women involved in prostitution, Harris's answer was chilling – 'It would be soon known to the police; every woman has a place of resort and I think the police could find out any woman's history in London if they chose.'

While the committee ultimately rejected Harris's proposal for the de facto registration of sex workers, it did propose the extension of the contagious diseases legislation and warned of the dangers posed by the women concerned if it was not carried out:

> *To deaden her feelings, she lives in a whirl of drunkenness and debauchery, delaying her cure and spreading the disease to the utmost of her power ... it is impossible that the full benefit of the Act can be reaped until it applied to the United Kingdom generally, or at least, to much larger districts.*

Let us pause and consider what the proposed extension of the contagious diseases legislation would have meant. It would mean that on any street, in any town or city in the country, any woman could be stopped by the police on suspicion of being involved in prostitution. She need not be doing anything illegal or even suspicious. This discretion was extraordinarily wide-ranging and based on nothing other than the suspicions – or prejudices – of the officers involved, which were often far from infallible.

In early legal history, prostitution was lumped in with adultery and fornication, part of the 'moral' crimes punishable under ecclesiastical law. By the sixteenth century, the sale of sex had instead become a public order matter, now categorised alongside vagrancy and other behaviours which interfered with people's enjoyment of public spaces. As the capital, London was the nexus for most of these legal developments. According to historian Julia Laite, from

> *the seventeenth century ... prostitution in London came to be increasingly – though not straightforwardly – criminalised. While the actual buying and selling of sex was not (and as of the time of writing is still not) illegal in Britain, over*

> *the four hundred year period in question, prostitution was separated from other forms of moral offence and public disorder, authorities found ways to more effectively identify women as prostitutes and there was a marked increase in statutory laws, regulations and licensing restrictions designed to suppress commercial sex.*

This growing enthusiasm by the law to legislate in order to protect the public – and public spaces – from private immorality created an increasingly complex web of criminal offences surrounding the sale of sex, while the transaction at the heart of this web remained legal itself.

The law's treatment of both the sale of sex and the people who sell it has always been a mass of contradictions and inconsistencies. But a campaign of social and legal censure gathered pace during the nineteenth century, as reformers, politicians and campaigners sought to stamp out vice and debauchery in all its forms. The term 'common prostitute', on which so much of the law's criminalisation of sex work would hang, first entered the lexicon in the Vagrancy Act 1824, 'an act for the punishment of idle and disorderly persons and rogues and vagabonds'. The list of people and behaviours prescribed by the act was long, encompassing beggars, street gamblers, fortune tellers, flashers and pedlars. But specifically – and for the first time in English law – it criminalised 'every Common Prostitute wandering in public streets or public highways or in any place of public resort and behaving in a riotous or indecent manner'. Offenders faced a sentence of a month's hard labour in a house of correction.

The lawmakers and law enforcers saw little point in outlawing commercial sex per se; after all, prostitution hasn't survived as the world's oldest profession for nothing. But they began to develop an increasingly complex system of criminal offences around the transaction itself. Overwhelmingly, the risk of criminalisation fell on those selling, rather than buying; the Contagious Diseases Acts were the apogee of this, with women subject to forcible examination and detention without being convicted of any crime. And while the policy underlying the legislation spoke to the wider attitudes to sex and morality of the time, it is in the personal stories of those subjected to the acts – and the attitudes of those enforcing them – that we learn most about their effect on women's lives.

The expansion of the contagious diseases regime throughout the 1860s led to the gradual formalisation of a protest movement against it into an organised campaign. At the forefront of this were Josephine and George Butler, the founders of the Ladies' National Association for the Repeal of the Contagious Diseases Acts. The couple were both committed campaigners for the abolition of the legislation, but it was the spirited and charismatic Josephine who would become the public face of the movement. Following the passing of the 1869 act, Butler and the Association set out the aims of their campaign in a manifesto, which attracted two thousand signatories including Florence Nightingale, Harriet Martineau and many others 'well-known in the literary and philanthropic world'. A significant driver behind their cause was religion. Butler herself believed that the regime amounted to state regulation of vice and encouraged, rather than deterred, immorality.

This, she believed, was against all Christian teachings. However, the manifesto itself centred the legal and jurisprudential arguments against the laws. As a campaigning move, it was a canny one; it encouraged opposition to the acts on the basis of natural justice, for those who might otherwise have felt squeamish about the subject matter of the legislation.

Under the headline 'The Women's Protest', the *Daily News* published the signed statement on the first day of 1870. The 'Protest' pointed out that the regime represented a 'momentous change in the legal safeguards hitherto enjoyed by women in common with men' and, crucially, that it permitted detention without defining any criminal offence which it sought to punish. Most powerfully, the manifesto stated that 'so far as women are concerned, [the acts] remove every guarantee of personal security which the law has established and held sacred, and put their reputation, their freedom and their persons absolutely in the power of the police'.

The wording of the published manifesto was key to its impact in other ways as well. It referred only to 'women' and did not attempt to delineate groups to whom the laws were most commonly applied. Its meaning was clear – the law was an attack on the rights and safety of all women, lacking even the most basic safeguards to curtail the discretion of, or prevent exploitation by, the police. There was no room for any woman to feel complacent – the regime posed a risk to all. It succinctly described the faults inherent in the laws themselves. No crime was proscribed under the Contagious Diseases Acts; it was not an offence to either sell sex or contract venereal disease. But the mere suspicion of both was enough to permit a woman's detention. This detention was without any trial, conviction or even arrest. Even the long held maxim of innocent until proven guilty – a cornerstone of the English legal system for centuries – was negated by the acts. The onus was placed on women to submit to the medical examinations in order to prove they were free from disease, rather than on the police to justify their apprehension with any corroborating evidence that they were infected.

Writer Melanie Phillips described the 'Women's Protest' as a

> *foundation document of feminism. It declared that ... it was unjust not to punish the sex who were the main cause of vice while punishing women by arrest, forced medical treatment and where they resisted imprisonment, hard labour; it made evil easier for men as it provided a convenience for ... vice; it violated and further brutalised women; and it would not diminish disease, whose condition was moral, not physical.*

It would take another fifteen years for the campaign that was started with this publication to achieve its aims. In hindsight, Josephine Butler considered that the very duration of the campaign gave it strength and that a more easily won victory might not have endured. Public awareness and revulsion at the legislation needed time to incubate, in order to ensure that it would not be forgotten too quickly. But although the acts were repealed in the 1880s, the attitudes and prejudices that lay behind them would not disappear so quickly.

CHAPTER EIGHT

'NO MAN EVER INJURES AN HONEST WOMAN'

The women sitting together in the chapel of the Royal Albert Hospital, in the Devonport area of Plymouth, for Sunday service in May of 1873 numbered about forty. They were grouped into one half of the chapel, separate from the rest of the worshippers. They were each dressed in an identical uniform: a blue serge dress, a bright red neckerchief and a starched white cap, with long ribbons trailing back over their shoulders. The chaplain stood at the pulpit and preached of the hell and damnation that awaited those who indulged in the sin of fornication.

A woman sat alone at the back of the chapel, watching those in the blue dresses intently as the chaplain spoke. When the sermon ended, she slipped out of the chapel door and into the outer yard of the hospital, where she noted 'the height of the surrounding walls and the appearance of the buildings ... a combination of the conventional establishment, the military prison and the palatial hospital'. Through barred windows set close to the ground, she could see the hospital laundry down in its basement and, through the steam on the windows, noticed the women in the blue dresses filing into the room to begin filling the tubs with water and soap.

A little later, the woman sat in a parlour on the upper floors of the hospital. The large windows looked down on the hospital gardens and on to the Hamoaze, the wide estuary of the River Tamar. On the horizon was the far bank of the river, Cornwall green and wooded in contrast to the muscular granite buildings of the Devonport dockyard on the Devon side of the Tamar. Across a desk sat the hospital's president, a greying man of middle years. His lips pursed slightly as the woman began to speak: she protested that the women in the blue dresses were patients but treated as prisoners by the hospital, the victims of a law that was manifestly unjust. There was, she explained, warming to her theme, 'one law for men, one for women; one for rich, one for poor; one for strong, one for weak; one for the enfranchised and one for the enslaved. Would you treat "fallen men" in the same way?'

'Madam,' replied the president,

> *you are not a lawyer and so you cannot understand the question. These women are incomparably worse than the men for whose benefit the contagious diseases acts were designed. When anyone can show me a class of men trading in sin as these female prostitutes do, I will grant that the present law is unjust, as it applies to the one sex only.*

The hospital matron, sitting in the corner of the parlour now interjected. 'Whenever a ship comes in, would it not be a dreadful thing for the innocent wives and unborn children of the seamen, if the women with whom the men were sure to consort had not been treated in the hospital?' The woman sighed in exasperation. 'So you are preparing the women for the ships then!'

The matron and the president shared a look across the room. The hospital had, the president explained, invited the woman to visit in order to see for herself and her association the good that was being done at the Royal Albert under the Contagious Diseases Act. Perhaps, he said, she would be good enough to relay their discussion to her association so that they might better understand the benefits of the legislation for all involved. The woman assured them that she would be reporting everything she had seen to her colleagues, and with that the meeting closed.

The woman was as good as her word and wrote up a lengthy report entitled 'What I saw at the Royal Albert Hospital at Devonport on Sunday evening May 4th and on Monday morning May 12th 1873 by a Member of the Ladies' National Association for the Repeal of the Contagious Diseases Acts'. Rather tellingly, she did not put her name to it.

* * *

The 'Three Towns' of Plymouth, Devonport and Stonehouse, all now subsumed within the modern city of Plymouth, were an important hub for the British navy in the nineteenth century and home to a number of barracks around the large Devonport dockyards. The significant naval population around the towns made them a natural testing ground for the promotion of – and objection to – the Contagious Diseases Acts. The

Writer and campaigner Caroline Norton personifying *The Spirit of Justice* in Daniel Maclise's fresco, painted for the chamber of the House of Lords.

The abduction of Emily Jackson as depicted in *Illustrated Police News*. The illustration in the bottom right corner shows the provisioning of Rover Street during its 'siege', much to the amusement of the gathered onlookers.

Saint Mary's church in Clitheroe in the summer of 2022. Emily Jackson was bundled into a carriage at the gates of the churchyard in the middle of the picture.

Actress Julia Glover in character as Mrs Candour in Richard Sheridan's play *The School for Scandal*.

Georgina Weldon pictured in an advertisement for Pears Soap a couple of years after her legal battle with her husband. The stress of the litigation had not apparently affected her youthful complexion.

Publicity photographs taken to mark the stage debut of Countess Russell in *The Runaway Girl*. She is posing with her co-stars Harry Phydora and Bert Haslam.

A nineteenth-century engraving of a wife-sale in rural England. Note the observance of the supposed formalities – in public, in front of witnesses – that were believed to legitimise the sale. The halter was optional.

George Cruikshank's 1820 cartoon in support of Queen Caroline's fight against her husband's attempt to divorce her. Caroline is portrayed as Boadicea riding to victory and trampling her husband George beneath her chariot. In the bottom left corner, a member of the government scrambles to save the divorce legislation, known as the 'Pains and Penalties Bill'.

Marble bust of campaigner Josephine Butler by sculptor Alexander Munro.

The unlawful arrest of Elizabeth Cass by PC Endacott in Regent Street in 1887. Behind them can be seen the crowds gathered to celebrate Queen Victoria's jubilee.

It appears from the Handbills issued by MR. CHILDERS this morning, that

HE IS AFRAID TO MEET US,

And answer our questions on the Contagious Diseases Acts.

THEREFORE

MRS. BUTLER

REQUESTS THE

WOMEN OF PONTEFRACT

TO MEET HER AT THE

LARGE ROOM, IN SOUTHGATE,

(USED BY MR. JOHNSON AS A SPINNING ROOM),

THIS EVENING AT SEVEN O'CLOCK.

MRS. BUTLER will shew that the Bill of which MR. CHILDERS says he is now a supporter, while pretending to Repeal the "Contagious Diseases Acts" is an extension of their principle to the whole country.

MRS. BUTLER will shew that MR. CHILDERS belongs to a Government which has extended these Acts not only to this Country but to the Colonies and Dependencies of the British Empire.

JOSEPHINE E. BUTLER, Hon. Sec. of the Ladies' National Association.

Notice of Josephine Butler's ill-fated visit to Pontefract during her campaigning against the Contagious Diseases Act. She ended up speaking to supporters in a hay loft from which she had to flee for her life when it was set alight by opponents of her campaign.

Emily, or Phyllis, Dimmock modelling a sailor suit in a novelty snapshot taken a few years before her death in 1907.

Ruby Young, who testified against Phyllis's alleged murderer Robert Wood at his trial at the Old Bailey. For her troubles, Ruby was barracked by a hostile crowd as she left court.

An autumnal scene in Wolverhampton's George Street in November 2022 which is little changed since 1908, when Ruth Hadley was killed by Edward Lawrence in the house to the left of the picture.

Illustrated Police News's graphic illustration of the murder of Laura Glendell outside her home in Arthur Road, Windsor.

Writer Florence Fenwick Miller, who commented on women's issues during the nineteenth century, particularly the shortcomings of the courts in dealing with violence against women.

Maud Crofts, one of the first women to be admitted to practice as a solicitor after the passing of the Sex Disqualification (Removal) Act 1919. Crofts was also the author of *Women Under English Law*.

Shrewsbury Prison, where Thomas Cox was executed for the murder of his wife Elizabeth in 1917. The prison's appearance in the poetry of A.E. Housman influenced Oscar Wilde's 'The Ballad of Reading Gaol', itself based on the murder of Laura Glendell.

government allocated generous resources to the area to support enforcement of the legislation and considered the towns to be a model example of the proper application and rigorous upholding of the law. Conversely, this notoriety drew to the area those who were campaigning and lobbying for the abolition of the acts, to investigate and demonstrate against some of the most egregious examples of the law's cruelty.

In response to the extension of the acts in 1869, two organisations had formed in opposition: the Ladies' National Association for the Repeal of the Contagious Diseases Acts (headed by Josephine Butler) and the National Association for the Repeal of the Contagious Diseases Acts. The Ladies' Association had despatched their correspondent to Devonport in 1873 to report on the conditions at the Royal Albert Hospital. But they also employed more covert tactics, with whispers that there were paid agents of the Association at work in the Plymouth area, encouraging and assisting women who were being persecuted by the police.

From the inception of the contagious diseases regime, the police working in the Three Towns had developed a formidable reputation. This centred around one officer in particular, the notorious Inspector Silas Anniss. The dockyard and its environs had been Anniss's patch for a while, and when the acts came into force his name became closely associated with the legislation, due to what proponents of the regime praised as his diligent enforcement – and objectors condemned as unlawful overreach of his powers. Married with four children, Anniss took to his new duties of policing the contagious diseases legislation like a duck to water. He lived above the designated medical examination room in Octagon Street in Stonehouse; it was said that passing dockers could see into the room through the windows that faced onto the street.

In 1870, Anniss arrested John Marshall, a suspected agent of the repeal associations campaigning for the abolition of the acts. Marshall had intervened as the police were in the process of escorting Sarah Mack – 'a woman of ill-fame' – to the Royal Albert and was imprisoned for a month for his efforts. The following year, Anniss was also involved in the disturbing case of Bessie Bunker, a young girl from Bideford in north Devon who had come to Plymouth and become involved in prostitution. Her family had travelled to the docks to 'reclaim' her; but Bessie's name had already been inscribed on the informal list of sex workers kept by Anniss and his men. Such was the Plymouth police's reputation that Bessie and her family feared that they would continue to harass her even after she had left the area. So they applied to the magistrates to order that her name be removed from the list. Anniss's reaction was rather telling of his approach and attitude to the women he policed. He went to see Bessie and her family, to pressure them into dropping the court proceedings. He suggested that her parents would be fined for harbouring her if she did not drop the matter. When they remained undaunted, he upped the ante and alleged that he had received information suggesting that Bessie was suffering from venereal disease, which she vehemently denied. The police would therefore only agree to the removal of her name from their dossier if she submitted to a medical examination beforehand. Her lawyer, provided by the repeal campaigners, pointed out to the magistrates that there was no power for such an examination, even under the most stringent interpretation of the Contagious Diseases Act and requiring her to submit to one was a clear overreach of the police's powers. After some mumbling consideration, the magistrates announced their decision. They acknowledged the injustice of requiring Bessie to submit to an examination, 'but that they believed that it would be more satisfactory to the public, as it would be to them, that the girl should be examined before she was discharged'. Anniss had won; the case was adjourned so that Bessie could be examined by a surgeon, who pronounced her free of any sign of syphilis or indeed any other disease.

Even before his talents had turned to enforcement of the controversial legislation, Anniss was known and disliked around the dockyard for his sometimes over-zealous approach to his work. He frequently tried to enter premises without a warrant and 'on some occasions, this zeal had carried him on to the getting up of frivolous cases and to striving for convictions which the evidence on examination had failed to ensure'. Back in 1865, he had raided the warehouse of Edward Bunter looking for missing government property allegedly stolen from the dockyards. While he was poring over the store's logbooks, the disgruntled Bunter lunged at Anniss with a blade and stabbed him in the chest. A few days afterwards, Bunter took his own life while being held in a cell at the police station – 'he broke his breakfast basin and with the pieces cut the arteries of his arms and throat so severely that he afterwards died of the wounds'. Anniss wasn't expected to survive the attack, but against the odds he did and resumed his duties around the

Devonport docks. Shortly afterwards the first Contagious Diseases Act came onto the statute books and the infamous inspector found a new outlet for his detective skills.

The Rescue Society, dedicated to the redemption of 'fallen women', condemned the police's approach to the legislation in vituperative terms:

> *The uneducated, indiscriminating, over-zealous and mercenary spies employed to work this pernicious system, have brought many such to public infamy who would never have been so placed but for their interference. These men have gone into their homes, accused them of immorality, and by unjustifiable threats and intimidation, constrained them to attend the medical examination stations.*

Although intended as a general observation, it would certainly have chimed with the residents of Anniss' beat in Plymouth. As the acts were renewed and extended over the 1860s, Devonport became a battleground between those in favour of keeping and even extending the legislation to other parts of the country, and those who sought its complete abolition.

Things came to a head in the summer of 1870, a period which was later christened by those on both sides of the debate 'the Siege of Devonport'. In June, Anniss and his men had burst into the home of Harriet Hicks, where she lived with her partner of six years, Ebenezer Simmonds. Anniss didn't have a warrant but announced that he believed Harriet to be infected. As Simmonds watched on, the police took Hicks out of the house and to the Royal Albert. It was to be her third stay in the hospital's lock ward. Every couple of days, Simmonds would present himself at the hospital gates and ask to see Harriet; each time he was turned away unceremoniously. After a couple of weeks, the case came to the attention of the local repeal campaigners, who supported Harriet in bringing a case to court. Section 25 of the act permitted a woman to apply to the court to be discharged from hospital – when the hospital refused to do so – provided she could produce 'respectable evidence that she be free from contagious disease'. Even after several weeks of 'treatment', it was not even clear what disease, if any, Harriet was actually suffering from. Like many of the other patients there, she was forced to carry out hard labour during her time in hospital. The Royal Albert in particular used its lock ward patients as a free workforce, requiring them to carry out much of the grunt work involved in running the hospital and ministering to its other patients.

The magistrates accepted the medical evidence that Harriet produced, confirming that she was not suffering from any disease. They also heard the testimony of Ebenezer Simmonds, who maintained that he had never contracted any illness from his wife, despite the hospital doctors claiming she was highly contagious. Interestingly, it does not appear from reports of the case that Simmonds was required to undergo any examination to confirm this; the court was prepared to take his word that he was not suffering from any disease, in contrast to its treatment of Harriet. To cheers from the public gallery, the magistrates ordered the immediate release of Harriet from the hospital. Historian Judith Walkowitz's assessment of the case was valedictory – 'the Harriet Hicks case provided the subjected women of Plymouth with an important political education and touched off an avalanche of legal resistance'. Of all the individual stories of women affected by the over-zealous and sometimes downright wrong application of the law, by the police and by the courts, it is Harriet's case that best illustrates the fundamental legal problems with the acts themselves and demonstrates the flaws in pieces of legislation that remained on the statute books for almost two decades.

Harriet Hicks was guilty of being neither a sex worker nor diseased, neither of which were crimes in any case. Yet she was forcibly detained in an institution indefinitely and was required to perform hard labour, which was usually reserved as punishment for hardened criminals. She had not committed, yet alone been convicted of, any crime. Moreover, in order to be granted her freedom, the onus was on her to prove that she was not a prostitute nor diseased. In any other criminal case, the burden would be on the prosecution to prove the guilt of the accused, not for the accused to establish their innocence.

If the abolitionists had expected Inspector Anniss to be chastened by the result in the Hicks case, they were mistaken. He continued to terrorise the working-class women of Plymouth for years to come. In 1876, a young woman named Miss Murton accused Anniss of accosting her in the street, asking her 'indecent questions' and trying to force her to come with him to the examination office beneath his lodgings. Miss Murton resisted and managed to get away. She reported the incident to the authorities and Anniss was in fact charged. He claimed that it was a case of mistaken identity and produced witnesses to say that he had been walking on the Hoe, Plymouth's wide seafront promenade, at the time he was accused of harassing Miss Murton a couple of miles away. The magistrates were inclined to believe that, if the story were true, it was most likely a ne'er-do-well impersonating the well-known police officer, in order to be able to molest or do worse to women. They dismissed the charge against Anniss.

The reaction to this case was no less polarising than that which accompanied Harriet Hicks's release a few years earlier. Supporters of the acts and the police claimed that Miss Murton had either imagined the encounter as a result of her hysterical temperament, or that she was a stooge of the repeal campaigners, who had concocted the entire account in order to discredit the police. One newspaper dismissed the National Association as being made up of 'well-meaning dupes and designing knaves'; another suggested that the people heckling Anniss as he left the court building were most likely those who had a vested interest in his downfall:

> *Many scoundrels and shameless women, who formerly lived in a low beerhouse or worse, on the wages of other women's prostitution, have been compelled to work for their livelihood owing to their filthy dens being closed by the exertions of Inspector Anniss and his men.*

Throughout the era of the contagious diseases regime, Anniss remained a prominent but divisive figure, both within the Three Towns and nationally. He became something of a star witness at the various royal commissions and select committees that were convened to inquire into the operation and possible extension of the acts over the course of their lifespan. Figures quoted by Anniss to these committees, demonstrating an apparently remarkable decline in the levels of disease and prostitution during his tenure in Plymouth, were routinely taken as gospel by those keen to expand the acts across the rest of the country. Others were more sceptical of the inspector's claims, with one participant in the royal commission hearings saying that 'he would not hang a dog on [Anniss's] evidence'. Although Anniss became an emblem of the police's habit of blurring the lines between enforcement and harassment, his colleagues in other towns subjected to the legislation had learned much from his approach – sometimes with tragic consequences.

* * *

On Easter Sunday of 1875, three young lads were rowing a small boat down the stretch of the Basingstoke Canal that ran through the town of Aldershot in Hampshire. As they idled along, one of them spotted a woman's straw hat sitting on the tow path of the canal. A little further along, as they passed under a bridge, one felt the oar strike something solid in the water. The boys glanced down and saw a dark shape just below the surface of the water. With a prod from the oar, the object rolled over and they saw that it was the body of a woman. Peering closer, one of them recognised her face, not yet bloated from immersion in the water. 'It's Mrs Percy, Mrs Percy from the theatres!' he exclaimed.

A few days later, an inquest on the body of Jenny Percy was held in the Military Hotel at Aldershot. The jurors filed into the hotel's stable block, where she was laid out for their inspection. Then they began to hear the sad tale of how – and more importantly why – she had come to be found dead in the dank waters of the canal a short walk from her home near the army camp.

Jenny Percy was thirty-five years of age and had lived in and around Aldershot for twenty years. She and her husband Henry were both professional actors, and earned their living performing in shows and revues in the various music halls and theatres around the town. In the years following the Crimean War, a large army garrison had been established in Aldershot and the town itself had flourished to serve the needs of the soldiers that now called it home. There were several music halls to entertain the populace; some were large-scale theatres, others little more than the upstairs rooms above pubs. There was a certain shabby glamour to these entertainment palaces and, while they might have longed for a career on the West End stage, the theatres of Aldershot provided the Percys with a comfortable living. The couple had three children, two young boys and a daughter of sixteen.

In 1874, Henry Percy died, leaving Jenny a widow and responsible for their three children. To support them, the eldest daughter had followed her mother and taken up acting as well. For several months after Henry's death, Jenny was able to secure various short-term contracts for shows in the local theatres. She also began a new relationship with Edward Ritson, a singer who she had met on the theatre circuit around the town. The couple could not marry as Edward was still married, although his wife had deserted him to bigamously marry another man. But he saw himself as something of a protector to Jenny and her children, and was determined to look after them.

But in March of 1875, Jenny and her daughter came to the attention of the police officers assigned to enforce the contagious diseases legislation around the garrison. As one of the biggest barracks in the country, Aldershot was another prominent town for the promotion of the regime. What exactly drew the police's suspicions to the Percys was not clear. Perhaps it was Jenny's living arrangements with Ritson, as they had not regularised their relationship by marrying. There were suggestions of insidious reports of her being seen around the town in the company of soldiers; without any doubt, she was a popular and well-known figure in the town – many people, soldiers included, paid to watch her perform almost every night. Whatever the reason, an officer visited her at home while Edward was out and presented her with a notice summoning her to attend the town's lock hospital for medical examination on Easter Monday. She tossed the paper on the floor in anger and hotly denied that she was either a prostitute or diseased. The constable shook his fist in her face and said he would return with a magistrates' warrant. The next day, Jenny and her daughter left for Windsor where they hoped to find work away from the prying eyes of the police in Aldershot. But none of the theatres were hiring and they returned shortly after, downcast. One music hall in Aldershot engaged her for a show, but the proprietor suddenly withdrew the offer soon afterwards. The rest seemed reluctant to take her on and she was convinced that the theatre owners were being pressured by the police, under threat of losing their licences.

The last few days of Jenny Percy's life, pieced together from the testimony of her friends and acquaintances at the inquest, appear to have been sad and desperate ones. She wrote a letter to the *Daily Telegraph* complaining at her persecution by the Metropolitan Police, their disgusting allegations against her and their attempts to stop her earning an honest living on the stage. She visited her friend Harriet Stynan, who kept the Artillery Arms on the town's high street. Over tea and buttered bread, Jenny wept at the scandal engulfing her and said she would rather drown herself than submit to the medical examination. As she was taking her leave of Harriet, she said forlornly, 'I am come to bid you farewell, for I will never live to go to the hospital.' To her regret, Harriet dismissed her friend's words as the dramatic statement of a theatrical personality.

On Saturday evening, Jenny went back to the Red, White and Blue music hall, from where she had been recently dismissed. She had been drinking and was tearful. Private Joseph Kivers, who knew Jenny from around the town, came across her leaving the hall and was concerned. He began to walk her home but was seen by an army official, who told him to go no further with her. Jenny was left to walk home alone, with part of her way lying along the canal.

The inquest jury reached an open verdict on Jenny's death, being unable to conclude whether she had thrown herself into the canal deliberately, had fallen in as she walked along it in the dark or had even been pushed into the water by persons unknown. But campaigners for the repeal of the Contagious

Diseases Act – and the newspapers that were supportive of them – had no such doubts. 'HUNTED TO DEATH' ran a prominent headline as the story became a national scandal. Those who opposed the acts presented the story as the ultimate example of police persecution and harassment under the cover of the legislation. The suspicions directed at Jenny Percy had cost her not only her career but her life as well. The National Association set up a subscription fund for the aid of her two young sons, now orphans who were themselves victims of the police's zeal as much as their mother had been. Her daughter, who had also been targeted by the police, was the recipient of more direct benevolence. The Butlers took her into their home to recuperate from her ordeal at Aldershot. Their association also launched its own inquiry into the case, which concluded that Jenny had died as a direct result of the police's intimidation and false accusations against her. They discussed the case at a specially convened 'Indignation Meeting' in London, where George Butler read out distressing testimony from Jenny's daughter, recounting the threats made by officers to her mother.

But even in death, Jenny Percy could not entirely escape the malignment of her reputation. Just three months after she had died, Sir Harcourt Johnstone MP presented to Parliament a bill for the repeal of the Contagious Diseases Acts in their entirety. He questioned the efficacy of the acts themselves and openly queried the veracity of statistics quoted by the likes of Inspector Silas Anniss in support of the legislation at the various commissions and committees that had been examining the act almost continuously since they had entered the law. The question of repeal was not a party political one, with supporters for the bill across both sides of the house. But the objections to the bill were vociferous. One MP balked at the citation of Jenny Percy's death as a case in point in support of repeal and claimed that 'he had made every enquiry into that case and he was able to state upon authority that she was not altogether what she was supposed to have been ... during the lifetime of her husband she gave him great anxiety by the manner in which she conducted herself'. He then proceeded to read out 'a detailed statement of the course of conduct pursued by her and her daughter from the time of her husband's decease until her own death', to some cheers in the chamber. The bill was defeated by 308 votes to 126.

* * *

In support of his ultimately futile attempt to strike down the hated Contagious Diseases Act, Sir Harcourt Johnstone MP hit upon the intrinsic injustice that lay at the heart of much of the opposition to the legislation:

> *I maintain that this House would not pass an Act that would compel the registration of men, and keep them on the register for a year – an Act that would arrest men coming out of brothels and require from them a voluntary submission, the refusal to sign which would render them liable to punishment.*

The other obvious question left unanswered by the legislation is why, when its express aim was to reduce disease among serving military personnel, was there no like requirement for these men to be examined for signs of disease. Periodic medical examinations for venereal infection did take place in some regiments, but it was not widespread. One army surgeon questioned at the 1868 select committee explained that the practice was repugnant to the soldiers and that the doctors themselves were not happy about carrying out such examinations. The navy introduced an inspection regime for unmarried sailors under the age of thirty-five before they left for shore leave, with the express instruction that the examinations 'should be conducted with all possible regard to privacy, decency and order'. A similar instruction for the examinations carried out on women under the Contagious Diseases Act does not appear to exist.

The Contagious Diseases Act remained part of English law for over twenty years. When the 1869 act was passed, increasing the period for which women could be detained in the lock wards to twelve months, it galvanised the nascent protest movement that had been quietly growing since the regime first came into force. The face of the movement and the woman that would remain most closely associated with it was Josephine Butler. She took charge of the Ladies' National Association and

by sheer force of personality, [she] was able to dominate the [Association] and guide its policy. Beautiful and histrionic, she was adored by men and women alike. A charismatic leader and a gifted speaker, she was able to capture the popular imagination and inspire a personal loyalty among her co-workers that bordered on idolatry.

Butler's campaigning career was colourful. It took her all over Europe as she collaborated with similar organisations in France, Germany and beyond. On a fact-finding mission to Paris in 1874, she had a heated interview with the head of the city's 'moral police' Monsieur Lecour. France had been an early adopter of a system of regulating the sale of sex ostensibly on health grounds, and Butler saw Paris as the root of the current evils in England against which she railed. At their meeting in Lecour's palatial headquarters, he laughingly dismissed her arguments around justice and equality: 'Madame, remember this, that women continually injure honest men, but no man ever injures an honest woman.' It amused Butler no end when four years later Lecour was forcibly retired from the police and became a bell ringer at Notre-Dame Cathedral.

Throughout the 1870s, Butler organised and attended meetings and congresses all over Europe to further her cause. She embarked on grand tours, visiting Lyon, Genoa and Rome, and travelled extensively in Germany, Switzerland and Belgium. But she was equally industrious at home and did not shrink from the sharp end of her activism. On a visit to the Yorkshire town of Pontefract, she was forced to address local supporters in a hay loft as the town's dignitaries had barred the Association from hiring public buildings for fear of disturbances. Not everyone in the town was sympathetic to the abolitionists' cause, and Josephine had heard that the owners of local houses of ill-fame had banded against her, fearing that repeal of the acts could harm their business. She persevered regardless and addressed a large group of women amid the dust of the loft. But the day nearly ended in tragedy when some of the mob set light to hay bales in the barn below. The Metropolitan Police – in town to observe the Association's activities – refused to intervene. Butler finally escaped from the loft by jumping out of a trapdoor and making a run for it.

Another meeting in Glasgow was disrupted by a group of medical students who had taken seats in the gallery of the hall where the meeting was being held. When Butler got up to speak, they began 'barking like dogs, mewing like cats, crowing like cocks, whistling and rattling their sticks'. This time the police were more helpful. Butler and her colleagues watched on from the stage as several burly officers entered the gallery and seized the unsuspecting students by their collars. They then proceeded to drop them one by one over the edge of the balcony and into the stalls of the hall below. The meeting proceeded without further incident.

Other campaigning groups formed a loose alliance with the repeal campaigners, as they saw parallels with other forms of social and sexual injustice. The Workingmen's National League viewed the acts as an element of class warfare, as they unfairly discriminated against working-class women who were more likely to attract the suspicions of the police when they were out on the street innocently going to work than those in the middle and upper classes. The League described the acts as 'a cruel and shameful evil and an injustice to working women ...

by placing their reputations and their persons at the mercy of an irresponsible secret police'.

Although the first act of 1864 had been passed with next to no parliamentary debate, this would not remain the case for the subsequent iterations. The 1870s saw successive inquiries into the operation of the acts and the twin questions of extension and repeal by firstly a royal commission and then a select committee. They were debated in Parliament every couple of years between 1870 and the mid-1880s. During the same period, organised opposition continued to grow and over 10,000 separate petitions, together containing two million signatures, were presented to the government calling for the total abolition of the acts. Gradually, elements of the regime began to slough away. The contentious periodic examinations were quietly scrapped in a partial victory for Butler and her association. Finally, in 1886, the Contagious Diseases Acts were fully repealed.

Just two years later, in 1888, *Punch* began to publish fictional extracts from *The Diary of a Nobody* by George and Weedon Grossmith. The eponymous Nobody, the comical hero Charles Pooter, came to represent the lower middle class as ineffectual, pompous and dull – but ultimately harmless. Pooter lived a middling life, in a middling house and went out to work at a middling job as a clerk in the city. 'Clerk' became a byword for this new urban mediocrity, mostly lived out in neat terraced villas in the developing suburbs of the large cities. Historian Peter Bailey summed up the popular image – and underlying tensions – of the clerking class in an essay entitled 'White Collars, Gray Lives?': '"Born a man, died a clerk". The arbitrary assertion of authority in the home may have been some compensation for the diminished masculinity in the wider world ... Conventional manliness could not be sustained in the unheroic, non-manual occupation of clerk ...'

This hint of something darker behind the net-curtained bay windows of Pooter and his ilk was not without foundation. The shocking criminal trial of a provincial clerk in 1888 passed largely unnoticed by much of the country, distracted that year by the murderous horrors unfolding in the Whitechapel area of London. But this case, coming just a couple of years after the final repeal of the contagious diseases legislation, was its own disturbing legal landmark for women and demonstrated that the same hypocrisies over the treatment of sex and its less savoury consequences were still alive and well.

CHAPTER NINE

'VERY SUBTLE METAPHYSICAL QUESTIONS'

Shortly before Christmas of 1887, twenty-eight-year-old clerk Charles Clarence visited his wife Selina at their home in Alcester Street, in the Digbeth area of Birmingham. The couple were married but unhappily, and had been estranged for a short while. They had a four-year-old daughter, Ethel. The Victorian sense of propriety makes it a little tricky to piece together exactly what happened during Clarence's visit to his wife and daughter on that December evening. But a couple of months later, Clarence was arrested in Birmingham and, so serious was the allegation against him, he was taken to London to be charged. The short newspaper report in the *Lichfield Mercury* summarised the awful 'arbitrary assertion of authority' that had taken place in the Clarences' home that night:

HORRIBLE CHARGE AGAINST A BIRMINGHAM MAN

> At the Thames Police Court, Charles John Clarence (28), clerk, of 1 Alcester Terrace, Alcester Street, Birmingham was brought up in custody of Detective-Sergeant Bradshaw, charged with carnally knowing his daughter, Ethel, aged four years. It was alleged that the prisoner, who had been separated from his wife for some time, visited her about the 20th December last, and communicated a frightful disease to her. It was also alleged that he committed the offence with which he was charged, and communicated the disease to his little daughter. The accused was committed for trial.

Clarence's trial took place on 23 April 1888 at the Old Bailey. Between his appearance at the police court and the trial, something had happened. The charge was now in relation to unlawfully assaulting and inflicting grievous bodily harm on his wife Selina. The record of the trial was expunged from the official publication of the Old Bailey, with a brief note under the case heading simply stating that 'the details of this case were unfit for publication'. The jury found Clarence guilty but with a recommendation to mercy. The case might have disappeared into obscurity – certainly the conviction attracted little press attention. However, the trial judge was sufficiently perturbed by the verdict that he reserved his judgment on sentencing while he referred the case to the Court of Crown Cases Reserved. Until the formation of the Criminal Court of Appeal in 1908, this was the only method of appealing a criminal conviction. Few cases were accepted for such review, and generally only cases that involved a complex point of law would be heard by the court. It was this decision to appeal the assault conviction that would make the case a legal landmark and create such far-reaching implications for successive generations of married women in England.

Charles Clarence had been charged with two offences under the Offences Against the Person Act 1861, namely the unlawful and malicious infliction of grievous bodily harm on his wife, and assault occasioning actual bodily harm. Both offences carried maximum sentences of up to three years in penal servitude. He remained in custody until the case was heard by the panel of thirteen judges in the Court Crown Cases Reserved later in 1888. The question the judges had to determine was whether the conviction was properly in accordance with the law on assault as it stood at the time. The reason for doubt on this point was the fact of Clarence's relationship to his victim.* It was the fact that Charles was married to his victim that was to go to the heart of the case and form its most controversial element.

The two key questions in the case for the judges were, firstly, had Charles assaulted Selina in legal terms; and did the transmission of venereal disease, namely gonorrhoea, to her constitute either grievous or actual bodily harm. The second

* It should be pointed out here that there is no reference to his assault upon Ethel in either the trial proceedings or the appeal case. It is one of the mysteries of the case that the little girl disappears from sight in all official records of the case after the initial charge. Was this for reasons of Victorian delicacy, or did the accusation turn out to be false?

question was the easier to answer. Even at the height of the contagious diseases regime, the actual transmission of infection was not made a criminal offence – despite the urging of certain elements of the expansion lobby to make it so. As one of the judges put it,

> *the worst of the contagious diseases of this class has ... been known in this country for close upon four centuries. The circumstances which have happened in this case cannot have been of infrequent occurrence during that interval, and cannot have failed justly to give rise to the bitterest resentment. It seems to my mind a very cogent argument against the conviction that, if the view of the law upon which it is founded be correct, thousands of offending husbands, and as I think also of offending wives, must have rendered themselves amenable to the criminal law.*

Nevertheless, there had been some attempts in the nineteenth century to make wilful transmission of 'dangerous infectious disorder' a criminal matter. The Public Health Act 1875 imposed a penalty of £5 on people who went about in public while knowingly suffering from infection without taking proper precautions or notifying the owner of any premises of their illness. But it was not the transmission of infection that was caught by this provision, but rather the failure to guard against transmitting it.

The extension of the criminal law to include the transmission of sexually transmitted disease within the categories of harm adjudged to be either actual or grievous bodily harm was a step too far for the judges. This alone was enough to negate Clarence's conviction. But it was their discussion of the question of whether Charles had committed an assault on Selina that was to make the case notorious.

Clarence's lawyers harked back to the legal writings of Sir Matthew Hale, the influential seventeenth-century lawyer and judge, who wrote extensive legal textbooks which remained judicial gospel for centuries after his death. In order to be an assault, said the defence, Charles must have committed an unlawful act against Selina. The only act he had committed was to have sex with her; and how could sexual intercourse between a husband and wife be unlawful? For Lord Hale himself had written 'the husband cannot be guilty of a rape committed by himself upon his lawful wife, for by their mutual matrimonial consent and contract the wife hath given up herself in this kind unto her husband, which she cannot retract'. In Clarence's submission, marriage itself bestowed a blanket consent upon all sexual relations and acts between husband and wife, regardless of the circumstances. While this may seem to be positively medieval even by the Victorian era, some of the judges in the Clarence case were perfectly happy to restate this archaic legal principle for contemporary ears, in perhaps even more chilling terms:

> *the wife submits to her husband's embraces, because at the time of marriage she gave him an irrevocable right to her person. The intercourse which takes place between husband and wife after marriage is not by virtue of any special consent on her part, but in mere submission to an obligation imposed upon her by law. Consent is immaterial.*

Ruling on the circumstances in which a wife's consent may be revoked, said the judge, required consideration of 'very subtle metaphysical questions'.

If Selina had been seeking a divorce from Charles, the fact that he had infected her with gonorrhoea would have been relevant to establishing the required legal cruelty and she would undoubtedly have got her divorce on the basis of it. The issue was whether the criminal courts were prepared to read across this into the law of rape, so that the concealment of his infection from her was sufficient to vitiate her marital consent. While the bench was divided on this point, the majority decision was to overturn Charles Clarence's conviction. His infliction of disease upon his wife via sexual intercourse was neither bodily harm nor an assault. He was a free man. And his acquittal had reasserted a seventeenth-century legal myth that would now persist until almost the end of the twentieth century.

There are plenty of reasons that the decision in the Clarence case was controversial, both at the time and for many years afterwards. It came just two years after the Contagious Diseases Acts were finally repealed and was a lived example of the social evil that the acts had been intended to address, chiefly the infection with disease of innocent wives by faithless husbands. Much of the discourse around the legislation when it came into force centred around the 'social contagion' of syphilis, spreading to unborn children from their unconsciously affected mothers. The circumstances of Charles Clarence's arrest – if true – posed a disturbing variation on this: a child infected not by genetic inheritance but directly, in the most heinous of circumstances, by her own father.

All of which makes the case difficult to reconcile with the rationale behind the earlier legislation. When the court had the opportunity to directly protect a wife infected by her husband, it chose not to do so. Indeed it reinforced the double standard inherent in the repealed acts, even after their abolition – one of the judges remarked that any extension of the law to make spreading of disease a form of bodily harm must apply equally to both men and women, for 'it is a great mistake to look at questions of this kind as if sexual faults and transgressions were all on the side of one sex', apparently heedless of the fact that for the previous few decades the Contagious Diseases Acts had done exactly that.

The so-called 'marital rape exemption' traceable directly back to Hale's writings in the 1600s and tacitly endorsed by the Court of Crown Cases Reserved in the Clarence case would continue to arise in a string of cases over the next hundred years. It was not until 1991, in a decision from the House of Lords,* that English judges gave an unequivocal ruling that rape could take place within marriage and waved away four hundred years of damaging legal myth.

* * *

Of course, with the abolition of the contagious diseases legislation, the likes of Inspector Anniss and the rest of the Metropolitan Police officers charged with enforcing it were relieved of their duties. But for women living in certain areas

* Then the ultimate appeal court in England, now replaced by the Supreme Court.

of Plymouth and Devonport, Anniss's reputation lived on – historians have found reference to his 'sinister presence' and reputation as 'a petty tyrant ... whose name may still convey a thrill of horror' as late as the turn of the twentieth century. But if it was hoped that the abolition of the legislation would change the attitudes of the police towards women and sex work, this was perhaps premature.

The phrase 'common prostitute' was a term of art rather than science; there was no detail in the legislation to define the activities, behaviour or conduct caught by it. For the police tasked with enforcing the law, it was a case of knowing it when they saw it, giving them considerable latitude. The application of this discretion was subject to public and press scrutiny in the 1880s, when two shocking cases called into question the Metropolitan Police's policing of the laws around commercial sex and its wider attitude towards women.

In 1887, Elizabeth Cass had been arrested on Regent Street on the evening of the Queen's Golden Jubilee by Constable Bowen Endacott. Elizabeth was a dressmaker and had been out to see the festivities around the West End with a couple of friends. Spotting her amongst the crowds near Oxford Circus, Endacott had arrested her for soliciting. At court, Endacott had alleged that he had seen her approaching men around Regent Street over a long period but Cass was able to call witnesses to testify that she had only moved to the capital a short while before and was not in the habit of visiting the area at night. The case against her was dismissed; but Elizabeth Cass was determined not to let the matter drop. With the support of her employer Mrs Bowman, she made a formal complaint to the Metropolitan Police and also persuaded MPs to take an interest. The upshot was that her case was discussed in Parliament and the Commissioner of the Met, Sir Charles Warren, was forced to open an inquiry into PC Endacott's conduct. When Warren's inquiry exonerated Endacott, there was uproar. Undaunted, Elizabeth Cass brought a prosecution against the constable for perjury.

Her case centred around Endacott's allegation, made under oath at the magistrates' court, that he had seen her soliciting on Regent Street on previous occasions. Cass maintained that this was not and could not be true, as she had only recently moved to London. In making such an accusation, in order to bolster the case against her, Endacott had deliberately perjured himself. And while the case was against the police officer, Elizabeth Cass could have been forgiven for thinking it was she who was in fact on trial. She was cross-examined at length by the defence barrister, who took the opportunity to undermine her account that she was a respectable young woman who had been subjected to a malicious accusation by an over-zealous police officer. Under close questioning, she had to account for her movements throughout her time in London and endure the raking over of her romantic history, such as it was. At the conclusion of the evidence, the judge stated that the prosecution had failed to produce any evidence that Endacott's statement was wilful, as opposed to a case of mistaken identity or otherwise innocent error. The jury were ordered to acquit the police officer.

The fury about the Cass case as it became known had barely begun to abate when another of Scotland Yard's officers became the subject of a very similar – but more disturbing – allegation. Late on a January evening in 1888, Annie Coverdale left her house in Hack Road, Canning Town, to fetch some milk for her elderly father. Annie was twenty-one years old and worked as a servant. As she walked down Hack Road, 'a quiet respectable bye-way lined by two-storeyed, bay-windowed houses, the occupants belonging to the struggling lower middle-class', she noticed a small group of young men huddled together. Drawing closer, she recognised one as her boyfriend, John Savage. He was the worse for drink and the other men seemed to be pulling at his clothes and pushing him around. When Annie tried to intervene, one of them snatched John's watch from his pocket and ran off. Unfortunately for her, Annie's cries for help were answered by Police Constable Bloy. When the officer arrived on the scene, rather than chasing after John's attackers, he tried to break into John's lodgings and threatened to arrest the couple. Annie concluded that she would be best off dealing with the situation herself and managed to get rid of Bloy.

But later, as she was walking home – without the milk that she had been sent out to fetch – she came across the constable at a street corner. Her temper got the better of her and she went up to him, shouting that he had made a mistake and should have pursued the men who had robbed John. In an interview with a journalist shortly after, she recounted Bloy's reaction:

He then began to push me about. I said 'You ought to be ashamed of yourself, you are drunk; and if I knew your number, I would report you.' He then caught hold of me by the arm, thumped me and kicked me until I hardly knew where I was.

Residents of Hack Street saw the attack from their bedroom windows and shouted at Bloy to stop. Realising he had been seen, Bloy pulled Annie to her feet and took her to the police station, where she was charged with being drunk and disorderly. After Annie was bailed and was awaiting her court date, Bloy made a habit of walking past her house in Hack Road. He would step up to the bay window of the front room and peer in, in a clear attempt to intimidate the Coverdales.

When Annie's case came before the magistrates, Bloy didn't simply stick to his story; he elaborated upon it. He now claimed that he had seen Annie regularly around the streets of Canning Town for the previous three years, often 'walking about with sailors or seafaring men' from the nearby docks. His suggestion was clear – as well as being a drunkard, Annie was a prostitute. But the magistrate, a Mr Baggallay, robustly questioned Bloy's testimony. In particular the policeman's account was flatly contradicted by evidence from the Coverdale family that they had only moved to the area a year before. Baggallay immediately dismissed the prosecution, going as far as to say that he did not believe the sworn evidence given by the police officer.

As in the Elizabeth Cass case just a few months before, Met Commissioner Warren launched his own inquiry. The press and the public were quick to join the dots between the two cases. But Warren was apparently heedless of the condemnation that had followed Endacott's acquittal. His report declared that Mr Baggallay was wrong in questioning Constable Bloy's testimony and that Annie Coverdale should have been convicted. Bloy was reinstated to his job, but moved from Canning Town to a different beat. The magistrate himself was furious that Warren had seen fit to publish this conclusion without even discussing the case with him first. For the second time in less than a year, the Metropolitan Police force's treatment of women, specifically working-class women, was the subject of public and parliamentary debate.

One magazine ran a spoof advertisement lambasting Warren's handling of the affair:

> *The stock of whitewash at Scotland Yard, in consequence of the extraordinary demands made upon it in connection with Endacott [and] Bloy ... having been exhausted. Tenders are now invited for the supply of a quantity sufficient for the coming year. Samples must be submitted to Sir Charles Warren, and must be guaranteed to be of a consistency which will readily cover up the blackest case.*

While it was Elizabeth Cass's case which attracted the most attention, Annie Coverdale's experience at the hands of the Met was more chilling. Warren took almost no interest in the allegation that Bloy had assaulted Coverdale, in spite of the fact that this was backed up by witnesses. The internal investigation into the case was done almost entirely in secret by the

Met and its conclusions were not supported by evidence. The act of whitewashing threw up uncomfortable questions around whether Endacott and Bloy were typical of the Met's pool of officers. Were they a couple of bad apples or the tip of an iceberg? Certainly Warren's rush to exonerate his men was seen by many as a tacit endorsement of their approach. Writing about the cases in 2015, academic David Taylor noted that:

> *As several contemporary commentators observed, there were fundamental questions to be asked about the right of women to be in the street without being seen to be prostitutes and thus about the way in which women were treated by the police.*

* * *

The Contagious Diseases Acts did not apply to London, much as some may have wished that they did. However, it was the city's Metropolitan Police that was entrusted with enforcing the legislation in the areas where it was in force. Officers were parachuted into the garrison and coastal towns, or recruited from the local constabulary to police the acts against a truculent populace. Annie Coverdale and Elizabeth Cass could not be taken away to suffer the indignities of the medical examination, but the officers involved were still able to trump up enough allegations to justify their apprehension, for simply being a woman in a public street.

Over twenty years after the repeal of the Contagious Diseases Acts, and also the controversies surrounding the Elizabeth Cass and Annie Coverdale cases, the Met was once again embroiled in a controversy over its treatment of women. In 1907, it was itself being investigated by a royal commission tasked with inquiring into the conduct of its officers towards women on the streets, following reports of threats and extortion of money or sex among the capital's constabulary. The commissioners heard harrowing accounts from women who had been wrongly arrested for prostitution, propositioned (sometimes violently) by constables when simply walking along a street alone, and worse.

The commission was examining the operation and enforcement of the laws around prostitution, which at the time was split across several pieces of legislation. The Vagrancy Act of 1824 remained in force and in London the Metropolitan Police had additional powers to fine 'every common prostitute or nightwalker loitering or being in any thoroughfare or public place for the purposes of prostitution or solicitation to the annoyance of inhabitants or passengers'. A new Vagrancy Act, which came into law in 1898, also made it an offence for men to live on the earnings of prostitution or to 'persistently solicit or importune for immoral purposes' in public. While this new offence was specific to men, it applied only to those who were engaged in the selling, rather than the buying, of sex. The complaints against the Met in this regard chiefly related to their enforcement of the laws. Some women complained that they were harassed by constables, who then falsely accused them of being involved in prostitution as grounds to arrest them. Other women had reported police officers blackmailing them, seeking bribes of money or sex to avoid an arrest under the vagrancy legislation. By contrast, there were also complaints that the police did not exercise their powers harshly enough and that solicitation was still too prevalent in London's streets, particularly around the West End.

The manager of upmarket department store Swan & Edgar, on the corner of Piccadilly Circus and Regent Street, testified that the store's female clientele were regularly subject to 'molestation by well-dressed men' propositioning them in the streets of the West End shopping quarter. When they had complained to the police, they had simply been told that the police had no power to deal with the men's behaviour and the risk of erroneously accusing a gentleman of such conduct was too great. The commission was also in agreement with the police's stance, concluding that

> *though of course the law might be amended to make the matter more clear, there is really ... no inequality created by the law itself. It is not the fault of the legislative or the fault of the Police that unchastity on the part of a woman, as compared with unchastity by a man, is looked on with much more gravity.*

This inequality in the law was not in fact corrected until the 1980s, when new offences targeting men soliciting for sex, including kerb-crawling, were created.

The most detailed testimony heard by the commission was that of a Mrs Louise Braham, a housewife from south London. She was returning from visiting a friend late on a June evening in 1903. As she was walking through Stockwell to catch a tram back to her home in Tooting, a man sprung out from a gateway and grabbed her around the shoulder, groping at her forcefully. In the darkness, she could just make out that her assailant was wearing a police uniform. He pushed himself against her while Louise struggled to break free. 'How dare you!' she cried. 'I'll show you what I dare do,' grunted the constable in reply. He then dragged her along the street until he found another constable, who helped him to take Mrs Braham to Clapham Police Station where she was charged with soliciting and being drunk and disorderly – on the sole testimony of the officer involved, Constable Walter Atkinson. Atkinson alleged that he had been watching Louise approach men as they waited for the tram – she vehemently denied this. The charge was subsequently dropped but Louise Braham's husband, who had collected his distraught wife from the cells on the night of her arrest, wrote to the Home Office to complain about his wife's treatment at the hands of the capital's constabulary. No action was taken at the time, but the case was referred to the commission when it came to inquire into similar issues that were continuing to plague the Met.

The commissioners heard detailed evidence from both Mrs Braham and Constable Atkinson, each flatly contradictory of the other. She was questioned repeatedly about her accusation of assault, a topic which she found acutely distressing. The commissioners allowed her to testify in private about the details of what Atkinson had done, even though they ultimately chose not to believe her. The commission concluded that while there were no grounds to suspect Mrs Braham of solicitation and so her arrest had been unlawful, her allegation of assault by Constable Atkinson was contradicted by the evidence of her alleged attacker and his colleague. They concluded that it was therefore untrue. Going further, the commissioners saw fit to criticise the Brahams for their pursuance of the complaint to higher authorities, when it would have been fairer to raise the issue in front of Constable Atkinson at the police station, so that he could respond immediately.

At least Louise Braham was invited to tell her story to the commission. When it came to accusations of extortion and blackmail of sex workers by police, the approach to evidence-gathering was more opaque. The commission concluded that 'it does not seem practicable to obtain direct personal testimony from any women of this class as to their relations with Constables [because] it would be open to such plausible suspicion as to be practically worthless'. Instead the commissioners spoke to charitable groups that worked in the field of social reform and philanthropy. From this, it was satisfied that the accusations against the police were groundless and concluded that the Met exercised its powers regarding street solicitation with 'a high degree of intelligence, caution and gentleness'; all without speaking to a single woman who was directly involved.

* * *

In *Personal Reminiscences of a Great Crusade*, Josephine Butler reflected on her efforts to abolish the Contagious Diseases Acts a decade on from their repeal. The book began with a note of warning:

> *Our long years of labour and conflict on behalf of this just cause ought not to be forgotten. A knowledge of, and a reverence for, the principles for which we have striven ought to be kept alive, for these principles are very far from being yet so clearly recognised as that our children and our children's children may not be called upon to rise again and again in their defence.*

The campaign to repeal the legislation is often a footnote in histories of the campaigns for women's suffrage, a prototype or a practice run for the bigger political battles that would be waged as the nineteenth century gave way to the twentieth, and the Victorians made way for the Edwardians. But the tactics of the campaign – and its ultimate success – helped to pave the way for the next generation of women fighting political battles:

> *since sexual injustice for women had been created by a political arena which excluded them, it was an obvious next step to conclude that sexual justice for women could only be achieved if they were allowed to enter the political arena to speak up for their rights.*

Suffrage campaigners would also grow increasingly willing to take on the causes of individual women to speak to wider issues about gender equality and violence. Women like Selina Clarence, who fought an ultimately unsuccessful battle against her husband through the courts, would come to be held up as shocking examples of the bias of the courts and the law against female victims of violence. And the campaign groups would continue to champion these causes as the end of the century approached.

The final repeal of the contagious diseases legislation in 1886 was a victory for Josephine Butler and the other campaigners who had banded together to fight against the regime for almost twenty years. From the outset, they had focussed on the legal as much as the moral arguments against the legislation. The acts were bad pieces of law smuggled in under a cloak of moral and sanitary outrage. They permitted detention without trial, conviction or even arrest. In fact, they did not create a criminal offence; it was not a crime to either sell sex or contract venereal disease. However, the legislation's effect was to criminalise women on the mere suspicion of each of these. The regime also circumvented that most ancient bastion of the English law, the presumption of innocence. It was for a woman to prove her health by submitting to the medical examination, not for the police to corroborate their suspicions with other evidence.

The stories of Annie Coverdale, Elizabeth Cass and Selina Clarence all occurred a very short time after the repeal of the acts and reveal darker legacies that were overlooked by the abolition campaigners as they celebrated their success. It is hard not to see the continuance of the sexual double standard in the outcome of Selina Clarence's prosecution of her husband for infecting her with disease. The contagious disease legislation had sought to protect virtuous wives like Selina from the trespasses of their husbands; it did this by targeting women who were deemed less righteous. But when faced with the very outcome it had intended to prevent, it offered no justice to a woman suffering through the actions of her husband. Throughout the period, the legal consequences for men were conspicuous by their absence. It was women that the law made responsible for transmitting disease to men, yet when a man passed on the same infection, it cleared him of any culpability. In doing so, it left damaging ambiguities in the laws of rape and sexual assault that would have ramifications for generations of victims of sexual assault and which are still being felt today.

As the statutory enforcers of the regime, London's Metropolitan Police were brought to national attention by the campaigns around the acts. For the first time, public focus was on the behaviour of the force's officers towards women; it would not be the last. During the lifespan of the acts, the Met's conduct was regularly examined by the various select committees and commissions. After the repeal, the experiences of Elizabeth Cass and Annie Coverdale brought further notoriety. The remit of the contagious diseases legislation had gone, but the police's attitude towards and mistreatment of women remained. The Met's tin-eared handling of the affairs, apparently oblivious to rising public anger, showed that it had not kept pace with changing attitudes. Had Elizabeth or Annie been apprehended while the Contagious Diseases Act was in force, it is doubtful that they would have attracted much attention beyond the repeal campaigners. Following abolition, their stories became a national scandal. But the force was determined to leave lessons unlearned. Less than two decades later, the royal commission was set up to inquire into the Met's activities following complaints about the behaviour of officers towards women. Once more, the force was under the official spotlight but would emerge unscathed yet again.

The police are only part of the justice system. At the same time as the Met was under investigation by the 1907 royal commission, it was investigating a particularly horrible murder in north London. In the story of the death of a young woman, the trial of her killer and the frenzy surrounding it, there is much to learn about the treatment of female victims of violent crime by the legal system. This story, along with others of the same era, occurred at a time when women could not serve on juries, act as lawyers or sit as judges, all on account of their sex. How was justice served when the chief place for a woman in the courtroom was as a victim?

PART IV

FOR RICHER, FOR POORER

CHAPTER TEN

'SUCH AN IDLE HOUR IS CARELESSLY SPENT'

If you had been in the Rising Sun pub on Euston Road late on a September evening in 1907, you might have seen Phyllis Dimmock, sitting in the 'bottly glitter' of the bar with a young man. He was of medium height and slight in build, with dark brown hair and a pale, pimply complexion. His eyes were small and close together, and he was dressed in something of a 'shabby genteel' style, enough to stand out among the pub's usual patrons of railwaymen and shore leave sailors. Phyllis and the young man chatted and laughed, and at one point he drew a postcard out of his pocket. He took down her address and wrote a message to arrange another date at the Rising Sun. Instead of writing the pub's name, he drew a little cartoon of a sun, peeping over a horizon and winking.

If you had been walking up Royal College Street in Camden the following evening, perhaps hurrying to catch a train from the station at the crossroads with Camden Road, you might have seen Phyllis and the shabby genteel man again, chatting in the street before slipping into the bar of the Eagle, across the road from the station. And if you had been in the Eagle a couple of nights later, on the evening of 11 September, you might have seen Phyllis come rushing in, dressed in a brown skirt and jacket, with her dark hair pinned up in curlers. The shabby genteel man was waiting for her at a table. Later in the evening, you might have seen them get up and leave together. But did you see where they went? Did they part in the street outside, with the man walking back down towards Euston while Phyllis crossed the road alone, heading home? Or did you see the man walk with her, through the darkened streets towards her lodgings in St Paul's Road?

If you had been standing in the snow at the top of George Street in Wolverhampton, late on an evening in the dead days between Christmas and New Year's Eve of 1908, you might have seen a light on in the window of one of the houses in the redbrick Georgian terrace. The portico of the house was garlanded with icicles and the wrought iron railings were tipped with snow. Cutting across the snow-muffled quiet of the street, you might have heard noises from the lit window; and if you had drawn closer, you might have seen Ruth Hadley and Edward Lawrence in their front parlour, she dark and pretty, he ruddy and bloated. You might have caught snatches of their argument; you might even have seen the light glint off the barrel of the revolver they were grappling with. But when the shot rang out and Ruth fell to the floor, did you see who fired it? Did she hold the gun to her temple and pull the trigger or was it pulled by accident as they tussled for control? Or did you see Edward grab the gun, step back and shoot?

What follows are the stories of two women who died between the autumn of 1907 and the end of 1908. Each was killed at the hands of another; but in the eyes of the law, neither of them was murdered by the man suspected. Each story is an individual tragedy, but taken together they paint an equally dark picture of the law's treatment of female victims of violent crime. Our collective response to these crimes, embodied most directly in a jury's treatment of those accused of them, reveals much about contemporary attitudes and shortcomings in the legal system that persisted long after their deaths.

The murder trials in each case shed light on the operation of the justice process for female victims of violent crime in the early years of the twentieth century and how this was still informed by the attitudes of the nineteenth. This was a system in which women played no part other than as victims or witnesses. The lawyers prosecuting and defending the case were men, the judge presiding over the trial was a man and the jurors who determined the fate of the accused were all men. How far did this lack of gender parity influence the law and wider public attitudes at the time? And how do the narratives of these cases, which were perpetuated in the courtroom, contribute to a collective obsession and glamorisation of violent crime and homicide, particularly involving female victims, that persists to the present day?

The popular press, emerging in the late nineteenth century, has undoubtedly played a role in driving our collective fascination with murder. But sensational coverage of these killings, focussed as much on the accused as on the victim, obscure the disturbing realities that these deaths epitomise. The murder of Phyllis Dimmock shocked Edwardian London; such cases always do. But when the initial disgust at how she met her death wore off, it was replaced with an equally prurient fascination with how she had lived her life. These attitudes infiltrated the courtroom and informed the presentation of the case against her suspected killer. The trials of the killers of Phyllis Dimmock and Ruth Hadley coincided with the battle to ensure that a woman's place was indeed in the courtroom. Organised campaigns to change the law to allow women to practise as solicitors and barristers, as well as serve on juries, were gathering pace at the time.

Historian Judith Walkowitz christened the London of this era the 'city of dreadful delight' and the Camden murder was just one of several cases that occurred around the same time, all of which combined a potently grubby mix of mystery, sex and death. The fact that these cases, all involving the murder of a woman, remained unsolved speaks to the risk to women's safety endemic at the time and reflects the attitudes of the police and the courts. And while some of them take on a life after death of their own, lasciviously memorialised in art, music and literature, the real people, stories and issues behind these cases are obscured. In the Camden case, as in so many others, the man suspected of the murder became more famous than the woman who was killed. And the woman who was killed is more remembered for how she lived than how she died.

* * *

Emily Dimmock, better known as Phyllis,* lived at the house in St Paul's Road with her boyfriend, Bert Shaw. The couple were young, aged just twenty-one and nineteen respectively. They had met in the saloon bar of the Rising Sun pub on Euston Road a few months prior. The Rising Sun is on a street corner, almost exactly halfway between Euston and King's Cross stations. In the early years of the twentieth century it was, like much of the Euston Road area, rather raffish. The pub was 'generally frequented by the demi-monde' of this part of London.

Bert worked as a chef on the trains that rolled north from King's Cross Station, a short walk from the couple's lodgings. On the morning of 12 September 1907, he was returning from an overnight journey up to Sheffield. He disembarked at King's Cross and walked up through the streets of Somers Town towards Camden. The couple rented rooms in the home of Mr and Mrs Stocks at 29 St Paul's Road. The house was an end terrace, set back a little way from the road and with a short flight of steps up to the front door. Phyllis and Bert lived in the ground-floor rooms, and had a parlour to the front with a view out onto the street. The walls were covered in floral wallpaper and Phyllis's sewing machine table stood before the large fireplace. Folding double doors across the back of the parlour led through to the couple's bedroom. The walls were covered in the same flowery pattern as the parlour, but the

* For consistency, Phyllis is used throughout the story that follows as this seems to have been her preferred name, although contemporary reports used 'Emily' and 'Phyllis' interchangeably.

bedroom was altogether sparser. The window was draped in net curtains and in the corner of the room stood a washstand. Tucked in another corner close to the window was a thin mattress atop a brass bedstead.

When Bert arrived home that morning, he was surprised to find his mother waiting for him in the hall with his landlady. Mrs Shaw had arrived to visit the couple earlier that morning and Phyllis had been due to meet her from the train, but she had not arrived. Her mother-in-law had managed to find her way to St Paul's Road; but neither she nor Mrs Stocks had been able to get any answer from Phyllis. Puzzled, Bert let them into the rooms with his key, and they soon discovered the reason for Phyllis's absence at the station. They found her lying dead in the bed, her throat sliced from ear to ear and the bedclothes saturated with blood. Bert ran from the house and round into Camden Square, where he found a police constable. Mrs Stocks led his mother down into her kitchen, away from the horrific scene in the bedroom.

Murders were not uncommon in the less salubrious areas of this part of north London, rent apart by the train tracks and cloaked in coal dust and smuts from the trains ploughing in and out of Euston and King's Cross. But something about Phyllis's death caught the interest of the press very quickly. A reporter from the *Pall Mall Gazette* spent most of that same day in Camden, speaking to neighbours and poking around in the local pubs. By the time the evening edition of the paper went to press, conclusions had been drawn – not about the killer, but about the victim. Phyllis's murder was 'the terrible sequel to an irregular life' ran the paper's headline. The anonymous hack had spoken to several people who had all told him the same story. Phyllis had many 'male friends' and had frequented the public houses around Camden, often arriving with one of her 'friends' in tow. Before living with Shaw, she had roomed in a succession of flats and boarding houses around Euston Road and its environs. While the paper stopped short of saying it explicitly, the implication was clear – Phyllis was involved in prostitution. How, then, asked the *Gazette*, could the police be expected to solve the case when the pool of potential suspects was so large?

Other newspapers expanded on this these innuendoes in the following days. One reported on the album of postcards found in the bedroom of St Paul's Road, many of which had been sent to Phyllis from naval or garrison towns around the country. She clearly had many 'friends' in the armed forces, the paper drily noted. Yet another reported that Bert Shaw was 'respectable' but Phyllis 'had been "hail-fellow-well-met" with a host of men' before their relationship. The papers recounted how the couple had first met one evening outside King's Cross, when Bert was walking home after a shift on the trains, before repairing to the bar of the Rising Sun to become better acquainted. Again, the inference to be drawn from Phyllis walking along Euston Road after dark was unsaid, but obvious nonetheless.

These reports sowed some dangerous seeds and reflected some unpleasant truths about society's attitudes to women and violence – which still echo in cases today. The suggestion was that Phyllis's mode of life must naturally have contributed to her death. Even her own sister said as much to one reporter just a couple of days after the murder: 'I often warned her of what might happen if she played with the feelings of any men in the way she did.'

A few weeks after Phyllis's murder, Bert Shaw was packing to leave the lodgings in St Paul's Road. While emptying the chest of drawers, he found a postcard, poking out from under the liner paper. It was addressed to Phyllis and was adorned with a little picture of a winking, rising sun. Based on the descriptions already given by those who had seen Phyllis with a man in the Rising Sun and the Eagle in the days before her murder, the police were now satisfied that the man who had written the postcard knew something about Phyllis's fate. What's more, another witness had come forward to say that he had seen a man coming down the front steps of the lodgings early on the morning of 12 September, as he was walking to work. As he watched the man stroll off down St Paul's Road the witness, named Macowan, had noticed that his gait was rather odd; one of his shoulders rolled forward with each step that he took.

The final piece of the puzzle that the police had slotted together fell into place a few days later, when they published an image of the 'rising sun' postcard in the press. The picture was thus broadcast across all of London and among those who saw it was a woman named Ruby Young. She immediately recognised the handwriting on the card: it was that of her former lover, Robert Wood. Wood was in his late twenties and worked as an artistic designer at a glass factory. His relationship with Ruby had come to an end some months earlier, but when he contacted her soon after the publication of the postcard, she was not surprised. When they met at a Lyons Corner House near Piccadilly Circus, he tearfully explained that he knew Phyllis from the Euston pubs and had written the card to her as a jape. But although there was nothing more to it than that, he had been wandering around the streets on the night she was killed and so had no alibi. In response to his pleading, Ruby agreed to say that he had been with her until midnight. But shortly afterwards, her conscience got the better of her. She contacted Scotland Yard to tell them that Wood had told her that he had written the card and asked her to lie for him. As Ruby watched on, Wood was arrested as he left his workplace one evening. 'Be true, Ruby, be true!' he shouted as he was led away.

Although he quickly became the prime suspect, Robert Wood was not the first or the only man of interest in the murder of Phyllis Dimmock. The police's list of potential suspects was as indicative of their view of Phyllis as it was of her killer. Summarising the investigation's progress to date, Met Inspector Arthur Neil's report damned the victim as much as the killer:

> *The number of [her] acquaintances has made the enquiry a most difficult one, added to which is the fact that she suffered from venereal disease to a considerable extent. Even this did not stop her lustful habits and in consequence, numbers of men contracted the disease which no doubt made her many enemies among men.*

It had been thirty years since the Contagious Diseases Acts had been abolished, but the attitudes they embodied still ran deep in the Metropolitan Police. In an echo of the rationale underpinning the contagious diseases regime, it was Phyllis that the police held responsible for the spread of the disease and they concluded that this could well have been sufficient motive for someone to murder her.

The police traced a man in Portsmouth who claimed he had married Phyllis a few years before and she had lived with him there before returning to London. A marine in Chatham told a similar story, and it seems improbable that both were true. However, the most famous picture of Phyllis, published alongside the story of her murder, shows her in a sailor suit with the wide navy flap collar around her neck and her dark hair tucked under a cap bearing the name HMS *Prince of Wales*. There was in fact another sailor who was of more immediate interest to the police. Robert Roberts was a ship's cook spending his leave at a hostel near the Rising Sun. He had met Phyllis in the pub and had spent three consecutive nights with her at St Paul's Road over the weekend before her death. He had also spotted her with the shabby genteel man, whom he later identified as Robert Wood, in the Rising Sun. But Roberts the cook had an alibi for the night of the murder, as he was waiting for Phyllis in vain at the Rising Sun while she spent the evening with Wood at the Eagle.

Then there were the reports from witnesses who saw Phyllis walking the streets of Somers Town, between Euston and Camden, on the afternoon before she died, arm in arm with a tall, well-built man with fair hair, smartly dressed in a blue serge suit and bowler hat. Two men, Henry Sharples and Frederick Harvey, claimed to have seen Phyllis with the same man late on that evening. The couple were, claimed Sharples and Harvey, standing out on Euston Road just down from the Rising Sun, near the corner of Ossulston Street.

Phyllis's own sister told the police about a disturbing encounter Phyllis had experienced with Arthur Hassop, who lived a short walk from her lodgings in Camden. She had known Hassop a little while and he had turned up at the house in St Paul's Road just three weeks before the murder, threatening that 'if he did not have [Phyllis], no-one else should'. Inspector Neil even ventured into Pentonville Prison to interview John Crabtree, who had been Phyllis's landlord at a house near King's Cross the previous year. But Crabtree was more than a landlord – he was also a pimp, and was part way through a sentence for brothel-keeping. He said that he had regularly seen a man, bearing a strong resemblance to the 'shabby genteel' man already connected with the killing, visiting Phyllis at the house. Crabtree didn't ask for names, but he did remember that the man had been much more than a passing acquaintance. He described a particularly grim encounter, when he had followed Phyllis along Euston Road and watched as she had sex with a man at the rear of St Pancras Station. Shortly after, according to Crabtree, the shabby genteel man had appeared and led Phyllis away. Crabtree also recalled hearing arguments between the couple at the house and claimed that the man had assaulted Phyllis, threatening to cut her throat in one row.

Although the police were reluctant to rely on the evidence of a convicted criminal, Crabtree's evidence clearly pointed to a relationship between Phyllis and Robert Wood that pre-dated her murder by some considerable time. Some of her friends also corroborated Crabtree's account, saying that they had seen Phyllis and the artist in the Rising Sun as well as the other pubs around Euston and King's Cross on several occasions prior to September of 1907. But Wood told the police that his drink with Phyllis at the Rising Sun, when he had written the postcard, was their first meeting. He admitted to meeting her again at the Eagle the next day, having bumped into her as he was walking up Royal College Street. And he belatedly accepted that he had been with her at the pub on the night before her death – but he claimed that he left her at the pub to return home alone, and denied he had ever visited St Paul's Road or even been intimate with Phyllis. Their entire association, Wood maintained, had been the couple of evenings they had spent together in the Rising Sun and the Eagle. But when he had seen her picture in the newspaper following the murder, he had realised how things would look for him if this was revealed. Of most concern to Wood was preventing his elderly father and respectable brothers from finding out the kind of company he kept outside of work and home; he had asked Ruby Young to lie for him because '[he] swore that he had not been immoral with Dimmock; but even the most casual association with a prostitute like Dimmock was disgusting in the eyes of good-living people'.

* * *

Just twenty years after Phyllis's murder, her brutal death was already being described as 'the classic British crime of [the twentieth] century'. In no small part, this was due to the sensational trial of Robert Wood, which took place at the newly opened Old Bailey shortly before Christmas of 1907. Even the prosecution had to accept that the case against Wood was mostly circumstantial; there was no physical evidence linking him to the crime and he disputed the testimony of both the eyewitnesses who identified him as a long-term acquaintance of Phyllis and those who placed him at the scene of the crime on the September morning.

In accounts of Wood's murder trial, both contemporary and more recent, there is one standout star. It is not the defendant but his barrister, the famed Edward Marshall Hall. It was Marshall Hall's presentation of the case – of the accused, the victim and the circumstances that led inexorably to the murder – that secured the reputation as a 'classic' that it so quickly earned in the years after the trial. But it also helps to reveal much about the treatment that female victims of violent crime could expect to receive at the hands of the British justice system in the early twentieth century.

The case against Wood rested on the testimony of two key witnesses: his former girlfriend Ruby Young and the man named Macowan, who was passing St Paul's Road in the early hours of 12 September and claimed to have seen Wood leaving number 29 shortly before dawn, walking along the road with a distinctive gait. The formidable Marshall Hall devoted his cross-examination of Macowan to discrediting him, questioning his eyesight, the street lighting and the weather in an effort to sow doubt in the minds of the jury.

In court, Wood cut an interesting figure: 'this slim young fellow of nine and twenty, with his long delicate hands and tapering fingers, with his deep set cavernous eyes and glistening eyeballs, his high cheek bones, his broad mouth with its twitching lips'. He took the witness stand himself, which was a privilege only recently afforded to defendants in criminal trials. Until the turn of the twentieth century, those on trial in the English criminal courts were not allowed to testify in their own defence; and while giving the defendant a voice may seem now to be essential to a fair trial, this was far from accepted wisdom at the time of Wood's trial. A poor performance in court could turn a jury against a defendant, and Wood's tendency to effusiveness and self-importance was a risk that Marshall Hall had decided to take. Wood snorted in derision when asked if he had killed Phyllis, and had to be pushed to give a definitive answer to a straightforward question that he clearly considered beneath his dignity. When asked what time he had left the Rising Sun on one of his meetings with Phyllis, Wood airily replied 'such an idle hour is carelessly spent and I could not speak definitively as to the time'.

Phyllis has to be pieced together from the statements of her friends, who were keen to counter the portrayal of her in the newspapers. Mrs Stocks, her erstwhile landlady, said she had no inkling that Phyllis was involved in sex work and found her to be a model tenant, houseproud and industrious. She knew that she supplemented Bert's wages by taking in sewing from local ladies, sitting at the treadle machine in the front parlour and singing to herself as she worked. Emily Lawrence, a friend from the pubs, defended her reputation from the slurs in the papers – 'she was a very nice, respectable, clean and tidy girl' – but Lawrence acknowledged that Phyllis could be timid and scared easily. This is all somewhat at odds with the portrait of Phyllis that the public would have gleaned from the many newspaper stories about her murder.

As well as Phyllis's background, the lives of her friends who had come forward to testify at the trial were also subject to scrutiny. Emily Lawrence found herself under fierce questioning from Marshall Hall about her past. She was forced to admit that she herself had dabbled in sex work before her marriage but was fierce in support of her dead friend, whom the barrister contemptuously described as 'the lowest type of prostitute'.

The malignment of the women involved in the trial was not just the preserve of the defence. Inspector Arthur Neil, who had been so involved in building the case against Wood, remained suspicious of the prosecution's own star witness. He explained to the jury that he had made extensive enquiries into Ruby Young's background and was sad to report that she had also been involved in prostitution before and during her time with Wood. She had been seen, Neil noted, frequenting the streets around Piccadilly, Charing Cross and Leicester Square. The fact that the police saw it necessary to provide such a caveat to the character of their own witness – and one upon whom much of the prosecution case hinged – echoed the attitude taken by the royal commission into the operation of the Metropolitan Police that was conducting its inquiries at the time of the murder: that the evidence of such women was to be mistrusted.*

* See Chapter Nine.

The character of all of the women involved in the case – the victim, her friends and key witnesses – was subject to as much scrutiny in court as the defendant's. Both sides were aware of the risk that a mere acquaintance with a woman like Phyllis could post to a man like Robert Wood. Central to the presentation of the case, in the press and by the police, was Phyllis herself. Not who she was, but rather what she did; although to most, the two were one and the same. Even the counsel charged with prosecuting Phyllis's murderer in court could paint no better picture of her than 'she belonged to the "unfortunate" class and to the lowest class of unfortunates'. While Marshall Hall was seeking his client's acquittal because of the victim's character, the prosecution were seeking a conviction in spite of it.

On the final day of Wood's trial, a crowd of ten thousand people massed in the street outside the Old Bailey to await news of the verdict. At eight o'clock in the evening, after just a quarter of an hour's deliberation, the jury returned. Robert Wood was, the foreman announced, not guilty of the murder of Phyllis Dimmock. Inside the courtroom

> *men and women seemed to lose control of their emotions. Hats and handkerchiefs were waved frantically; women cried for joy … [outside] the long pent-up feeling burst out. Cheer upon cheer rolled along the streets. Traffic was stayed. Hats and sticks were waved in unison as ten thousand throats voiced their sympathy with the verdict.*

Before Wood left the court, his father was brought out in front of the crowd to address them from the balcony of a tea shop opposite the court. When the acquitted defendant finally appeared, he was hailed as a hero. By contrast, Ruby Young had to be smuggled from the Old Bailey, her own clothes exchanged for a dark serge skirt and jacket to disguise her as a charwoman. The ruse failed, however, and the crowd smashed the windows of her cab as she was driven away from the court.

It is a cliché of the case that performances in the West End theatres were interrupted to bring news of Wood's sensational acquittal; but there is no doubt that public support for the accused murderer ran very high. Wood was quick to try to cash in on his notoriety. Just days after he left the court, it was announced that he would be appearing at theatres and music halls in Shoreditch, Woolwich and Rotherhithe. His 'turn' was to involve talking about his ordeal in court as he sketched some of the trial's key players live on the stage for the audience's amusement. Whether for reasons of good taste or the realisation of the limited entertainment value they offered, the performances were cancelled shortly after their announcement.

Notable from her absence in Wood's comments and interviews about the trial after his acquittal was Phyllis. Similarly, writer Sir Hall Caine, who had followed the trial from the public gallery of the Old Bailey, commented on its conduct in the *Daily Mail*:

Her [Phyllis's] dead body was there, indeed, with all the horror of its blood upon it, and the crime committed upon her we were always conscious of, but the woman herself seemed never for a moment to be present in our minds. That poor outcast of the streets, who was no vampire, no alluring temptress lying in wait to wreck the lives of men, but only an outcast girl, very poor, perhaps very worthless, though dowered with a little fatal beauty ... that poor crushed thing, whose existence as the victim of man's lust and the world's grinding poverty had been the prologue to the tremendous drama I had just seen.

* * *

In Walter Sickert's painting *What Shall We Do for the Rent?*, a nude woman lies in a narrow cast-iron bed in a dark garret room, her head turned towards the wall. A man, fully dressed, sits on the end of the bed; his hands are clasped between his spread legs and his gaze is fixed on the floor. The scene depicted had not sprung entirely from Sickert's imagination. Its inspiration was probably the bedroom of the house in St Paul's Road, Camden Town, not far from the studio where Sickert worked on his gloomy paintings in the first decade of the twentieth century. There is no violence depicted on the canvas, but as one art critic observed, a 'sense of menace ... is there in the fabric of the picture itself'. This menace is made more overt by the alternative title that Sickert chose for the work – *The Camden Town Murder*. And even though the murder itself is not depicted, he very clearly references the photographs of the crime scene published in the newspapers in 'the anecdotal elements of the composition – the discarded clothes, the shirtsleeves, the chamber pot, that particularly insistent wallpaper [and nevertheless] the slashing strokes of the brush ... already imply a kind of violence to the figure they represent'. And of course, the metal bedstead draws the eye in each of the scenes.

Sickert in fact christened three paintings after the case, all of which were painted between 1907 and 1909, along with various studies for the scenes. One sketch was actually inscribed 'Study for the murder of Emily Dimmock in St Paul's Road, Camden Town', suggesting that at some point Sickert intended to tell the story in less coy terms. An urban legend that Phyllis's partner Bert Shaw or even Robert Wood himself had modelled for the male figures in the paintings was not denied by the artist either. Murder was good for business. Sickert's name is now as closely associated with the case as those of Marshall Hall or Wood, but it was a story into which he had inserted himself. Nevertheless, his pictures summon up the Camden that Phyllis inhabited as truthfully as any photograph. He painted the smoky bars and shabby music halls that Phyllis and Robert Wood frequented, alongside the dark lodging rooms in the backs of terraced houses like the one where she died. Read together, Phyllis's story and Sickert's art tell of a place and a time; of a twentieth-century crime that took place in what remained

> *a Victorian neighbourhood at heart, with one foot in the city of dreadful night. The undercurrent of threat and the unknown gives Camden its allure. Generally, despite the*

> *poverty, the crowds, the drink ... Camden remains in balance. When it tilts out of alignment, it reaches back to its pre-history as treacherous territory.*

The paintings and the press gave the case a dark glamour and a shared vocabulary that Marshall Hall had exploited in presenting his case – and Phyllis – in court.

None revelled in the 'tremendous drama' more than Edward Marshall Hall. While Wood's questionable fame may have been fleeting, the case was the making of his counsel. His theatrical conduct of the defence made him a star and he enjoyed something of a professional renaissance on the back of securing his client's acquittal. He would deploy the techniques he had honed at the Camden Town trial in another grisly murder case just over a year later.

CHAPTER ELEVEN

DESPERATE, DEFIANT WOMEN

Christmas 1908 was a deeply white one in Wolverhampton. The snow lay in a heavy blanket through the streets, the trams were halted and motorcars stalled on the steep hill up Darlington Street towards Queen Square in the middle of the town. The town council found work for several hundred unemployed men, who were put to work clearing the snow from the streets and pavements. But still the snow continued to fall. As the old year drew to its close,

> *clean snow lay in deep drifts on roadway and pavement. It crowned the ivy which clings to [the] rather old-fashioned houses; it made the heavy iron fences around them look vague and indefinite, while whitened portico and gables increased the picturesqueness of the scene. Complete silence prevailed, and in [a] fine square beyond stood the historic church of St John ... In the solemn hush of this street, the residence of several doctors, and one of the most interesting residential quarters of Wolverhampton, death had reaped a harvest. The scene of the shocking affair was No. 2 George Street.*

Late on the evening of 29 December, Dr Galbraith popped out of the front door of his home in George Street to post a letter at the post box on the corner of the road. As he walked back to his house, he was startled by a figure emerging from the passageway which ran between the houses of the terrace. It was his neighbour, Edward Lawrence, looking flushed and dishevelled. 'Come with me,' he said to the doctor. 'I have shot a woman.' Galbraith followed Lawrence down the passage and round to the back door of his house. Upon entering the downstairs parlour, he found a young woman lying in front of the window. She was smartly dressed in a coat and hat, but bleeding from a wound at her temple. An ambulance and the police were called to the house while Dr Galbraith tended to the woman, who was unconscious but barely alive. Lawrence paced the room agitatedly, muttering more to himself than to the doctor, 'You do not know what a bad woman she was and what a life she has led me during the last two months.' He kept shouting, half to himself, that 'she's best dead' and he had 'done it in self-defence'.

The ambulance managed to make its way through the snow from the nearby General Hospital and the crew loaded the woman into it while a couple of police officers questioned Lawrence in the parlour room. His garbled explanation shifted again as he told the constables that the woman, who he explained was his girlfriend and named Ruth Hadley, had held the gun to her head and shot herself after the couple had argued. Upon inspection, the policemen noted that the bedroom of the house was in complete disarray and Dr Galbraith pulled them aside to explain something that he had noticed as he had tended to Ruth before the ambulance arrived. She had suffered two gunshot wounds, one to the arm and the more serious one to the temple. In Dr Galbraith's opinion, it seemed unlikely that these could both be self-inflicted. The police duly arrested Edward Lawrence for attempted murder. When Ruth died just before midnight on that evening, alone in the cavernous ward of the General Hospital, Lawrence was re-arrested for her murder.

The tale of Ruth Hadley and Edward Lawrence, which was to culminate in her violent death in the front parlour of his home, had begun a few years earlier when they met in one of the pubs that Lawrence owned around the town. Ruth was in her early twenties and had lived all her life in Wolverhampton. Before meeting Lawrence, she had been in service with a local family. She had two sisters and two brothers, one of whom kept a pub. By contrast, Edward was in his late thirties, married with several children. As the owner of one of the town's breweries, he was an apparently respectable businessman who was rapidly becoming one of its most notorious residents. He had embarked on a string of extra-marital affairs, seemingly heedless of whether his wife found out about them or not.

In 1905, Ruth gave birth to Edward's daughter, whom she named Dorothy. A few weeks later, his wife Margaret gave birth to their seventh child, also a daughter. Shortly afterwards, she finally tired of her husband's behaviour and left him; a divorce suit followed swiftly afterwards. Shortly before the divorce, Margaret had prosecuted him for assaulting her. Standing before the magistrates with her eye still black, she testified that Edward had attacked her twice, the first time just a month after she had given birth to their youngest child. In the second assault, he had beaten her about the head while she was working in the kitchen, forcing her to run to a neighbour's house for safety. It was this final attack that had made her leave him; on both occasions, he had threatened to kill her. Edward was initially sentenced to a month's imprisonment with hard labour but, following a plea by his lawyers, the magistrates reduced the sentence to a five-pound fine.

While the breakdown of his marriage might have been expected to chasten Edward, his private life remained as colourful as before. Ruth moved into the Lawrence family home almost immediately upon Margaret's departure. But the relationship was tempestuous and was broken off, on both sides, several times. Little Dorothy did not live with her parents and was under the guardianship of Ruth's sister. But by early 1908, Edward was living with a young woman named Emma Stacey who was herself expecting a baby. His affair with Ruth had, it appeared, come to a decisive end. But they continued to run into each other around the town and in Edward's pubs, in particular the Board Inn. The Board was the most prominent of Edward's premises and was a squat building jutting out into Queen Square. There had been an inn on the site since 1600, which had been refashioned in the Georgian era. The name 'Lawrence' was proudly proclaimed across the parapet of the roof and the grimy windows looked across the square to the statue of Prince Albert astride a horse. Edward was a particularly hands-on landlord and Ruth knew that she could often find him at the Board when she needed to track him down, usually to ask for money for their daughter. But the pub's regular patrons were often treated to the spectacle of their host arguing with the pretty young woman who called in at the pub, their tongues loosened by alcohol; on one occasion, Ruth was reported to have smashed a window at the Board in fury at Edward's intransigence towards her.

In the autumn of 1908, Edward and Emma Stacey moved to the house in George Street, an upscale terrace on the edge of the town centre. But shortly before Christmas, Emma had had enough and left the house. When Edward ran into Ruth outside the Board shortly afterwards, they were reconciled once more and Ruth moved her belongings into his new home. They spent Christmas together, mostly snowbound in George Street, but did manage to venture out to the Board on a couple of occasions. At around 5 o'clock on the afternoon of 29 December, an acquaintance of Edward's saw the couple leaving a pub on Dudley Street and stopped to chat. Edward looked to the darkened skies and remarked that he thought more snow was coming. But Ruth hustled him away, in the direction of the Board. It was later that same evening, after an argument back at the house, that Ruth had been shot.

That Edward Lawrence was a violent man was not in question. He had been convicted for assaulting his wife a couple of years earlier and Emma Stacey had fled from George Street after being threatened by Edward just days before his reconciliation with Ruth. When she argued with him over something, he responded, 'If you don't be quiet, I will quieten you for good.' Ruth's sisters had seen him wave a revolver at Ruth when trying to get her to leave after an argument. In the hours before he killed Ruth, he had groped his fifteen-year-old servant Kate Maddox as she worked in the kitchen and drunkenly tried to kiss her. Kate's matter-of-fact recounting of the incident to the police constables suggested that it was not the first time that her employer had abused his position towards her.

While Edward sat in the padded cell of Stafford Gaol awaiting his trial, Ruth was buried in a quiet way little noticed by the town. Just twenty people, including her siblings and little Dorothy, attended the funeral, where 'the body lay in a coffin of polished elm, on which lay four wreaths of sweet white flowers. The inscription on one furnished the most pathetic note of the tragedy: "In remembrance of happier days; from two school chums."' The small cortege made its way to the town cemetery, a classic Victorian necropolis on sloping ground to the west of Wolverhampton. The tiny procession wound its way along the cemetery's tree-lined avenues, past the weeping angels and Gothic monuments which stood out black against the snow, to a quiet corner where Ruth was laid to rest. Her small headstone read simply: 'Hadley, Ruth. 25 years. 2 January 1909. Hospital All Saints. Spinster.'*

* * *

* It is puzzling why Ruth's headstone gives an incorrect date of death. It may be that although she was killed on 29 December, her death was not registered until 2 January.

There were some remarkable parallels between the trials of the alleged murderers of Phyllis Dimmock and Ruth Hadley. Both cases involved the death of a working-class woman at the hands of a middle-class man, with the reputation of the victim impugned by both sides of the legal process. Pubs featured prominently in the stories of each tragedy, lending colour and a whiff of grubby debauchery to newspaper coverage which was already tending towards the lurid. And both trials ended in an acquittal of the man accused. The link between the cases was made flesh in the barrister that each defendant chose to represent them: the famous Edward Marshall Hall KC. His appearance in the Camden Town murder trial (and his successful result for his client Robert Wood) had resurrected his professional fortunes after a few years in the legal wilderness; and Edward Lawrence was keen to secure his services.

The arguments advanced by the barrister in each case were notably different. Wood had claimed that he had nothing to do with Phyllis's death; Lawrence accepted that he had but denied it was murder. Marshall Hall's plan was to persuade the jury that the gun had gone off accidentally while Lawrence grappled with Ruth to seize the gun from her. As he had done with Robert Wood, Marshall Hall decided to take the risk of putting his client on the witness stand. Before doing so, he outlined the defence's 'theory' of the case to the courtroom:

He would call witnesses, he promised, to show that Ruth was a violent woman, that she had often threatened Edward, and that she had become more aggressive still after he had replaced her with another woman. Ruth's death, he reiterated, was a fatal accident, the result not of murder, but of a drunken brawl.

Edward's story to the court was markedly different to his original statements to Dr Galbraith and the police on the night of the shooting. He now said that Ruth had discovered his gun in his bedroom and was pointing it at him at the denouement to their row.

She was pressing the trigger and I could see the hammer rising. I knew my only chance then was to go for her. I dashed in and got the revolver with my left hand by the barrel, and turned it from me just as it went off ... She fell.

This testimony was the culmination of Marshall Hall's efforts to portray Ruth as the author of her own demise. As he had with Phyllis Dimmock's friends and relatives, he cross-examined the prosecution's witnesses in order to debase Ruth and paint her as the aggressor in the relationship, to whom Edward was in thrall against his better judgment. She was, thundered the barrister, 'a reckless, violent, impossible woman, dangerous to the last degree, of a nature which brooded in secret over fancied wrongs, and finally blossomed out into violence which makes resistance impossible'. Her death was, concluded Marshall Hall, the tragic climax of Edward's 'terrible struggle with a desperate, defiant woman'.

Marshall Hall's approach to the case built on the tactics he had used in the Wood trial, where he had made Phyllis

Dimmock's life central to the question of her death. But here he refined it still further, playing to the psychology of the jury. In her biography of the barrister, lawyer Sally Smith pointed out his manipulation of the jury and its devastating effectiveness.

> *It was terrible to attack poor dead Ruth's character, he said. He had had to do it. And the jury, touched by the grave contrition with which he had humbled himself, quite forgot the relish with which he had approached the task and remembered only the evidence he had by this means elicited: the violent drunken jealous woman revealed.*

So compelling was this depiction of Ruth and her relationship with Edward that before the conclusion of the trial the prosecution made a dramatic announcement. They would not push for a murder conviction but would instead accept a lesser verdict of manslaughter. The judge nodded sagely and intoned that he agreed with their proposed approach.

After a short deliberation, the jury returned with its verdict. Edward Lawrence was guilty of neither murder nor manslaughter. He was acquitted entirely and was a free man. The reception that greeted him afterwards was certainly more muted than the outpouring of support from the public towards Robert Wood. Many in Wolverhampton believed that he had got away with murdering Ruth and his social standing never recovered. Edward left the town shortly after the trial and moved to Kidderminster in Worcestershire; he died just three years later.

Weaving together the stories of Phyllis Dimmock and Ruth Hadley produces a portrait of the inadequacies of the law and the justice system for women who were victims of violent crime – particularly homicide – in the early years of the twentieth century. Firstly, there was the attitude of the law in general to female victims of crime who did not conform to the social expectations of the day. For Phyllis, this was her involvement in sex work. The law's treatment of prostitution ebbed and flowed, driven by the waves of public pressure and reform campaigns that became more prevalent in the second half of the nineteenth century. But this attitude started to harden and, starting in the 1880s, the government and the courts began a further official crackdown on the sale of sex in England. In 1885, the law was changed to make brothel-keeping a criminal offence, alongside the introduction of a host of other new crimes around the selling and buying of sex.* The outcomes of this were finely balanced, but historians have noted that this resulted in a raft of laws that were intended to protect the morals of the middle classes, often at the expense of the safety of working-class women for whom prostitution was the only means of support available. Brothels were outlawed and women soliciting on the street faced harassment from patrolling policemen.

The Whitechapel murders had occurred shortly after the reforms of the Criminal Law Amendment Act of 1885 and historians have noted that 'it is officially a coincidence that, three short years after an almost unprecedented crusade

* See Chapter Six.

against commercial sex had begun in London, during which brothels were shut down … women were evicted from their homes and street solicitation became an increasing focus for public condemnation' that Jack the Ripper struck. And while the case is the archetype of its era, there was in fact nothing typical about it.

> *Whoever the Ripper was, he was only responsible for the deaths of between five and nine women … Hundreds of poor working-class women prostituted themselves and suffered more mundane deaths than the victims of the Ripper … if the Ripper had chosen to butcher the wife of a wealthy banker … then rewards would have been offered and the entire effort of the police in the capital directed towards his capture.*

This was a theme that Marshall Hall himself had propounded in the trial of Phyllis Dimmock's alleged murderer:

> *Is it not much more probable that the crime is the work of a sexual maniac – a murder similar to the murders which paralysed all London many years ago? Is it not possible that this woman, who had descended to the lowest depths of prostitution, should have been acquainted with some maniac … seeking his prey?*

The reference to the Whitechapel murders in Marshall Hall's speech was a calculated one. The so-called 'Jack the Ripper' murders were never solved but the mode of life of the victims was inextricably linked with how they had died. The Whitechapel murderer was never put on trial and Marshall Hall's plan was to contrast the monstrous creature who had stalked the slums of East London with the mild-mannered clerkish designer that sat in the dock.

Secondly there was the threshold of culpability accepted by the courts in murder trials. In Ruth's case, the question of whether a killing was murder or the lesser manslaughter – and the combination of circumstances that determined this – had a significant influence on the outcome of the trial of her killer. Edward Lawrence argued that his shooting of Ruth was excused by self-defence or was even accidental.

At both trials, the final obstacle was in the courtroom itself. The men who had allegedly murdered these women were facing an exclusively male jury. When Edward Marshall Hall invited the jury at Stafford Assizes to acquit his client Edward Lawrence of the murder of a 'desperate, defiant woman', he was preaching to the choir. It would be a further decade before women would be entitled to sit on juries. In both cases, the character and behaviour of the victims feature heavily in the courtroom, and was fundamental to the outcome of the trial. And while they are undoubtedly stories of their time, they still resonate with the challenges faced by our legal system today.

CHAPTER TWELVE

THE UNWRITTEN LAW

Dawn was just beginning to break over the city of Cardiff as the railwayman walked the line a little to the west of the city on the morning of 12 September 1907. When he reached a level-crossing, near the engine sheds at Canton, he saw a dark shape lying across the rails. As he approached, he realised that it was the body of a man, smartly dressed in a light grey suit and brown shoes. The man's head lay a little way from his body – he had been decapitated by a train that had passed over him as he lay across the line. When he had recovered his composure, the railwayman checked the man's pockets for any clues as to who he was or how he came to be in such a desolate spot. All he could find was a postcard on which was written an address on Montpelier Road, in London's Kentish Town.

The man was soon identified as Charles Panther, a jeweller from Tooting. He was due to be married and his fiancée, a Miss Appleton, had recently moved into the Montpelier Road flat in anticipation of the wedding, which was to take place very shortly. She had last seen him a few days earlier, when all had seemed well. Unbeknownst to her, he had travelled to

Cardiff after their last meeting and had taken a room at the Angel Hotel. He did not bring any luggage with him. He checked out of the hotel on the Tuesday of that week and nothing further was heard of him until the railway worker found his body on the level-crossing two days later. It was presumed that he had fled to Cardiff to take his life because of some desperate reason known only to himself.

The story attracted a little attention in the London press as well as the Welsh papers, largely due to the mystery of why Panther would have travelled 150 miles from his home in order to end his life. At the inquest into his death, neither his parents nor his fiancée could shed any light on why he had done so. But the coroner's jury returned an open verdict, as there was nothing found to indicate how he had come to be on the railway line or that he had intended to kill himself.

A couple of weeks after Charles Panther's body was found, his sad story took an extraordinary turn. The editor of the *Morning Leader* newspaper received a postcard containing a message made up of words clipped from press articles, like an old-fashioned ransom note. The postcard read as follows:

CAMDEN TOWN MURDER
The Murderer
Committed Suicide
At
Cardiff
12 Sept

The card was postmarked from north London and had been sent in the previous evening's post. A few hours after the discovery of Charles Panther's body in Cardiff, Phyllis Dimmock had been found dead in her bed in Camden – just a mile from Charles's new home in Kentish Town.

The police soon dismissed any suggestion that he was involved in Phyllis Dimmock's murder. The timings simply didn't add up, as to be found dead in Cardiff shortly before six o'clock in the morning Panther would have had to have left London on the last train going west from Paddington at one o'clock. Based on the medical evidence which put Phyllis's time of death at around 3 a.m., it was not possible that Panther could have been both committing a murder in Camden and on a train bound for Cardiff at the same time. The police concluded that, as many newspapers had featured reports of the deaths of Panther and Phyllis on the same day, this had inspired a hoaxer to connect the cases and send the incriminating postcards.

The timing of Phyllis's murder had been crucial to Robert Wood's defence as well. On his own admission, he had asked Ruby Young to give him an alibi until around midnight on the evening that Phyllis was killed. Marshall Hall had pointed out at court that this was in fact useless as an alibi for the murder, as that took place a couple of hours later. If Wood was indeed the killer, why concoct a false alibi that didn't cover the time in question?

Most of the conclusions about the case flowed from Phyllis's time of death, given by the police surgeon as around three hours or so after she had last eaten. As her usual habit was to eat a late supper at around 11.30 p.m., the investigation concluded that she must have been murdered at around 3–4 a.m. the following morning. But the police reports contained evidence from one witness not called at the trial. The owner of a fish shop in Camden, a few streets away from St Paul's Road, claimed that Phyllis came into his shop at around 9–9.30 p.m. on the night before her body was found. She was with a man and the two of them ate some fish and potatoes at the shop's counter before leaving. If the fish man's account was true, this may well have been Phyllis's last meal, putting the time of her murder much closer to midnight than three o'clock in the morning and therefore within the time period that would bring both Robert Wood and Charles Panther back into the frame for it.

While the shadow of doubt has hung over Wood for more than a century, the identity of Phyllis's killer is still formally a mystery. But if the police did harbour suspicions about the jeweller from Tooting or the acquitted artist, they took them no further. After Robert Wood's exoneration, the murder of Phyllis was once again officially unsolved. In the weeks and months after the trial, questions began to be asked about the resolution rate of murder cases particularly in the Metropolitan Police area. *The Times* ran an article listing six recent murders of women in the city that still remained open on Scotland Yard's books, including the killing of Phyllis Dimmock. Sir Herbert Stephen, himself a criminal judge and writer of legal books, was moved to defend the police in public: 'the liability of such women as Dimmock to be murdered, in circumstances highly unfavourable to the detection of the murderer, is a commonplace too obvious to require the support of argument'.

Perhaps stung by the criticism it had received, the Met allowed it to be known in the days after Wood's acquittal that they were working on a new theory about the case. They explicitly linked the Camden Town Murder with the death of Dora Piernick, who had been killed three years earlier in remarkably similar circumstances. Like Phyllis, she was found dead in bed in her room, on Whitfield Street, off Tottenham Court Road. Like Phyllis, her throat had been cut. The press were quick to pick up on further similarities between the victims as well, noting that they 'both led lives which rendered them liable to the dangers that beset women of their class'.

Dora was born in Poland in 1875. She had married her husband Mendel in the city of Lodz aged just nineteen and by the turn of the twentieth century the couple had moved to London. In 1903, the Piernicks were prosecuted for brothel-keeping under the Criminal Law Amendment Act. They were convicted of procuring a young girl named Marjem Gick into prostitution. Mendel was sentenced to two years' hard labour while his wife served six months in jail. After her release and without the protection of her husband, Dora had turned to street prostitution. On the evening of 29 December 1904, she was seen talking to a man in Tottenham Court Road. The man was dressed in a light grey suit, of medium height and build, with a thin face. It was an almost identical description to the one issued after Phyllis Dimmock's murder and which led to the arrest of Wood.

The investigation into Dora Piernick's death quickly floundered and no serious suspects were identified. It was languishing in Scotland Yard's files until raised again by the press in the aftermath of the Camden Town case. Other killings were linked with the case as well: a few weeks after Phyllis died, seventeen-year-old Esther Praeger was found dead in her lodging room near Russell Square; a year later, Lily Templeton was murdered in her small flat in Brixton, found by a servant the following day with her throat cut. The newspapers tried hard to connect these cases, knowing a Ripper for a new generation would push sales. But the theory never really took off and the police quietly dropped the re-opened investigation into Dora Piernick's murder, while the links between the other cases didn't get beyond newspaper speculation.

It was the tag of 'unsolved' that drew the press to seek out the stories of Phyllis, Dora and the other women who were brutally but anonymously murdered in London in the first decade of the twentieth century. It is the reason that the Camden Town Murder case is still notorious in its own right as a mysterious homicide which has never been solved. Ruth Hadley's death, for which Edward Lawrence took responsibility but denied it was murder, lacks this mystique and so her death is more often relegated to a footnote in the accounts of Marshall Hall's glittering legal career. But the question of law raised at Edward Lawrence's trial was in fact more significant. The fault lines between murder and manslaughter had long been a difficult and controversial aspect of homicide law, particularly in cases involving women killed by their partners. The question of whether a victim's behaviour should excuse their murder was a difficult one, as shown by the prosecution's willingness to accept a lower verdict of manslaughter at Lawrence's trial.

* * *

Late on the evening of New Year's Day of 1909, young John Fallon was dozing in front of the fire at home on Hannahgate, in the slums of Bradford. He was awakened by the front door opening with a bang, as his mother Elizabeth came into the house, accompanied by a man that John didn't recognise. Elizabeth sent the boy out on some spurious errand and, as he wandered the streets, he came across his father William, walking home from his sister's house. When William asked why John was out at such a late hour, John blurted out that his mother had brought a man back to the house. William marched his son back home and burst into the front parlour, only to find Elizabeth laughing loudly while the strange man stood in front of the fire, casually filling a pipe with tobacco. The stranger looked on unabashed when William ordered him to leave and said jovially, 'Let us not fall out, let us shake hands.' William was taken aback by his rival's insouciance and dumbly shook his hand, before recovering his ire and throwing him out into the chilly night. As his warring parents began a familiar round of recriminations about drinking, men and money, John once again slipped out of the house to walk the streets. When he returned a little while later, hoping that the row would have died down, he found a policeman and his father bending over the prone figure of his mother, who was lying in front of the fireplace in a pool of blood.

Before an inquest jury a week or so later, the Bradford coroner summed up the unhappy history of the Fallons. They had been married for over twenty years and most of those years had been miserable. William said that Elizabeth had been repeatedly unfaithful to him and their arguments had been exacerbated by her fondness for drinking. He had been out of work for several months and Elizabeth had jibed him for his inability to provide for the family. She returned to this theme in their argument on New Year's night and, in fury, William had thrown a kettle at her head. While she was still stunned from this, he had struck her on the temple with a broom handle. Despite the efforts at first aid by the policeman, the blows had proved fatal. Elizabeth was, pronounced the coroner, 'of low character', while William should be given credit for his initial self-control when confronted by the strange man in his front parlour. The jury's task was to decide whether her death was murder, manslaughter or some lesser category of homicide. Evidence of provocation by Elizabeth towards William could be sufficient to reduce the crime from murder to manslaughter but the jury could also conclude that Elizabeth's behaviour was so bad that it excused her husband's reaction altogether.

The inquest jurors – all of them men – deliberated for just 25 minutes before returning with a verdict. The appointed juryman pronounced that

> *they believed that for years Fallon had had a terrible life with his wife, and had stood it as few men would have done. On account of the woman's remarks, the jury thought that Fallon was justified in acting as he had done.*

The jury gave an unexpected verdict – Elizabeth Fallon's death was excusable homicide. The excuse was her infidelity. Press reports of the case called it 'the unwritten law' and, in truth, the idea that infidelity could explain – or even excuse – murder was a longstanding legal myth. The inquest verdict did not preclude a separate criminal trial as it did not convict Fallon of any offence but rather reflected the jury's conclusion as to the cause of Elizabeth's death. However, given the unusual nature of the inquest's conclusion, there was some surprise in Bradford when William Fallon was in fact charged with his wife's murder.

The trial of William Fallon at Leeds Assizes in February 1909 was not a long or dramatic one. But it provides a compelling snapshot of the law of homicide in the early twentieth century and some of the misconceptions that prevailed amongst jurors and even the judiciary at this time. Of the five murder cases listed for hearing at the Leeds Winter Assizes, four of them involved the murder of a woman by a man.

William's testimony focussed heavily on his wife's 'habits of intemperance'. He described how he had tried to leave her on at least six occasions but had always returned to the family home. On New Year's Day itself, he had gone to visit his sister and had a spent a sober evening in her nearby home. Elizabeth, by contrast, had been drinking with a friend in the Queen's Arms pub during the afternoon and returned again in the evening. Her teenaged daughter Nellie sneaked into the pub with a friend at one point and her mother asked for a glass of port for her, but the landlady refused to sell a drink to such a young girl. By the time she returned home with the mysterious stranger, she was apparently drunk. This time the jury did not even need to step out of the jury box to consider their verdict. They ruled that the killing was manslaughter, not murder, with a remarkable exchange between the foreman of the jury and the presiding judge: 'it is the unanimous opinion of the jury that the prisoner has had great provocation and it should be taken into account when he is dealt with.' The judge replied: 'It is a recommendation to which I shall be glad to give the greatest weight, because I entirely agree with it. You had the greatest provocation.' He sentenced Fallon to just six months in prison.

The press coverage of Elizabeth Fallon's death branded the case as vindication of the 'unwritten law' – the popular myth that a wife's infidelity excuses a husband of murder if he kills her upon discovery of it. There is no such law in England, written or unwritten. But it has long been assumed that sexual infidelity was the highest category of provocation, derived ultimately from the historical conception of wives as 'property' of a husband. Back in the eighteenth century, it was in fact ruled to be only manslaughter for a husband to kill his wife's lover, on the basis that such an affair was an invasion of his proprietorial rights over his spouse.

But the law had shifted over the intervening centuries, in light of which William Fallon's acquittal was a generous application of the law in his favour. In fact a close reading of the case reveals some inconsistencies with the law that suggest that the verdict itself was a miscarriage of justice. The presiding judge directed the jury that Elizabeth's verbal assault on her husband, chiding him for failing to provide for the family, could amount to provocation under the law. This was incorrect – words alone did not constitute provocation and in fact would not do so until the law was changed in the 1950s. He then went on to note that the fatal injury was inflicted by a blow from a broom, not in and of itself a deadly weapon, indicating that William had no intention to kill Elizabeth when he struck her.

From a legal point of view, the judge's statements are at variance with each other. If William had been provoked into killing his wife, then his lack of intention was not relevant as it would be manslaughter in any case. And if he had killed her accidentally, then her provocation held no weight because the crime could not be murder as the killing was unintentional. English juries are not supposed to comment on the reasons for their verdicts and so the foreman's comments to the judge were something of a liberty, albeit a revealing one. Clearly the jury considered that Elizabeth's behaviour towards her husband, including her final taunting of him, was sufficient to exonerate him for her murder, and the judge wholeheartedly agreed with them. A murder trial in a provincial assize court* was not going to set much of a legal precedent, but the comments on and reports of the case illuminate damaging misconceptions about the provocation defence that have persisted well into the twenty-first century.

So the trials of the killers of Phyllis, Ruth and Elizabeth, although they differed in many respects, all resulted in the same outcome – no one was convicted of murder in any of the three cases. William Fallon may have received a conviction for manslaughter, but was given a notably short spell in prison for it especially when contrasted against the death sentence he would have received if he had been found guilty of murder. All of the trials took place before an exclusively male jury. The role of the jury in criminal trials in England is an ancient one

* Assize courts were the predecessors to today's Crown Courts and tried serious criminal offences.

but it had been reformed to some extent in the 1820s. The Juries Act of that period specified that jurors must be male, aged between twenty-one and sixty, and be either a landowner or meet certain financial thresholds; the result being that, in the words of one legal historian, juries were comprised only of men who were 'middle-aged, middle-class and middle-minded'.

These middling men sitting in the jury at the trials of Robert Wood and Edward Lawrence had only to gaze out onto the benches of the court to see themselves reflected back on the lawyers' benches and the judge's chair. However, these cases where Marshall Hall's expansive oratory struck such a chord with the jurymen, took place against a backdrop of fomenting rebellion in the legal field. In 1903, twenty-two-year-old Bertha Cave had attempted to qualify as a barrister by applying for admission to one of the Inns of Court, a necessary precursor to a career at the bar. She was rejected on account of her sex but was undeterred. The following year, she made an application to the Law Society to take the required exams to practise as a solicitor. A special committee of the Society was convened to determine whether Cave's application was permissible under the Solicitors Act 1843, which governed the rules of admission to the profession. The inquiry hinged on the meaning of the word 'person' under the act, where it stated who was eligible to qualify as a lawyer. The committee was placed in the unique position of asking itself if a woman could be considered a person. Its conclusion was stark:

having regard to the fact that from time immemorial there had been no question of a woman obtaining registration of articles or admission as a solicitor, it should be held that the legislature did not intend to authorise such applications, and it would be repugnant to the construction of the sections dealing with these applications to interpret the word 'person' as including woman.

Bertha Cave was not the first woman to try to gain admission to the hallowed professional precincts of the law. Back in the 1870s, Maria Gray had unsuccessfully tried to attend law lectures at one of the Inns of Court. She was followed a few years later by Eliza Orme, who was refused permission to sit the Law Society examinations. But Bertha Cave's attempt coincided with the growing strength of the women's suffrage movement. Bertha was a friend of Christabel Pankhurst, daughter of suffrage leader Emmeline and a prominent campaigner in her own right. Christabel had also studied law but had also been prohibited from pursuing a legal career because she was a woman.

Over the following years, there was a concerted effort to push for women lawyers, culminating in a landmark case against the Law Society brought by four women in 1913. Gwyneth Bebb, Maud Crofts, Karin Costelloe and Lucy Nettleford sought to overturn the Society's ban on women solicitors in a case that went all the way to the Court of Appeal. But once again their cause was unsuccessful, with the male judges ruling that as women had never been permitted to practise law in the past, then they could not do so in the present unless and until there was a legislative change from Parliament. The outcry at the outcome of the case – contrasted against the gathering momentum of the suffrage campaign – kept the issue in the public consciousness. Finally, in 1919 Parliament passed the Sex Disqualification (Removal) Act which formally lifted the ban on women's admission to a host of professions including the law. It also permitted women to serve on juries for the first time.

It is impossible to know whether the presence of women on the juries trying Robert Wood, Edward Lawrence and William Fallon would have changed the outcome of their trials. The first female jurors did not begin to hear cases until a couple of years after the act came into force. Women were still subject to the same property requirements as men to serve on juries, which operated to restrict the numbers of women eligible to take their place in a jury box. There remained provisions for defendants to challenge the appointment of women onto a jury and for judges to order single-sex (i.e. male) juries in cases which they deemed appropriate. Most often, this occurred in sexual offence cases where the parties were male. There were further complaints from the Home Office that a new flood of women barristers into the legal profession would push for all-female juries in cases involving female defendants, as they would expect a more sympathetic hearing.

However, this prediction did not come to pass. In the first decade of the new law, the average jury included just two to three women; but they made their presence felt. A 2016 study of the cases heard at the Old Bailey with juries including women between 1918 and 1926 concluded that the presence of female jurors accounted for an increase in conviction rates for cases involving female victims of violent crime. Some estimates put this at as much as 10 per cent. The researchers concluded that

> *female representation on juries substantially affects the likelihood of conviction for a subset of cases – sexual and violent crimes – in which female jurors might have viewed the alleged behaviour or its impact on the victim from a different perspective than their male counterparts.*

* * *

There was no legal precedent to be set in the trial of Robert Wood; it was a straightforward whodunnit, albeit enlivened by the gritty locale of the murder and the mode of life of its victim. It was the performance of Edward Marshall Hall, a legal showman operating at the height of its powers, that has elevated the trial above the usual and entered it in the annals of Edwardian legal history. It was one of the first murder cases to be tried in the newly opened Central Criminal Court at the Old Bailey, and so often features in the histories of the infamous courtroom and its denizens.

But the fascination for stories like the Camden Town case overlook the nuances of the laws around homicide and the potential for inequalities between victims and defendants. At its simplest, murder is the intentional killing of another human being, and there can be no doubt that whoever killed Phyllis did so intentionally. But in the stories of Ruth Hadley and Elizabeth Fallon, shades of grey begin to emerge. If, as he told the police officers that first attended the scene, Edward Lawrence had genuinely been in fear for his life as he grappled with Ruth for control of the gun, then he was not guilty of murder. Self-defence is a complete defence to murder, provided it can be shown that the killer was in genuine and reasonably held fear for their own safety, and that the level of force with which they responded was reasonable and proportionate to the threat in question.

It is the tragic story of the Fallons that best epitomises the complexities of the law of murder, many of which seem to flummox even those entrusted with upholding the law. As we shall explore further in Part Five, provocation as a defence to murder is a controversial but venerable element of the law. If argued successfully, it will reduce a deliberate killing from murder to manslaughter. In the age of capital punishment for murder, this was a literal question of life and death. But it is a necessarily uncomfortable argument to make, resting as it does on the implication that a victim is to blame for their own murder. The terms of the provocation defence were not codified in statute until the middle of the twentieth century and so before this time the categories of behaviour deemed to amount to provocation were a moveable feast. The question of whether adultery (or rather the discovery of it) was provocation has recurred time and time again in murder cases involving intimate relationships between killer and victim. The myth of the 'crime of passion' is a particularly longstanding and persuasive one, even though it has no basis in English law. But a hardening of the law towards men who abused women during the latter half of the nineteenth century might have been expected to result in the eradication of this damaging concept. Attitudes towards domestic abuse – particularly abuse which culminated in the death of a victim – were finally changing. But how successful had these changes to the law really been?

PART V

'TIL DEATH US DO PART

CHAPTER THIRTEEN
ARTHUR ROAD

At the jangle of the little bell over the door, the postmistress looked up from her ledger. She smiled a hello when she saw that it was her assistant Laura Glendell who had entered the post office on Eton High Street. Miss Glendell returned the smile quickly, but dipped her head and hurried through the back of the shop to take off her coat and bonnet. When she returned to take up her place behind the counter, her employer looked up in readiness to exchange their usual morning pleasantries. But the words dried on her tongue when she finally looked properly at Laura's face. Her left cheek was swollen and bruised, and her eye was black. 'What an earth has happened to you, Miss Glendell?' asked the astonished postmistress. Laura busied herself with some papers on the counter and avoided her superior's eye. 'Oh goodness, I had a dreadful accident last night. I fell down the stairs and frightfully bruised myself. But I am feeling better today.' To Laura's relief, after a further protest that her injuries were the result of her own clumsiness, the postmistress seemed to accept the explanation and probed no further.

At the end of the day, Laura put on her coat and tied the ribbons of her bonnet under her chin, adjusting them to cover as much of her left cheek as possible. As she left the post office, she slipped an envelope into the bag of mail awaiting collection by the door. She made her way down Eton's narrow high street, over the footbridge across the Thames and towards her home in Arthur Road in Windsor. Her route took her around the precincts of Windsor Castle and past the railway station. As she walked, she checked frequently over her shoulder, but the streets were quiet. At last she reached her home, one of the neat little villas that lined Arthur Road. The front of the house was separated from the street by a low wall and a gate, and Laura paused there to take a final look up and down the road, before pushing the gate open and entering the house.

She shared the house with Alice Cox, who had kept house for Laura since she had moved into Arthur Street. But Alice knew Laura by another surname; for the Miss Glendell whom her colleagues assumed was still unmarried at the age of twenty-three was in fact Mrs Wooldridge. Laura was estranged from her husband Charles Wooldridge, a trooper from the barracks at Windsor.

Laura, originally from Bath, had met Wooldridge in Windsor and they had married, in no little secrecy, at St Martin's Church in Kentish Town in October of 1894. Charles had not sought his commanding officer's permission to marry and Laura had continued to use her maiden name when working at the post office. Shortly after their marriage, Charles's regiment had been moved from Windsor to the Albany Street barracks at Regent's Park while his wife remained in Windsor. The details of the deterioration of the Wooldridges' marriage were scant, but something had triggered suspicions in Charles's mind. He became consumed with the thought that Laura was being unfaithful with other soldiers still stationed in Windsor, and returned as often as he could to check up on her. By the early part of 1896, Laura was sufficiently concerned by her husband's behaviour that she had moved to the house at Arthur Road, which she rented under her maiden name. She had also asked Charles's cousin Alice, who had become something of a confidante, to move into the house with her.

And if the postmistress had apparently been taken in by Laura's story of how she sustained the injuries to her face, then Alice knew the truth. The previous evening, Charles Wooldridge had come to the house, ostensibly to make amends with his wife. Alice had left them to talk things over and had taken herself upstairs to her bedroom, where she was disturbed by a loud cry from the room below. When she came downstairs, she found Laura lying on the floor of the front parlour, her hand to her face and blood dripping from her nose. Wooldridge was pacing the room shouting, 'Why do you try my temper so?' Alice ushered him out of the house and slammed the door. She fetched a basin of water from the kitchen and returned to Laura, who was sitting up and quietly sobbing. As Alice bathed her face, she could see the bruises beginning to bloom. 'He's going to kill me, he's going to kill me,' Laura muttered. She explained that the quarrel had blown up when she had asked Charles to stop coming to the house. If he did not, she had threatened to report him to his senior officers over his behaviour towards her. He had pleaded that this would ruin him, and when Laura refused to back down, he had knocked her to the floor with a blow to the face.

The letter that Laura had posted from her workplace the following day was her cry for help to her husband's regiment and was addressed to his commanding officer:

My Lord,

Pardon my troubling you. I would not do so if I could avoid it. I wish to tell you about Charles Wooldridge. He came down a fortnight ago and behaved in a most strange manner and had some sort of fit. Friday he came down again in the evening and we disagreed and he struck me as violently as he could in the face, blackening my left eye and causing my cheek to swell and become discoloured, and it is most painful now. I told him I should complain to his officers about and he promised he would never come near me again. May I ask you to make him do this and send me, [sic] as I feel far from safe he might come again and repeat the treatment and as I am in business in Windsor I should lose my situation if I prosecuted him and of course he knows that. I had to tell my employer this morning that I had fallen down stairs and so disfigured myself. I do not write this to you to get Wooldridge punished I want him to sign that paper so that I may have a safeguard against his coming. May I implore you never to let him come down here again. If you would grant me an interview I could explain everything to you, which I cannot do by writing. Please allow me to see you, I could come on Friday next if that would suit as it is a holiday. If you reply to this letter,

kindly address to Miss Glendell at the above address.
Again, asking your pardon.
Believe me to be yours very respectfully,
Miss L. E. Glendell

Laura was not granted her requested interview on Good Friday of 1896; in fact by the time she posted her letter, she had just a matter of hours to live. At around 9 o'clock that evening, just twenty-four hours after she had been assaulted by her estranged husband, there was a knock on the door of the house in Arthur Road. Laura was upstairs and Alice, believing it to be the lodger that also lived there, opened the door only to see Charles Wooldridge standing on the front step. When Laura came downstairs, he was stood in the narrow hallway looking abashed and clutching a piece of paper in his hands. Before she could ask him to leave, he said that he had come to give her the assurances that she had requested and, without waiting for an invitation, went into the front parlour. Laura followed him and gestured to Alice to leave them together. Charles sat himself down at the little table and took out a pen from his pocket. As he wrote, he read aloud in a calm and measured voice: 'I hereby promise never to come near or in any way molest Laura Ellen Glendell.' Laura watched warily as he signed the paper with a flourish.

A few minutes later, Frederick Davis was disturbed from his evening doze in his front room a few doors along Arthur Road by the sound of screaming from outside. He jumped up from his armchair just in time to see a man run past his window. By the time he got out into the street, the man had gone; but he saw Laura Glendell lying prone in the middle of the road with a razor blade dropped on the asphalt beside her. As Alice came running from the house, Fred crouched down and cradled Laura's head in his hands, aghast at the savage wounds to her face and neck. There was nothing that he could do and a few seconds later Laura died in his arms.

But Charles Wooldridge had not gone far. Before Fred and Alice had even had time to gather their wits sufficiently to call for help, Wooldridge appeared from around the corner accompanied by an officer. He had handed himself in to the first policeman he had found and the constable, now satisfied that the soldier's garbled report of killing someone was indeed true, promptly arrested him for murder. Wooldridge said little, muttering only 'she has been carrying on a fine game' as the policeman began to lead him away.

The next day 'early passers-by through Arthur Road ... were able to see the great pool of blood which marked the spot where Mrs Wooldridge fell, while there was a smaller blood-stain by the garden gate'. A day or so later, a small crowd gathered outside the grand entrance to Windsor railway station that Laura had passed on her walk home the previous evening. After a few moments, their patience was rewarded when a black brougham pulled up outside the station. Flanked by police constables, the tall figure of Charles Wooldridge stepped down from the cab and was led through the station to board the train bound for Reading – and its gaol. A short distance away on Arthur Road, another small procession set off to follow a glass hearse as it set off from the little house, bound for the parish church up the river at Clewer.

* * *

Laura's story – of injuries passed off as accidents for fear of bringing further trouble down on her head by taking action against her attacker – still chimes with any contemporary account of domestic abuse today. Her plight had failed to muster any sympathy from the only people able to provide immediate assistance by preventing Charles Wooldridge from leaving his accommodation at the barracks and returning to Windsor to harass his wife. How far did the law of the nineteenth century protect women like Laura?

Just two months before Charles Wooldridge murdered Laura Glendell outside her home in Windsor, there had been another strikingly similar tragedy in west London; and while the women involved shared the same tragic fate, the outcomes for the men who had killed them were markedly different.

Number 37 William Street was one of a row of terraces near Ladbroke Grove in the Notting Hill area of London. Today, these pastel coloured townhouses are worth millions, but at the end of the nineteenth century, the area was little above a slum. The houses were split into tenement rooms and rented out by the week, month or whatever period tenants could afford. Number 37 housed several families over three floors, and was overseen by a deputy, who lived in a room in the adjacent property. The ground-floor rooms of the house had been recently rented by Thomas Cripps and Elizabeth Biles, a couple in their twenties with a young baby. Thomas was a ship's fireman and was well known in the pubs of the area, particularly the Earl of Zetland that stood at the top of

William Street. Elizabeth was also a regular and the pub's patrons had often seen the couple's evening descend into recriminations after a few drinks.

The events of the night of 30 January 1896 give a flavour of what life was like for those living in the tenements and garrets of Victorian Notting Hill. Jane Madigan had a room upstairs in the house and had known Elizabeth for a number of years. The two women had often gone drinking together in the back-street pubs of the area. Madigan was a hawker, scratching a living from selling any bits and pieces that she could put her hands on. On that evening, she heard the couple arguing from her own room. Unable to resist her curiosity – and emboldened by some Dutch courage herself – she knocked on their door under the pretext of asking for some lamp oil. When Thomas threw open the door, she could see that the room was in disarray and the baby was crawling on the floor crying. He was bleeding a little from a scratch on his face. Jane needed little encouragement to enter the room and began to remonstrate with Elizabeth and Thomas in turn.

Such was the noise coming from the row in number 37 that it woke Amy Godwin, the deputy charged with keeping the tenants in order, who was asleep in her bed in the neighbouring property. The walls between the houses were thin and she could clearly hear another argument between the young couple on the ground floor. The rows had become a regular occurrence during their short time in the property. Amy hurried round and as she opened the front door she saw Jane Madigan sat on the stairs wrapped in a shawl. She was clutching a flask of oil and was shouting words of encouragement – or admonishment, it was difficult for Amy to catch – at the closed door of Cripps's room, from which Amy could still hear the row continuing. She ordered Madigan to go back to her own room and hammered on Cripps's door, telling the couple to keep it down or else. Madigan slunk away up the stair but only went as far as the top step, and continued to watch through the bannister. Amy Godwin went back to her own bed, slamming the front door of the house hard behind her.

Just moments later, Charles Garner – who occupied the room across the hall from Cripps and Biles – heard the row start up again. He heard the sound of crockery smashing and furniture thudding; above the noise of the row he could also hear Jane Madigan taunting Thomas Cripps from the top of the stairs: 'Don't just stand there arguing. Go down and fight her if you want to!' Garner heard a scream followed by a thud on his door, as if someone had fallen against it. There was a gurgling sound and then the creak of the front door opening.

From across William Street, John Willoughby had also been listening to the commotion from number 37. He watched as a woman stumbled out of the front door, lent briefly on the front gate before staggering a little way along the middle of the road and collapsing. He briefly thought about going outside to check on the woman but thought the better of it when he saw two women running over to her. It was probably just an ordinary row, he thought. Best not to interfere, he thought. After all, in this neighbourhood, it's not safe to stick your nose into a row, he thought.

When Metropolitan Police Sergeant Everett arrived on the scene shortly afterwards, he found Elizabeth Biles bleeding to death in the middle of William Street from a gash to her throat. Her head was cradled in the lap of a postman. He entered number 37 and found Thomas Cripps inside the front room. The room was upside down and the baby was still crying as it crawled around on the floor, now splashed with bloodstains. Cripps himself was holding a razor from which blood was dripping. In response to Everett's questions about what had gone on, he was almost offhand. 'Is she dead? I hope she will die. I mean it. I paid 4 shillings out of my pocket for her yesterday. I meant to do it. The cow.'

* * *

The coroner's jury that had first listened to the tale of the death of Elizabeth Biles had returned a verdict of 'manslaughter under great provocation'. This was following the dramatic account given at the inquest of Elizabeth's behaviour towards Thomas during the course of their relationship, their frequent drunken arguments and the verbal abuse that she had inflicted upon him. But he was nevertheless tried for murder and the full troubled history of the relationship was played out at his trial for her murder, which took place at the Old Bailey at the end of February. The couple were not unknown to the police. Biles herself had previous convictions for assaulting Cripps's parents; when he had left her after a previous row, she had followed him to their home in Chelsea and had become violent when they tried to get her to leave. She had smashed the windows of their cottage and assaulted both his mother and father. She had been sentenced to a couple of months' hard labour. Cripps had been convicted of aggravated assault on

Elizabeth two years earlier and had received a similar sentence. And just two days before the killing, he had been arrested after she called the police and accused him of attacking their baby. He denied doing so but was fined four shillings for a breach of the peace and released. The police officer had noticed that he was carrying a razor with him when he was taken into court. Drinking pals of Cripps from the Earl of Zetland also recalled him making muttered suggestions of doing something to solve his 'woman' problems a few days before Elizabeth was killed.

In the stories of Laura Glendell and Elizabeth Biles, there is a feeling of grim inevitability as the tales progress towards their grisly ends. In both cases, the focus was on the actions of the woman killed as much, if not more than, those of the man who killed them. The provocation defence had long been wrapped up in a romanticised concept of the so-called 'crime of passion'; even if – as pointed out by academics Jeremy Horder and Kate Fitz-Gibbon in a 2015 paper – that this is more a figment of 'folk memory' than legal reality. Horder and Fitz-Gibbon point to a hardening of judicial attitudes towards the provocation defence in domestic killings during the latter half of the Victorian era. But an alleged murderer's fate ultimately rested in the hands of the jury and their interpretation and application of the law to the facts of the cases coming before them, subject of course to all of their prejudices and preconceptions. All in all, the testimony paints a far less sympathetic picture of Elizabeth Biles than that of Laura Glendell, who died just a matter of weeks afterwards in eerily similar circumstances. And while they were simply two of many cases of fatal violence against women in the closing years of the nineteenth century, they reveal much about the trials and errors in the fight against such crimes and the failures of the law and society to prevent them from happening. Furthermore, the cases reveal troubling questions, as to whether the two killers had in fact committed the same crime and so were deserving of the same punishment, which go to the heart of nineteenth-century concepts of gender, violence and intimate relationships.

Both Charles Wooldridge and Thomas Cripps would seek to rely on the behaviour of their victims as mitigation for their crimes. This concept of 'provocation', which would operate to reduce a killing from murder to the lesser charge of manslaughter, had long been one of the most controversial aspects of the law of homicide. For a killer on trial for murder, a successful argument of provocation was a matter of life and death, as after the 1860s a verdict of manslaughter carried a custodial – rather than capital – sentence. The types of the behaviour that the law considered sufficiently provoking to save a killer from the gallows had been the subject of legal debate ever since the defence had first emerged in the sixteenth and seventeenth centuries. It rose to prominence with the popularization of duelling, as the courts sought a way to excuse the nobility from the consequences of their actions when they killed an opponent in a duel. By the early eighteenth century, a succession of cases had considered the issue, and an ever-widening list of behaviours had been caught within the term of 'provocation' and been recognised by the courts as an acceptable defence to a charge of murder.

The question of whether the discovery or the admission of sexual infidelity amounted to provocation was a particularly difficult one for judges and juries. As far back as the early 1700s, a court had ruled that a husband's killing of his wife's lover could be excused by provocation for

> *when a Man is taken in adultery with another man's wife, if the husband shall stab the Adulterer, or knock out his Brains, this is bare manslaughter, for jealousy is the rage of a Man, and Adultery is the highest invasion of property.*

But as we have seen, the changing legal status of women during the nineteenth century had begun to undermine some of these old legal certainties. The argument carried less weight when a wife was no longer seen as a husband's chattel. As for Thomas Cripps, he stood on slightly firmer legal ground. It had long been settled law that provocation had to consist of actions, not merely words; and he had evidence of an apparent litany of abuse and assaults against him by Elizabeth. But there did seem to be precious little to substantiate what had actually triggered the fatal fight on the January night, other than Jane Madigan's suggestion that Elizabeth had physically attacked Thomas as shown by the scratches on his face. Most troublingly, the deployment of a defence of provocation in domestic homicides inevitably turned the focus on to the heat of the moment, rather than all that had gone before it.

To convict Cripps of Elizabeth's murder, the prosecution had to show that he had intentionally killed her, which certainly seemed to be borne out by his conduct and statements both before and after the killing. But, like Charles Wooldridge, Cripps relied on a defence of provocation based on Elizabeth's treatment of him. He was successful and was ultimately convicted of manslaughter. Cripps was sentenced to seven years' penal servitude, most of which he served in the remote and forbidding prison at Princetown, deep in the heart of Dartmoor. On his release, he returned to London but moved away from Notting Hill. He lived in Holborn and was last recorded as working as a painter.

As spring turned to summer in 1896, the trial of Charles Wooldridge for the murder of Laura Glendell took place at the Berkshire Summer Assizes and lasted just one day. His prompt confession of murder at the scene of the crime had been superseded by a plea of not guilty. His defence was that he had been provoked into killing Laura and thus the crime should be reduced from murder to manslaughter. Charles's own violence and threats were dismissed by his lawyer in favour of a tale of infidelity and betrayal by Laura. Her husband had become fixated on the idea that their estrangement was not due to his abuse and attacks, but because Laura had begun a relationship with another soldier from the Windsor barracks. Taking the witness stand against her uncle, Alice Cox testified that Laura had friends in the town but denied that the relationships were anything other than platonic. There was also produced to the jury a letter from Charles, found among Laura's possessions. The letter was undated but seemed to have been written in the fraught few days leading up to Laura's death. It was by turns apologetic, rambling and self-pitying. 'My darling,' Wooldridge began, 'you need not get any Police or anyone else to look after your house – you are perfectly safe my dear you know my darling

I will never molest you or do you any harm nor I would come near you without you asking me my dear. It's very hard lines for me but I must try and put up with it.'

Tellingly, there was no reference in the letter to the infidelity that Wooldridge now said had provoked him into killing Laura. His lawyer bolstered this flimsy defence as stridently as he could, thundering to the jurors that

> *this woman was undoubtedly carrying on, if not an immoral, a wicked and unrighteous connection with some man or the other ... there was no doubt that from the 1st of March onwards this woman was doing that which she ought not to do.*

The paper that Laura had insisted that her husband sign, promising to keep away from her, was dismissed by the lawyer as 'that wicked document'.

The jury deliberated for only a short while before returning with a verdict of guilty of murder, albeit with a recommendation of mercy. Wooldridge was said to have appeared unperturbed as the sentence of death was passed and smiled at someone seated at the back of the court as he stepped down from the dock towards the cells. His solicitor organised a petition for clemency, which had garnered over 10,000 signatures by the time it was sent on to the home secretary, who was the ultimate arbiter of whether condemned prisoners should be reprieved. But he saw no reason to interfere with the capital sentence and Charles Wooldridge's execution was scheduled for the morning of 7 July 1896. The

Evening News reported the proceedings of the execution in sombre tones:

> *Many persons, including a number of factory hands, assembled in the vicinity of the prison long before the hour appointed for the execution. The great bell of St Lawrence's Church, which is close to the gaol, commencing tolling at a quarter to eight and continued to 8.15. As the last chime of eight was heard from the municipal clock, the fact that Wooldridge had paid the penalty of his crime was announced to those outside by the unfurling of the black flag.*

And there the story of Charles Wooldridge might have ended, but for the fact that he happened to have been waiting for his appointment with the hangman at Reading Gaol, at the same time as the prison's most famous inmate. Oscar Wilde, whom we last encountered in Part Two, had been left dangerously exposed when his libel prosecution of the Marquis of Queensberry failed. The police had begun to investigate Wilde's private life in the wake of the libel case and in 1895 he had been jailed for two years for committing acts of gross indecency. After spells in other prisons, he had been sent to Reading Gaol to serve out the remainder of his sentence and his sojourn coincided with the time that Wooldridge spent there while awaiting firstly his trial and then his execution. The legend goes that from his cell window, Wilde's eye was caught by Wooldridge's military bearing as he paced around the prison's exercise yard. Following his release, Wilde composed *The Ballad of Reading Gaol* and the opening stanza was eerily familiar to anyone with a passing knowledge of the Wooldridge trial:

He did not wear his scarlet coat,
For blood and wine are red,
And blood and wine were on his hands
When they found him with the dead,
The poor dead woman whom he loved,
And murdered in her bed.

Yet each man kills the thing he loves,
By each let this be heard,
Some do it with a bitter look,
Some with a flattering word,
The coward does it with a kiss,
The brave man with a sword!

Wilde took some artistic licence when composing the poem; the description of the murder is considerably more lyrical than the true, grim story of Laura's killing in the middle of Arthur Road. It romanticised both Wooldridge and what was in reality a terrifying story of suspicion, obsession and violence. But the poem's popularity has ensured that Charles Wooldridge's name has endured, after a fashion, far longer than that of 'the poor dead woman whom he loved'. But like the death of Phyllis Dimmock would do just over a decade later, the murder of Laura Glendell had inspired an artistic response which surpassed the interest in the real story of the real woman behind the poem or the painting. To understand the complex relationship between the Victorians and violence against women, the law's response to it and its interaction with the issues already explored, we must go back several decades, to another slummy street in the dark side of London.

CHAPTER FOURTEEN

A WOMAN, A DOG AND A WALNUT TREE

On a November evening in 1852, PC Bardell was walking his beat along Princes Street in London's Spitalfields. From a window on the first floor of one of the narrow houses, he heard a cry of 'murder!' The constable barged through the front door and up the stairs to a small shabby parlour at the front of the house. There he found a sobbing woman, crouched in front of the fire with two other women kneeling next to her. The woman's tears escaped through eyes that that were swollen shut and she was bleeding heavily from a wound on her forehead. The woman herself was unable to speak and seemed to be struggling to breathe; her friends haltingly explained to the policeman that she had quarrelled with her husband, over what they didn't know. He had dragged her from their bed, thrown her onto the floor and jumped on her several times.

A month later the man from Princes Street stood in the dock in the police court on Worship Street in Shoreditch. His wife was brought to court from London Hospital in Whitechapel. Doctors found that she had sustained seven broken ribs in the assault and she had defied their predictions by surviving the attack. She was still unable to sit or stand unassisted and had to be held up by a policeman as she sat in the witness box. The magistrate listened to the accounts of the attack from the constable and neighbours, confidently pronouncing it one of the worst cases of its type he had ever seen in his court room. He proceeded to fine Jeremiah Donovan, 'a tall, muscular fellow', the sum of £5 and set him free from the dock. His wife, on whom he had inflicted this dreadful assault, was not named in any of the newspaper reports of the case.

A few months after Donovan's brush with the law, over the Thames in Southwark, Mary Coghlan faced her husband James across another magistrates' court room. When Mary had begged her husband not to go drinking with his friends one night, he punched her in the face before seizing a pair of coal-tongs from the grate and beating her about the head with them. Mary's evidence to the court outlined the quandary faced by women like her and the nameless Mrs Donovan. If she left her husband or he went to jail, she faced financial ruin and the prospect of the workhouse. If she stayed with him, she feared for her life. But like Jeremiah Donovan, Coghlan walked free from court with a £5 fine to pay. Mary's subsequent fate was not recorded.

This failure of the law to protect women from being 'ill-used' by the husbands or partners had not gone unnoticed. Henry Fitzroy, MP for the Sussex town of Lewes, made a study of the court reports and press accounts of these and other similar cases. In March of 1853, he rose to his feet in the House of Commons and made an impassioned speech in support of the Aggravated Assaults Bill. This landmark legislation was the first time that the law had recognised a specific offence of violence against women.

Speaking in the bill's debate, Earl Granville drew attention to the comparatively harsh punishments of whipping and imprisonment meted out for offences against property or animals, as against the mere fines awarded to wife-beaters like Donovan and Coghlan. Perhaps, he thought, this failure to take the issue seriously could be explained by prevailing attitudes towards women, summed up in a popular proverb of the day:

A woman, a dog and a walnut tree,
The more they are beaten, the better they'll be.

For some women, like Mary Coghlan, the home itself was a place of mortal danger. For others, simply walking the streets left them running a gauntlet of harassment, assault or worse. The hand-wringing in the press and the solemn pronouncements of politicians on the issue were of their time, but echo with uncanny familiarity even today. Violence against women, and the response of the law and society to it, is a concern that is both shockingly contemporary and depressingly historic.

Such violence had been around since long before the Victorians, but this era saw the first substantive attempts of government and the law to address these concerns and offer some protection. Concerns about the rise of violent attacks on women, both by partners within the home and by strangers on the streets, had prompted a groundswell of concern for women's safety. At the same time, reforms to the law of marriage opened up the possibility of divorce to more than the privileged few. In theory at least, women were no longer tied to husbands who 'ill-used' them or worse – but the reality was often terrifyingly different.

Historian Martin Wiener points to an absence of domestic violence cases from the court records of the eighteenth century. English law of this era was focussed on the protection of property and money; it was the time of the so-called 'Bloody Code' under which a record number of crimes attracted capital sentences. Many of these were more material offences, relating to theft or forgeries. Violent crimes were not viewed as being any more or less serious than a host of property crimes – all attracted the same lethal sentence.

From the very end of the eighteenth century a wider change in the attitude of the law began to emerge. As we have seen in Part Two, the 1790 divorce suit between Mr and Mrs Evans first set down the standard of cruelty which entitled a spouse to terminate a marriage. This hinged on physical violence or the reasonable fear of it. It would take longer for the criminal courts to catch up with the divorce court. And it is only as one area of the law began to harden its attitude towards domestic abuse that the way was paved for the criminal law to do the same.

Fitzroy's speech to the House summed up the public and political concern about the issue. He too recognised the power of an emotional reaction. The stories of a few individuals said more than dry statistics ever could.

> *He rose for leave to bring in a bill for the better prevention and punishment of aggravated assaults upon women and children ... [an] evil ... so generally felt, so universally acknowledged, so rapidly growing and constituted such a blot upon our national character that he was convinced that any measure ... would meet with general favour ... he would read one or two cases which had been brought before the magistrates of the metropolis in the last few years and in which a most inadequate punishment had been inflicted ...*

The Aggravated Assaults Act was passed into law in 1853. It was – and remains – a legal landmark as the first time that the criminal law had created a specific offence of gender-based violence. The provisions of the act expressly prohibited assaults upon women or children, punishable by a sentence of up to six months in prison. The proverbial tolerance of domestic abuse seemed to come to a decisive end and 'wife-beating now joined the ranks of other newly discovered and officially recognised evils'. But by 1860, there were concerns that the act was not operating sufficiently effectively to stamp out the ills of domestic violence. Parliament debated an amendment to the act, which would make an offender convicted under the legislation liable to a corporal sentence, rather than a custodial one. The arguments for and against the changes to the legislation were finely balanced – and passionately argued. Supporters of the new bill were adamant that the act had not proved to be a sufficient deterrent, as evidenced by the continuing prevalence of shocking newspaper reports like the cases cited by

Henry Fitzroy in the original debate. Others dismissed this as simply 'the evidence of notoriety' and disputed that the criminal statistics bore out the alleged increase in violent assaults upon women.

There were practical, as well as judicial, arguments in favour of replacing a spell in prison with a flogging. Many women were often inadvertently penalised themselves when their husbands or partners were sent to prisons, as it left them without financial support. At the same time, debate around the twin issues of crime and punishment was ongoing, particularly around the continued use of the death penalty. In the second half of the nineteenth century, a serious abolition movement began to grow against capital punishment and in a similar vein some campaigners and legislators were nervous about extending, rather than reducing, the use of corporal punishment as well. In response to this, one MP pointed out that, 'Flogging was objected to as a degrading punishment. What was there in the punishment of flogging more degrading than in the act of assaulting women and children?'

But those against the bill cited other concerns as well as the principle of the punishment. One objection raised in Parliament was the possibility of vexatious claims by women against men:

> *But though there were many cases in which delicate women came forward and claimed protection against brutal husbands, it must be remembered, on the other hand, that a mischievous and ill-tempered woman could very easily impose on a magistrate, and by aggravating her husband until he struck her, might contrive to bring him to a police*

court, rid herself of his society and disgrace him by the punishment which this Bill proposed to inflict.

This worry for men being fined or worse on scurrilous pretexts by vengeful women was still prevalent at the time of Elizabeth Biles's murder. A police witness at Cripps's trial told how when Cripps had been charged with assaulting her previously Elizabeth had turned up at court with her head wreathed in bandages. According to the officer, he later saw her celebrating Cripps's fine in the pub with the bandages nowhere to be seen.

There was also a class dimension to the objections to corporal punishment as well, reminiscent of much of the debate around the reforms to divorce, which had come into the law in the 1850s. The suggestion was that, while middle- or upper-class men were just as likely to beat their wives, the reality was that it would only be those of lower social standing that would be subjected to flogging for it. What magistrate would possibly be expected to order the flogging of a gentleman? In truth if not in law, the punishment would not be applied equally and so would create 'an invidious distinction' on the basis of class. There were further misgivings around whether a magistrate alone should have the power to inflict corporal punishment upon an offender or whether this should be the preserve of a jury only. These doubts were sufficiently fatal to the bill and it failed.

The aggravated assaults legislation did not exist in a vacuum. As we have seen, defining the concept of marital cruelty and the level of it sufficient to allow a divorce was also a struggle for the law at this time. The obvious interplay between the criminal law of assault and the civil law of matrimony was finally united towards the end of the nineteenth century. In 1878, a new Matrimonial Causes Act was passed. One of its provisions enabled a wife to seek a separation order against a husband who had been convicted of assaulting her; such an order could be issued by the magistrate dealing with the assault case and it could also make provision for a husband to pay maintenance and award custody of young children to a wife. In effect, such separation orders were a de facto divorce on the grounds of cruelty, but without the costs involved in trekking to London's divorce court to seek a *decree nisi*. It was intended to ameliorate the hardship experienced by poorer women who could not afford to leave abusive marriages. But there were still caveats which, again, operated to the disadvantage of a wife. A magistrate would not grant a separation order if a husband could prove that a wife had committed adultery. There was also the stigma involved in bringing such a case to court, as alluded to by Laura Glendell, who was firmly convinced that her employers at the post office would dismiss her if she attempted to bring an assault charge against Charles Wooldridge.

The issue of violence against women – and the measures taken to prevent it – became something of a legal and political football during the latter half of the nineteenth century. Proposed extensions and reforms to the aggravated assaults legislation were repeatedly tabled in Parliament, but were not taken forwards. In 1861, the offence of aggravated assault had been subsumed into the new Offences Against the Person Act which covered all crimes of violence and did not distinguish these on the basis of sex. The legend of English men selling their wives like cattle in the marketplace was widely believed abroad during the eighteenth century. By the nineteenth century it had been replaced by that of them beating their wives:

> *it would be a great thing to have put an end to a practice which was a disgrace to this country in the eyes of all Continental nations, who believed that if the English people could not sell their wives, they could beat them to death almost while they were alive.*

* * *

In the autumn of 1888, writer and campaigner Florence Fenwick Miller sat down at her desk and began to compose a letter. Strewn in front of her were pages and pages of press cuttings, carefully clipped from newspapers from across the country and with sentences underlined and names encircled in black ink. She re-drafted the letter several times until she was happy with it, cross-checking her paragraphs against the newspaper sheets and carefully copying out the names she had underlined. Finally, she placed it into an envelope, addressed to the Editor of the *Daily News*.

A couple of days before Florence posted her letter to the *Daily News*, the paper had – like its competitors up and down the land – splashed across its front pages the story of two shocking murders in the Whitechapel area of London. Elizabeth Stride and Catherine Eddowes had both been murdered on the night of 30 September in what was believed to be the latest attack by 'the wild beast … running loose in Whitechapel'. As any student of true crime will know, the story was referring to a series of horrific killings that took place over the autumn of 1888 in the Whitechapel area of east London. The most famous of the killer's victims were Mary Ann Nichols, Annie Chapman, Elizabeth Stride, Catherine Eddowes and Mary Kelly, although students of the case have speculated that other murders around the same time and area were in fact the work of the same killer. Each of the five women was murdered within an area of a few square miles of each other over a three-month period. Their killer was never caught but has of course gone down in history as Jack the Ripper.

And while it was these most recent murders themselves that had moved Florence to write her letter, she proposed a rather different thesis to explain the killings from that favoured by the authorities and the press. Since the spate of killings had begun in August 1888, much of the rhetoric around the case had focussed on the infamy of Whitechapel as an explanation for the horrors – its endemic poverty, vice and squalor. The suggestion was that the place itself had somehow given birth to, or irresistibly drawn in, Jack the Ripper. But the nineteenth-century hacks who sold so many papers on the back of the Whitechapel murders could little have imagined how long their words would endure. 'The Whitechapel murders have continued to provide a common vocabulary of male violence against women … its persistence owes much to the mass media's exploitation of Ripper iconography.'

But Florence Fenwick Miller took a view of the murders that was simultaneously wider yet more subtle. Published by the *Daily News* under the headline 'Woman Killing No Murder' just three days after the discovery of the bodies of Elizabeth Stride and Catherine Eddowes, the letter suggested that the authorities and the press should look a little closer to home for the origins of the monster now stalking the East End. Far from being a mindless beast, the Ripper himself must have made a careful study of the press and the law reports before embarking upon his spree of horror, wrote Florence. For how else would he have been sufficiently emboldened to start killing women, other than reading how lightly he would be punished if he was ever caught? Like Henry Fitzroy had done before her, she then proceeded to cite a grim list of cases where women had been violently assaulted by men who were then sentenced to either paltry fines or short spells of detention. The public imagination had been caught by the horrific attacks carried out in Whitechapel, by a perpetrator so brutally efficient that he could kill two women in one night without seemingly leaving any trace. But why, asked Florence, did we not feel the same revulsion towards men who assaulted and abused their vulnerable wives or partners over prolonged periods of time, until they eventually died after being 'beaten to death by instalments'.

Seen against the backdrop of these other crimes, wrote Florence, the Whitechapel murders bore a different complexion. 'These frightful murders are no isolated events. They are part and parcel of a constant and ever-increasing series of cruelties perpetuated on women … regarded so lightly by the public and treated so leniently by the judges.' And while the public and the press pored pruriently over the details of each of the Whitechapel killings that took place over a short period in the autumn of 1888,

> *yet week by week or month by month women are kicked, beaten, jumped on [until] they are crushed, chopped, stabbed, seamed with vitriol, bitten, eviscerated with red hot pokers and deliberately set on fire – and this sort of outrage, if the woman dies, is called manslaughter; if she lives, it is a common assault. Common indeed!*

Florence's letter ended with a question, no less effective for being rhetorical:

> *What are men going to do? Now, when their consciences and their imaginations are aroused by the stealthiness and barbarous sequels of the Whitechapel murders, I ask them what are they going to do to check the ever-rising flood of brutality to women, of which these murders are only the latest wave?*

To the credit of the *Daily News*, the letter was published prominently and in the days following they ran a series of the replies that they had received, most of which supported and even elaborated upon Florence's arguments. In her letter of reply physician Kate Mitchell expanded on Florence's key theme of public and judicial laxity when dealing with violent crimes against women, particularly when contrasted against the current sensationalism of the Whitechapel killings:

It would almost seem as if magistrates and jury alike were in league with the prisoners against the protection of the assaulted women. And yet these men must have hearts and feelings, for we see the universal indignation aroused in their breasts by the present horrible succession of murders. The same men who have been settling a case of wife-beating, almost amounting to murder, by three months' imprisonment in the morning, are throwing themselves heart and soul into vigilance committees in the evening, to unearth the greater monster.

The solution as Mitchell saw it was a familiar refrain from the debate on the varying aspects of the law which impinged on women throughout the nineteenth century – suffrage. Things would only improve once women were involved in making the laws and sitting on the juries that applied them.

* * *

With the benefit of hindsight, legal historians now consider that the aggravated assaults legislation was in reality of limited effect. Under the regime, prosecutions were still dealt with in magistrates' courts, where sentencing powers were limited. As a result 'whenever a crime of violence was committed against a woman, whatever its features, however serious or life-threatening, it was unlikely to be referred higher'. The statute itself acted as filter to prevent cases of serious assault, attempted murder and even sexual attacks from getting in front of judges and juries in the higher courts, who were likely to hand out stiffer sentences. Overall, comparatively low numbers of prosecutions were brought under the act and cases declined over the second half of the nineteenth century.

When charges were brought against violent husbands and partners, the deterrent effect of sanctions was not always as effective as hoped. Three years after Florence Fenwick Miller's letter to the *Daily News*, campaigner Matilda Blake asked, 'Are Women Protected?' in an 1892 essay for the *Westminster Review*. She concluded that the answer was no. Blake referenced a return collated by MP Walter McLaren on convictions for assaults against women for the year of 1891. According to McLaren's data, out of the 8,075 assault cases that were successfully prosecuted, only forty-three attracted a custodial sentence of more than two years. When such violence culminated in the death of a victim, the sentences handed down still failed to acknowledge the seriousness of the crime.

The muted effect of the Aggravated Assaults Act was of a piece with the general trend of the legal system's failure to properly address male violence against women as highlighted by Fenwick Miller and Blake. Where men's violence turned fatal juries often looked for ways to mitigate or excuse it in order to avoid convicting of murder. Growing squeamishness at the death penalty meant that reducing a killing from murder to manslaughter was a matter of life and death for the person on trial – and the jury trying them. Wiener notes that where a woman was killed by blows or kicks, the jury men often excused the defendant's crime on the basis that no weapon had been used and therefore the killer could not have intended to kill.

In 1889, John Matthews was tried for the murder of his wife Mary. After celebrating New Year with a day of drinking around the Lancashire town of Bacup, the couple had argued and John had kicked out at Mary, striking her in the shin. The blow opened up a varicose vein in Mary's leg. During the night, she bled to death. Matthews was charged with murder; the jury returned a verdict of manslaughter on the basis that he did not intend to – nor foresee that he would – kill Mary from a relatively minor assault. The jury also made a strong recommendation to mercy. Ordering Matthews to serve just two months in prison, the judge stated that he was prepared to sentence as if the crime was an assault, rather than a homicide.

Locally, the case attracted a large public outcry, for Matthews was well known to the town and its magistrates. He had twenty-three previous convictions, three of which were for previous assaults on Mary. He had also been sent to jail for six months for breaching maintenance orders that Mary had obtained against him. The local newspaper commented that

> *there is abundant food for reflection in the fact that a man should suffer six months' imprisonment because he would not contribute towards his wife's maintenance, and yet only get two months for taking her life. This should be good news for ruffian wife-beaters.*

The disquiet at Matthews's sentence spread beyond Bacup. MP Charles Bradlaugh raised the case in the House of Commons and pointed out that the jury were not made aware of his earlier convictions for assaulting Mary. It was Bradlaugh's intervention that had brought the case to Matilda Blake's attention and she cited it in her essay. Her damning conclusion on the question that she had posed herself was summarised thus:

> *Their so-called protectors daily beat, torture and violently assault them, often with such violence that death results; while male judges, appointed by a Government chosen by an exclusively male electorate, punish the offenders in a most inadequate way, holding a woman's life at a less value than a purse containing a few shillings.*

CHAPTER FIFTEEN

THE WHISTLES BLOW FORLORN

When viewed from the air or on a map, the town of Shrewsbury resembles a noose, the medieval heart of the town caught in a loop of the River Severn as it flows through Shropshire. At the neck of the town, a little above the tightest snare of the noose, sits Shrewsbury jail. It is high on a bluff over the Severn and is cut off from the centre of the town by the railway line. The squat stone gatehouse and the high redbrick walls of the prison can just be glimpsed from the platforms of the town's station. In the same year as Charles Wooldridge was executed, poet A.E. Housman published *A Shropshire Lad*, a cycle of verses set in the eponymous county where England rolls into Wales.

Shrewsbury was long a hanging town. From their cell windows, some of the prisoners would see the trains pull into the station and chug away to freedom. Until the late nineteenth century, executions would take place on the roof of the gatehouse, with the townsfolk gathered in the street below or watching from the grounds of the castle, across the railway line from the prison. In the early 1900s, the gallows was moved into a new execution suite, the windows of which afforded a glimpse of the town's castle and the hills on the far horizon.

Over the course of the twentieth century, eight men were executed at Shrewsbury Jail. All had been convicted of the murder of a woman. In accounts of the prison's history, this fact is often listed as an aside, a quirk of the jail's history worthy of note but little more. The women killed had little in common, being of varying ages, occupations and locations. The majority were killed by a husband or lover; just two were murdered by strangers, both in botched burglaries.

The story of one of these murders, which bore uncanny similarities to the killings of Laura Glendell and Elizabeth Biles, occurred on the eve of the suffrage campaign's victory. And so, just as it seemed that there would be a change in the making of laws which so affected women, the rural peace of Housman country was shattered by another horrible crime of violence against a woman.

Elizabeth Ellis was born in the Shropshire town of Bridgnorth, a few miles down the Severn from Shrewsbury, in 1868. By the age of eighteen she was living in Ludlow, an ancient town deep in Housman country, to the south of Shrewsbury. On 23 June 1886, at St Laurence's Church, she married Thomas Cox. Despite its apparent gentility,* Ludlow was no stranger to poverty. By the turn of the twentieth century, it had several slum districts and the Coxes' situation was typical of many families in the town and the outlying area. Thomas worked as a hawker,

* In the 1940s, poet John Betjeman famously called Ludlow 'probably the loveliest town in England'.

selling odds and ends of meat, fish, tools and anything else he could lay his hands on. Hawkers had to be licensed by the town's police and, from time to time, Elizabeth and their older children assisted him with his sales. The family lived an itinerant lifestyle among the 'blue remembered hills' of Housman's landscapes. After their marriage, they stayed in Ludlow for a time before moving to a small cottage in the hamlet of Abdon, on the slopes of Brown Clee Hill. They later roamed to Clungunford, a tiny village going west into Wales. Another *Shropshire Lad* couplet describes the area: 'Clunton and Clunbury, Clungunford and Clun, are the quietest places under the sun.'

By 1913, the family were back in Ludlow. They first lived in Frog Lane, a dingy thoroughfare underneath the crumbling town walls lined with cramped cottages and apparently so named because the dampness of the properties attracted frogs inside the dwellings. It was one of Ludlow's poorest streets, yet immediately behind it lay the palatial Georgian houses that fronted onto the town's handsome Broad Street. After Frog Lane, the Coxes moved to another cramped slum house at the top of the town on Upper Galdeford. This was a warren of narrow streets and courts near to the town's railway station. The family moved into a tiny three-storey house, with a single room on each floor. Thomas and Elizabeth shared a bedroom with their younger sons Henry and Benjamin. Their eldest son Thomas had volunteered with the Ludlow Pals on the outbreak of the First World War and was fighting in the trenches on the Western Front.

Living in such close quarters, there were no secrets between neighbours, and from the adjoining property William Watts frequently overheard Thomas and Elizabeth's quarrels late at night. On occasion, he had heard Elizabeth cry out 'Murder!' but he had always seen her alive and well on the following morning. He was not the only one to have observed the Coxes' woes. Elizabeth's sister Mary Ward also lived in Ludlow and had little time for her brother-in-law. She had been a regular witness to their arguments and the threats of beatings that Thomas made to his wife.

The Shropshire constables were also well aware of Thomas Cox's treatment of his wife. The villagers at Abdon had often called the police to the couple's small cottage when rows had turned violent and had tried to persuade Elizabeth to bring charges against her husband, but she always refused to do so. Cox was in court a couple of times in Ludlow, for being drunk and disorderly on one occasion and using abusive language on another, but never for his threatened or actual attacks on Elizabeth.

One afternoon in August 1917, Mary Ward walked from her house on Old Street to visit her sister. She skirted the Bull Ring, a junction of roads surrounded by tall dour buildings which was home to many of the town's shops. When she arrived at the cottage on Upper Galdeford, she could hear raised voices from inside. She stopped at the door and listened. 'You've been following me about!' shouted Thomas, banging his hand on the dirty table. 'Of course I haven't,' shouted back Elizabeth. 'I never have the chance, you're always watching me.' Mary could hold her tongue no longer. She opened the front door and gestured to Elizabeth to follow her out. 'Come on. If I was you, I wouldn't stand for this no more.' Shooting a look at Thomas, she pulled the door closed behind them and the sisters walked towards the town. They had not gone far when Thomas caught up with them in the Bull Ring. He pulled at Elizabeth's arm and told her to come home with him. He did not want, he said, to be left on his own. When she resisted, he pulled harder and began to shout. Mary, finally tiring of her sister's treatment, stepped forward and slapped Thomas sharply across the face. He reeled back and dropped Elizabeth's arm in surprise. The two women rushed off, away from the Bull Ring down the narrow street towards St Laurence's Church. Cox stood and watched them for a moment. Then he turned and stepped into one of the shops. A few minutes later, he came out clutching his purchase, a new razor with a white enamel handle. He stood and looked around the Bull Ring once more for his wife and sister-in-law, but could not see them. He turned and walked back towards Upper Galdeford.

Later that night, thirteen-year-old Henry Cox was awoken by a ghastly cry from his parents' bed. As he fumbled for a candle and a match, he heard groans and a thud of someone falling on the floor. In the dim light, he saw his mother lying on the floor with a dark wound across her throat. His father was still on the bed, tossing from side to side with his hands over his ears, as if to shut out his wife's cries. 'This! This is what you and your companions have brought me to,' Cox moaned. As Henry bent over his mother, his father grabbed at his shoulder. 'She's been lying, telling lies about me all around the town,' he offered by way of further explanation. Henry backed out of the room and ran out of the cottage and through the town, amidst the moonlight pale, towards his aunt's house.

Together, they went to call the town constable, who had seen the aftermath of several of the Coxes' fights. But this time was different. The policeman found Elizabeth dead on the floor of the bedroom, which was covered in bloodstains. Thomas, seemingly insensible, was still rolling around in the heavily spattered bedsheets.

Thomas Cox was swiftly convicted of Elizabeth's murder at the next Assizes and was sentenced to death. He was held in Shrewsbury jail while solicitors worked on an appeal against his conviction. The ground for the appeal was his insanity, and a brace of Home Office appointed doctors travelled to the town to examine and interview him as part of the case. His discussions with the doctors revealed the further horrors of the Cox family's miserable existence in Housman's corner of England. They had had seven children, four sons and three daughters; but Cox revealed several other children had died in infancy and early childhood. Scratching a living as a farm-hand, rag and bone man and finally a hawker, Thomas had moved the family around regularly before they had finally settled back in Ludlow. While they were lodging on a farm in Herefordshire, one of their young sons was trampled by a horse and killed. Not long afterwards, a daughter had died in a fire on the farm. In the cottage at Abdon, Thomas had twice tried to hang himself – once in the stable and once in the kitchen – but was discovered by Elizabeth in the nick of time. While the appeal process was ongoing, Thomas received news that his eldest son had been killed in action in Flanders.

The doctors found no evidence of mental disturbance or delusions, such as would be necessary to prove that Thomas was insane at the time of killing Elizabeth. He continued to deny that he had ever been violent towards his wife, but the appeal judges were more persuaded by the testimony of young Henry and Mary Ward to the contrary. Cox's appeal was dismissed and he was executed at Shrewsbury a week before Christmas of 1917. It seems unlikely that he would have found much solace in Housman's rhyme about the jail and those who had faced the same fate before him:

They hang us now in Shrewsbury jail
The whistles blow forlorn,
And trains all night groan on the rail
To men that die at morn.

In truth, the tragedy of Elizabeth Cox's death could have sprung from the pen of A.E. Housman, not just on account of its setting. It bears all the hallmarks of his maudlin, morbid verses with their quiet brutality amid the hills and dales of this corner of England. The rhyme itself is often cited as another inspiration for Wilde's 'The Ballad of Reading Gaol', the true story behind which was similarly echoed in Elizabeth Cox's fate.

* * *

Less than a year after the execution of Thomas Cox, the Representation of the People Act became law. It gave the vote to women over the age of thirty who met criteria relating to property ownership and education. In a stroke, almost 8.5 million women were enfranchised. The electorate was no longer exclusively male, as Matilda Blake had protested almost forty years earlier. In November of 1918, just after the war had ended, Nancy Astor won a by-election in Plymouth to become the country's first female MP. Further change came very quickly in the wake of the eventual success of the suffrage movement, including the Sex Disqualification (Removal) Act. Women could practise as lawyers and sit on juries, as well as join other professions previously closed to them. The equality that Caroline Norton had warned against had begun to arrive.

EPILOGUE

TO LOVE AND TO CHERISH

On a crisp January morning in 1922, the thin winter sun was spreading across the great lawn in the middle of New Square, Lincoln's Inn. The square was quiet but behind the windows of its tall terraces, London's lawyers were busying themselves over papers and briefs. A workman was standing on the steps of one of the houses, affixing a plaque next to the front door. He tightened the final screw, gave the brass a wipe over with the cuff of his sleeve and stepped back to inspect his handiwork. The sunlight glinted on the yellow metal, on which was inscribed the name of the firm that had set up its practice in New Square. Below were listed the names of its three partners including, at the bottom of the plaque, 'Mrs M. Crofts, Solicitor'.

Following the passage of the Sex Disqualification (Removal) Act 1919, Maud Crofts was among the first group of women to pursue a career as a solicitor. She had passed her Law Society exams in December 1921 and had been formally admitted to the profession a few weeks later, immediately setting up a practice with her husband and brother in New

Square. As well as her burgeoning legal career, Maud was also in demand as a writer and commentator on the law, particularly in relation to women. In 1925, she published *Women Under English Law*, a slim but significant volume. It was the first such book to be written by a woman who was also a lawyer herself. Maud was writing around three-quarters of a century after Caroline Norton and, of course, the discrimination that she had faced from the law was professional rather than the more personal travails documented by her predecessor in the 1850s. The book is now largely forgotten; the Law Society library doesn't even hold a copy in its collection. Its tone is studiously neutral compared to Norton's personal and impassioned prose. But Maud's book was all the more remarkable for being written by a woman who spoke from professional as well as personal experience. On the law, Caroline was entirely self-taught as women were not permitted to study the subject in her time. Maud represented a new generation of women who could study, practise and engage with the law directly just over half a century later. Within that period, many aspects of the laws that both women had written about had changed for the better. And so if either Caroline Norton or Maud Crofts were to be brought back to life in the first decades of the twenty-first century, what would they make of the state of the laws that they pronounced so eloquently upon in their own times?

The legal landscape surrounding marriage has changed dramatically from the time of Emily Jackson and her infamous spousal abduction. The strict gender roles imposed on spouses for much of the history of the institution of marriage have shifted. In 2004, the Civil Partnership Act ended matrimony's monopoly on the state's formal recognition of relationships and introduced a new form of union into the law. Just under a decade later, the Marriage (Same Sex Couples) Act brought full marriage equality into the law for the first time. The ecclesiastical conception of marriage as an indissoluble sacrament between a man and a woman passed into legal history. The hierarchical gender roles inherent in marriage – epitomised in the Jackson case and the contemporary commentary that surrounded it – are now a thing of the past.

Divorce law was belatedly equalised in the 1920s, when a new Matrimonial Causes Act eradicated the requirement for women to prove an additional aggravating factor to their husband's adultery and entitling them to a divorce. The process itself remained unchanged, with the divorce court first adjudging whether the petitioning spouse had proved their case sufficiently to merit the awarding of a *decree nisi*. From the Latin word for 'unless', the effect of this order was to confirm that the marriage was to be absolutely dissolved in six months' time – unless during that period any reason could be shown why the dissolution should not take place. Once the six-month period had elapsed, the marriage was fully dissolved by the granting of a *decree absolute*. In 2020, the Divorce, Dissolution and Separation Act finally eradicated the central requirement of one party to marriage having to prove a 'fault' on the part of the other in order to secure a separation. In recent times, the law had changed to recognise only one basis for divorce, that of the irretrievable breakdown of the marriage. This breakdown must be established by satisfying the court that one of five matrimonial faults had occurred, namely adultery, unreasonable behaviour, desertion, two years of mutually agreed separation or five years of unilateral separation. However a divorce order can now be granted by a court on the application of one or both spouses confirming that the marriage has broken down irretrievably. This is now the era of 'no fault divorce'; the burden of proving wrongdoing on behalf of a partner which for so long fell unequally on wives has now gone. It is difficult to see how it could ever return, now that the law recognises a much wider concept of relationship and marriage. Over the coming years, as more couples take advantage of the changes in the law of marriage – and divorce – the law's historical allocation of roles of 'husband and wife' will begin to fade.

But in other areas, the law's protection of women had stalled. Crofts baldly stated that the law of rape remained as set out in the Clarence case over thirty years earlier, as

> *it has been held that a man cannot be guilty as a principal in the first degree of a rape against his wife, for she is unable to retract the consent of cohabitation which is part of the contract of matrimony.*

In fact, this statement of the law as it stood in the 1920s is more disturbing than that laid down in 1888; for not only does it suggest that marriage gives a blanket consent to sex, but that this consent is irrevocable during the course of the marriage. It would be another half a century before the English courts finally overruled the dangerous idea – prevalent for several hundred years – that a man had the right to rape his wife.

Over a century after the last royal commission into the activities and conduct of the Metropolitan Police, the force is still dogged by allegations around its attitude towards and treatment of women, both in the public it serves and within its ranks. In November 2021, the home secretary announced the commencement of an independent inquiry into the circumstances around the murder of Sarah Everard by a serving Met officer. Named the Angiolini Inquiry, after its chair the lawyer Lady Elish Angiolini, the probe's terms of reference for its first phase include examination of previous offending against women by the officer and the vetting procedures of the forces that employed him. A second phase of the inquiry, not yet commenced at the time of writing, will consider what 'further, broader, issues arise for policing and the protection of women' based on the findings of the inquiry's first phase. These will include

> *the extent to which systems, policies and processes for the recruitment, vetting and transfer of police officers are fit for purpose and help to identify those who display misogynistic and/or predatory attitudes and behaviours … the extent to which aspects of police culture observed across police forces enable misogynistic and/or predatory attitudes and behaviours … [and] the extent to which existing measures prevent sexually motivated crimes against women in public spaces.*

In February 2023, it was announced that the inquiry's remit will be expanded to examine the case of a Met officer convicted of multiple sexual attacks on women during service. Whether the outcome of the inquiry can avoid the accusations of white-wash that were levied at the Met during the nineteenth century remains to be seen.

The murders of Phyllis Dimmock and Ruth Hadley would be as shocking today as they were at the time. In 2022, there were retrospectives of Walter Sickert's paintings at both the Tate Britain and the Walker Art Gallery in Liverpool. The *Camden Town Murder* series and the killing that inspired the paintings featured prominently in both exhibitions, the draw of violence, sex and death seemingly undimmed. But it is the stories of Elizabeth Cox and Laura Glendell that resonate more closely with modern trends in domestic abuse that leads to homicide. For the year ended March 2022, there were 696 homicides in England and Wales; 70 per cent of victims were male and 30 per cent female. In 95 per cent of the cases involving a female victim, the suspect identified was male. Almost half of female victims were killed in a domestic homicide and a third were killed by either their partner or ex-partner. These figures go against the popular obsession with serial killers, random attackers and unsafe streets. For women, now as then, by far the most dangerous place to be is at home with a partner.

In 2021, the Domestic Abuse Act came into the law. Like its ancestor the Aggravated Assaults Act, it was hailed as a land-mark in the battle against gender-based violence. It contains the first statutory definition of domestic abuse which had hith-erto been – at least as far as the law was concerned – a term of art rather than science. It categorises domestic abuse as violent or threatening behaviour, controlling or coercive behaviour, physical, sexual, economic, psychological, emotional or other abuse which is carried out by someone personally connected to the victim. It does not make such abuse a standalone criminal offence, but permits the police and courts to issue protection notices and orders against perpetrators.

Just after this new law came into force, a letter landed in the inboxes of the home secretary, Lord Chancellor and attorney general. Signed jointly by the Domestic Abuse Commissioner Nicole Jacobs and the Victims' Commissioner Vera Baird, the letter echoed the concerns raised throughout the period of time covered by this book. The commissioners stated that

> *we have seen the effects of a culture of misogyny through the criminal justice system, to the detriment of women across England and Wales. This is evidenced by falling criminal justice outcomes for crimes that disproportionately affect women, particularly rape ... [Furthermore we] are very concerned that some sentences received by men who kill their female partners or ex-partners do not reflect the seriousness of domestic abuse, nor do they reflect the fact that these homicides often follow a period of prolonged abuse.*

The trigger for the letter had been the five-year jail term handed to Anthony Williams for the manslaughter of his wife Ruth at their home in March 2020. The commissioners were concerned that the case could set a troubling precedent and called for the government to conduct an appraisal of the sentences handed down in cases where women had been killed by current or former partners.

In response to the letter, Clare Wade KC was appointed to carry out a Domestic Homicide Sentencing Review; her report was published in March 2023. Wade's summary of the law's shortcomings echoes eerily with the writings of women like Matilda Blake and Florence Fenwick Miller, over a century earlier:

> *Women comprise the majority of victims in domestic killings. Their voices are silenced not just in virtue of their killing but because at present there is insufficient recognition in law of the harms which their killings involve. Not only are these women wronged by a breach of trust which is an integral part of domestic abuse, but the harms to them often extend to further harm to secondary victims in the form of the families (many of whom are children) and friends of the victims. There is then the harm to society in general which, to date, may not have been sufficiently considered.*

At the time of writing, the review's recommendations are being considered and debated in Parliament. It remains to be seen whether Wade's proposals for reflecting the particular complexities and aggravating features of domestic homicides and sentencing discrepancies due to gender will be brought into law.

Maud Crofts would struggle to recognise the landscape of the legal profession one hundred years on from her ground-breaking entry into it. According to the Law Society's own research, 53 per cent of all solicitors currently practising are women. For barristers, the gender gap is a little wider, with only 40 per cent of the profession made up of women. It is the judiciary that has most catching up to do; just over a third of court judges are female. But in October 2023, 800 years of precedent was overturned when Dame Sue Carr took up the position of Lady Chief Justice, the head of the judiciary in England and Wales, and the most senior judge in the country. She is the first woman ever to be appointed to the role, which was created in the thirteenth century.*

The stories we have seen reverberate through all of these contemporary developments and changes in the law. The current gender pay gap is less surprising when seen in the context of the history of the law around women's right to own property and earn their own money after marriage. The fact that it has taken until now for the English courts to allow couples to divorce without pointing a finger of blame at one of them is the natural upshot of a law of separation that for centuries favoured husbands over wives, with disturbing consequences. The history of the Metropolitan Police reveals that its current reputation, mired in accusations of misogyny, owes as much to its past as its present. Victorian concepts around sexuality and violence fed into modern laws around rape and sexual assault until frighteningly recent times. For

* All previous incumbents have been known as Lord Chief Justice. So novel was Carr's appointment that there was considerable discussion about the title she would assume.

much of our common history, these laws were debated in a Parliament that excluded women from its franchise and upheld in courtrooms that remained closed to them as well. Barred from practising as lawyers or sitting on juries, the hegemony of the English legal system has only just been consigned to history. Debates around domestic abuse and the law's failure to prevent it from escalating into homicide still adorn front pages when a particularly shocking case catches our attention. The women we have met in these pages all shaped, in large ways or small, these changes; how are they themselves remembered?

* * *

Number 3 Chesterfield Street in Mayfair was adorned with a blue plaque in 2021 in recognition of its most influential former resident. The handsome townhouse was Caroline Norton's home from 1845 until her death in 1877 and she lived there while writing her treatise on women and the law in the middle of the nineteenth century. The plaque describes her as a 'champion of women's legal rights' and serves as a memorial to her campaigning and the enduring nature of her reputation. But it is a little harder to find commemorations for the 'little hinges' that she referred to in her writing and whose stories had a more direct influence on the laws and precedents that Caroline railed against throughout her life.

As Caroline Norton recognised in her writing, the law is only ever half of the story. The black letters of the legislation that influenced and impacted on the lives of so many women during the Victorian and into the Edwardian era are, after all, only words on papers. It is the enactment and application of these laws – by politicians, police, judges and juries – that determines their course. Then it is also in the hands of those who challenge it; the campaigners who lobbied for change but, more importantly, those who directly tested it in court by defending themselves or pursuing their own legal fights. Most of the women we have met in these pages were not powerful or well connected. It is difficult to comprehend the bravery it took for Selina Clarence to prosecute her husband for sexual assault. For a middle-class wife at the end of the nineteenth century to make public the fact that she had contracted venereal disease from her own husband and to have her sexual relationship discussed in open court must have taken immense courage. For the case to end in the exoneration of her husband must have almost destroyed her.

But in truth it is impossible to say what happened to Selina Clarence following her husband's acquittal or indeed how she felt about it. Her thoughts were not recorded. Emily Jackson was unusual in being able to tell her own story. Searching for the afterlives of most of these women is a difficult task. Their legacies must be reconstructed from the changes that came afterwards. As for their memorials, they are few and far between. So I looked for what I could in the places associated with their stories.

I read the pamphlets published by Emily and Edmund Jackson sitting at a large round table in the reading room of Clitheroe Library. It was built a few years after the case had made the town famous, and overlooked the marketplace. The books were slim and bound in red leather, illustrated with pen and ink sketches of the key locations of the case. Later, I walked up the hill from the library to St Mary's church. It has changed very little since 1891 and the scene still matched the contemporary illustrations of the story I had seen earlier. From the churchyard, the views were expansive. The church stands on a hill and looks down the undulating high street and across to the castle at the other end of the town. Between the houses to the west were glimpses of the high wooded slopes of the Bowland Fells; to the east loomed Pendle Hill, a dark green table-top that even on a sunny day seemed to be partly in shadow. I walked down the church path towards the gate where Edmund Jackson's carriage had drawn up. Later still, I climbed up to the top of the ruined castle. From there I could see back to the spire of the church and then follow the route that the carriage had taken on that Sunday morning, running down the slope, past the library and through the marketplace to skirt the base of the castle and then away down the hill to the south.

The Rising Sun has not yet set, although it is now called the Rocket. The pub's former name is still visible on an ornate plaque that sits in a cornice above the doorway. I walked past the pub several times while writing this book, going to and from the British Library just a few steps further along Euston Road. One afternoon, late in the winter, the sky ahead was turning pink and the pub's windows glowed warmly from within, a cricket match on its big screen. It was already starting to fill up with Friday early-finishers and a few were spilling out onto the pavement on the corner of Chalton Street. A couple sat in the window at a high table, deep in conversation over a couple of drinks. More business casual than shabby genteel, they were not quite the ghosts of Phyllis Dimmock and Robert Wood.

I walked through rooms of Walter Sickert's paintings at the Walker Art Gallery exhibition – past music hall stages, Dieppe streets and forbidding Venetian canals – until I found what I had really come to see. The Camden Town paintings were in a claustrophobic corner of one of the galleries, appropriate to their subject matter. You couldn't walk past them; once you had stepped in towards them, you were surrounded by images that were no less violent for their complete absence of gore or blood. The dark and grimy paintings were set in bright gilt frames, and overlooked by a blown-up image of Sickert, shaven-headed and straddling a backwards-facing chair in a pose he may well have instructed his models to adopt. However tenuous the connection between the paintings and the crime, there was a visceral quality to the images that brought the story to life in a way that reading countless accounts of the case in newspapers and books had until then failed to do.

I also stumbled across Josephine Butler in the Walker Art Gallery. Among the collection of Pre-Raphaelite works, in the corner of one room was a bust of Butler, captured forever in white marble. Her eyes were almost closed and her gaze was downwards. Her force of personality, which had helped to galvanise her supporters and electrify her campaigns, did not shine through from the likeness. The most lifelike thing about the sculpture were the folds of her dress, gathered around her shoulders and collar.

In Eton, the high street was still bedecked in coronation bunting as I followed Laura Glendell's route home from the post office on a hot June day, over the footbridge to Windsor as the pleasure boats passed underneath on the wide lazy Thames. There was no pool of blood in Arthur Road when I walked along it. The houses themselves were little changed, the neat bay windows and tidy little walls still recognisable from newspaper illustrations. In the National Archives I read the files on Charles Wooldridge's trial and execution. There were handwritten copies of the Wooldridges' letters, transcribed for the court. There was a beautifully drawn plan of the little house on Arthur Road, delicately coloured to highlight the parlour and the front path. Such is the pull of the case's poetical associations that at some point a curious civil servant had noted a nugget of archival trivia on the front of the buff-coloured folder: 'this appears to be the case referred to in Oscar Wilde's "Ballad of Reading Gaol"'. Such is the extent of the memorial to the murder of Laura Glendell.

Parts of the Cox family's Ludlow have changed beyond all recognition since 1917, while the rest of the town remains reassuringly timeless. I read about the grimy underbelly of the picturesque town in its library, which sits above the railway station on an area of land now cleared of its ramshackle cottages and hovels. From the desk, I could see across the car park to where the Coxes' cottage had once stood, now replaced by modern flats. The Bull Ring, where Elizabeth stormed off and Thomas went to purchase the razor, looks much as it would have done then, and for years before that. Shrewsbury prison, where Thomas Cox was executed along with the other men who had killed women during the twentieth century, is now a tourist attraction. The prison was busy on the day that I visited, with tour groups and guides mingling on the cell-block landing. But when I got to the execution suite where Thomas Cox was hanged, down at the far end of the main block, it was deserted. Out on the corridor was the executioner's bedroom where the hangman slept the night before an execution. An innocuous looking door in the corner of the landing led through to a large room at the corner of the building, filled with light from the windows on all sides. These gave views of the castle across the railway lines. Looking out of the windows, on the far horizon and with a little imagination, I could see hills of South Shropshire towards Ludlow. The gallows have long gone but a noose still dangles from a beam above the trapdoors in the middle of the room. This area of the prison is rumoured to be the most haunted section and in truth there was something unnerving about being the only living person in a room designed for death.

Much of the streetscape around the fringes of Wolverhampton's centre has altered beyond all recognition since the turn of the twentieth century, swept away by an encircling ring road. But the terraces of George Street have survived and have changed very little, although they are now mostly occupied by offices. Number 2 looks as it must have done on that evening near the end of 1907; even down to the iron railings that were draped in snow and frost. On the other side of the town, in the cemetery where Ruth Hadley was buried on a cold morning in the first days of 1908, the trees are taller than they were then. The graves are packed in now, running down the slope in a mass of granite and marble. Many of the monuments are crumbling and tilted, the inscriptions faded almost to nothing. In a drizzling rain, I walked around the graveyard for some time, looking without success for the small corporation headstone that was supposed to still be there.

SELECT BIBLIOGRAPHY AND NOTES ON SOURCES

AUTHOR'S NOTE

London Labour and the London Poor (1851), Henry Mayhew

INTRODUCTION: FROM THIS DAY FORWARD

English Laws for Women in the Nineteenth Century (1854), Caroline Norton

'The Transfigurations of Caroline Norton', Kieran Dolin, *Victorian Literature and Culture* (2002)

'Are Women Protected?', Matilda Blake, *Westminster Review*, Vol. 137 (1892)

PART ONE: TO HAVE AND TO HOLD

CHAPTER ONE: 'YOU SHALL HAVE THE BODY'

R v. Jackson [1891] 1 QB 671

Criminal Conversations: Victorian Crimes, Social Panic and Moral Outrage (2005), Judith Rowbotham and Kim Stevenson (eds), Ohio State University Press

The True Story of the Clitheroe Abduction, Or Why I Ran Away with My Wife (1891), Edmund Jackson

Binding Men: Stories about Violence and Law in Late Victorian England (2014), Lois Bibbings, Routledge

The Clitheroe Times, *Leeds Mercury*, *Western Mail*, *Evening Standard*, *St Helen's Examiner*, *Northern Weekly Gazette*, *Lloyd's Weekly Newspaper*, *Pall Mall Gazette*, *The Globe*, *Morning Post*, *Sunderland Daily Echo*, *Daily Gazette for Middlesbrough*, *South Wales Daily News*, *Methodist Times*, *Blackburn Standard*, *Cardiff Times*, *Cambridge Chronicle and Journal*, *Liverpool Echo*, *Birmingham Daily Post*, *Lancashire Evening Post*, *Yorkshire Post*, *Leeds Intelligencer*, *The Statesman*, *Evening Mail*

CHAPTER TWO: *FEMMES SOLES*

Married Women's Property Bill parliamentary debates: *Hansard*, 21 April 1868, Vol. 191, 10 June 1868, Vol. 192, 18 May 1870, Vol. 201, 21 June 1870. Vol. 202

The Country Squire, or Two Days at the Hall, Prefaced by an Original Biographical Sketch of Mrs Glover (1837), Charles Dance, Chapman & Hall

The Case of the Married Woman: Caroline Norton (2021), Antonia Fraser, Weidenfeld & Nicolson

'Ideologies on Women in Nineteenth Century Britain 1850s–1870s', Sudesh Vaid, *Economic and Political Weekly*, Vol. 20(43) (1985)

'Class, Gender and Liberalism in Parliament 1868–1882: The Case of the Married Women's Property Acts', Ben Griffin, *Historical Journal*, Vol. 46(1) (2003)

Gloucester Journal, *Public Ledger and Daily Advertiser*, *Sun*, *Englishman*, *Evening Mail Bridgend Chronicle*, *Portsmouth Evening News*, *Stonehaven Journal*, *Weekly Dispatch*

English Laws for Women in the Nineteenth Century (1854), Caroline Norton

CHAPTER THREE: ABSOLUTE DOMINION

See Chapter One, ibid.

PART TWO: FOR BETTER, FOR WORSE

CHAPTER FOUR: LOT 29

Women's Legal Landmarks (2019), Erika Rackley and Rosemary Auchmuty (eds), Hart

'Equality from the Masculine Point of View': The 2nd Earl Russell and Divorce Law Reform in England', Gail Savage, *Russell: The Journal of the Bertrand Russell Society*, n.s. 16 (summer 1996)

A Taste for Poison: Eleven Deadly Substances and the Killers Who Used Them (2022), Neil Bradbury, HarperCollins

The Six Wives of Henry VIII (1992), Antonia Fraser, Weidenfeld & Nicolson

Pall Mall Gazette, *Yorkshire Evening Post*, *Northern Echo*, *Penny Illustrated Paper*, *Toronto Daily Mail*, *Maidenhead Advertiser*, *St James Gazette*, *Dundee Evening Telegraph*, *Bristol Mercury*, *Boston Guardian*

CHAPTER FIVE: PAINS AND PENALITES

Evans v. Evans [1790] 161 All ER 466

A Queen on Trial: The Affair of Queen Caroline (1993), E.A. Smith, Sutton

Minutes of evidence taken on the 2nd reading of the bill entitled 'An Act to deprive Her Majesty Caroline Amelia Elizabeth of the title, prerogatives, rights, privileges and exemptions of Queen Consort of this realm, and to dissolve the marriage between His Majesty and the said Caroline Amelia Elizabeth' (1820)

Cases illustrative of the conflict between the laws of England and Scotland with regard to marriages, divorce and legitimacy: designed as a supplement to an essay upon the law respecting husband and wife (1835), Henry Prater, Saunders and Benning

Exposition of the laws of marriage and divorce, as administered in the Court for Divorce and Matrimonial Causes, with the method of procedure in each kind of suit, illustrated by copious notes of cases (1872), Ernst Browning, William Ridgway

'One Must Ride Behind: Married Women's Rights and the Divorce Act of 1857', Mary Lyndon Shanley, *Victorian Studies*, Vol. 25(3) (1982)

The Life of Samuel Johnson (1791), James Boswell

Cruelty Without Culpability, or Divorce Without Fault, L. Neville Brown, *Modern Law Review*, Vol. 26(6) (1963)

'References to "Y Ceffyl Pren" (The Wooden Horse) in South West Wales', E. Scourfield, Folklore, Vol. 87(1), (1976)

Divorce and Matrimonial Causes Bill parliamentary debates: *Hansard*, 13 June 1854, Vol. 134, 3 March 1857, Vol. 144, 23 June 1857, Vol. 146

CHAPTER SIX: *SAEVITIA*

Russell v. Russell [1897] AC 395

'The Double Standard in the English Divorce Laws 1857–1923', Anne Sumner Holmes, *Law and Social Inquiry*, Vol. 20(2) (1995)

Curious and Surprising Victorian Derbyshire (2015), Glyn Jones, Halsgrove

Report of the Royal Commission on Divorce and Matrimonial Causes (1912)

Sunderland Daily Echo, *Barbadian*, *Bell's New Weekly Newspaper*, *Public Ledger and Daily Advertiser*, *Morning Gazette*, *Penrith Observer*, *Sheffield Evening Telegraph*, *York Herald*, *Western Morning News*

PART THREE: IN SICKNESS AND IN HEALTH

CHAPTER SEVEN: THE EXAMINATION PLACE

Report from the Select Committee on the Contagious Diseases Acts (1882)

'Opposition to the Contagious Diseases Acts 1864–1886', Margaret Hamilton, *Albion*, Vol. 10(1) (1978)

Selling Sex in the City: A Global History of Prostitution 1600s–2000s (2017), Julia Laite, Brill

Prostitution and Victorian Society (1980), Judith Walkowitz, Cambridge University Press

The Ascent of Woman: A History of the Suffragette Movement and the Ideas Behind It (2003), Melanie Phillips, Little Brown

Select Committee of the House of Lords on the Contagious Diseases Act 1866 together with the proceedings of the committee, minutes of evidence and Appendix (1867–8)

CHAPTER EIGHT: 'NO MAN EVER INJURES AN HONEST WOMAN'

'What I Saw at the Royal Albert Hospital at Devonport on Sunday Evening May 4th and on Monday Morning May 12th 1873 by a Member of the Ladies' National Association for the Repeal of the Contagious Diseases Acts' (1873), S.G. Pyke

'"We are not beasts of the field": Prostitution and the Poor in Plymouth and Southampton under the Contagious Diseases Acts', J. Walkowitz and D. Walkowitz, *Feminist Studies*, Vol. 1(314) (1973)

Manchester Courier, *Paddington Advertiser*, *Sheffield Daily Telegraph*, *Birmingham Daily Post*, *Reynolds Newspaper*, *Nottingham Journal*, *Western Morning News*, *Liverpool Daily Post*, *Aldershot Military Gazette*, *Hour*, *Evening Standard*, *Western Morning News*, *Kendal Mercury*

'White Collars, Grey Lives? The Lower Middle Class Revisited', P. Bailey, *Journal of British Studies*, Vol. 38(3) (1999)

CHAPTER NINE: 'VERY SUBTLE METAPHYSICAL QUESTIONS'

R v. Clarence [1888] 22 QBD 23

Report of the Royal Commission upon the Duties of the Metropolitan Police Vol. 1 (1908)

Personal Reminiscences of a Great Crusade (1898), Josephine Butler, Horace Marshall & Son

'Cass, Coverdale and Consent: The Metropolitan Police and Working-Class Women in Late Victorian London', David Taylor, *Cultural and Social History*, Vol. 12(1) (2015)
The Contagious Diseases Acts from a Sanitary and Economic Point of View, C.W. Shirley Deakin, paper presented to the Medical Society of University College London on 30 November 1871
The Contagious Diseases Acts, or A Few Suggestions for Controlling Men as well as Women (1873), John Moore
Criminal Conversations, ibid.
East London Observer, *Lichfield Mercury*, *Evening News*, *Justice*
National Archives file reference HO/144/474/X17970

PART FOUR: FOR RICHER, FOR POORER

CHAPTER TEN: 'SUCH AN IDLE HOUR IS CARELESSLY SPENT'

The Trial of Robert Wood (1936), Basil Hogarth (ed.), W. Hodge & Co.
Murder Mistaken (1963), John Rowland, John Long
The Camden Town Murder (2008), John Barber, Mandrake
Walter Sickert: The Camden Town Murder and Tabloid Crime (2000), Lisa Tichner, Tate
City of Dreadful Delight: Narratives of Sexual Danger in Late-Victorian London (1992), Judith Walkowitz, University of Chicago Press
London's Shadows: The Dark Side of the Victorian City (2010), Drew Gray, Continuum
Court Number One: The Old Bailey Trials that Defined Modern Britain (2019), Thomas Grant, John Murray

Camden Town: Dreams of Another London (2017), Tom Bolton, British Library Publishing

Pall Mall Gazette, *Lloyd's Weekly Newspaper*, *Cambria Daily Leader*, *Daily Gazette Middlesbrough*, *Reynolds Newspaper*, *Dundee Evening Telegraph*, *Daily Mirror*, *Northampton Mercury*, *Royston Weekly News*, *South Wales Daily News*, *Yarmouth Independent*, *The People*, *Exeter and Plymouth Gazette*, *Modern Man*, *Dundee Courier*

National Archives file reference MEPO/3/182

CHAPTER ELEVEN: DESPERATE, DEFIANT WOMEN

The Wolverhampton Tragedy: Death and the 'Respectable' Mr Lawrence (2009), John Benson, Carnegie

Marshall Hall: A Law unto Himself (2016), Sally Smith, Wildy Simmonds and Hill

Common Prostitutes and Ordinary Citizens: Commercial Sex in London 1885–1960 (2012), Julia Laite, Palgrave Macmillan

Express and Star

CHAPTER TWELVE: THE UNWRITTEN LAW

Men Of Blood: Violence, Manliness and Criminal Justice in Victorian England (2004), Martin Wiener, Cambridge University Press

Report of the Examination Committee as to a Woman Being Eligible to Become a Solicitor, 1st June 1904, Law Society Committee Reports 1903–4 (13)

Women's Legal Landmarks, ibid.

'The Significance of the Sex Disqualification (Removal) Act 1919', Mari Takayanagi, lecture for First Women Lawyers series, 25 January 2019

'Keeping Women Off the Jury in 1920s England and Wales', Kevin Crosby, *Legal Studies*, Vol. 37(4) (2017)

Hants and Berks Gazette, *Empire News*, *Cornishman*, *Leeds Mercury*, *Yorkshire Evening Post*

PART FIVE: 'TIL DEATH US DO PART

CHAPTER THIRTEEN: ARTHUR ROAD

Birmingham Mail, *Bristol Mercury*, *South Bucks Standard*, *Evening News*, *Echo*, *Globe*, *Sheffield Daily Telegraph*, *The Scotsman*, *Weekly Dispatch*, *Lloyds Weekly Newspaper*, *Illustrated Police News*, *Western Times*

National Archives file reference HO/144/268/AS8000

Old Bailey Online, 24 February 1896

West London Observer

CHAPTER FOURTEEN: A WOMAN, A DOG AND A WALNUT TREE

Criminal Conversations, ibid.

'Are Women Protected?', ibid.

Aggravated Assaults Bill parliamentary debates: *Hansard*, 10 March 1853, Vol. 124, 18 May 1874, Vol. 219

Globe, *London Daily News*, *Morning Post*, *Women's Suffrage Journal*, *Daily News*, *Bacup Times and Rossendale Advertiser*

CHAPTER FIFTEEN: THE WHISTLES BLOW FORLORN

'When Sexual Infidelity Triggers Murder: Examining the Impact of Homicide Law Reform on Judicial Attitudes in Sentencing', Jeremy Horder and Kate Fitz-Gibbon, *Cambridge Law Journal*, Vol. 74(2) (2015)

How the Other Half Lived: Ludlow's Working-Classes 1850–1960 (2016), Derek Beattie, Merlin Unwin

Rise Up, Women! (2018), Diane Atkinson, Bloomsbury

National Archives file reference HO/144/486351804

EPILOGUE: TO LOVE AND TO CHERISH

Women under English Law (1928), Maud Crofts, Butterworth & Co.

Domestic Homicide Sentencing Review (2023), Clare Wade KC, His Majesty's Stationery Office

Joint letter on domestic homicide from Victims' Commissioner and Domestic Abuse Commissioner to Home Secretary, Lord Chancellor and Attorney General (published 5 March 2021)

Trends in the solicitors' profession – Annual Statistics Report 2021 (2022), The Law Society

Diversity at the Bar 2022 (2023), Bar Standards Board

'Homicide in England and Wales: year ending March 2022', Office for National Statistics, February 2023

ACKNOWLEDGEMENTS

First and foremost, I have to say thank you to everyone who bought, borrowed or downloaded a copy of my first book, *Murder: The Biography*. As an author, the spring of 2021 was not the ideal time to make your publishing debut, and the support for my first book spurred me on while writing my second.

Thanks to all the booksellers I've met since *Murder* was published, who pressed it into customers' hands, allowed me to scribble on their stock or hosted events. From Waterstones, I'm grateful to Mark at Wolverhampton, Meg at Ipswich and Bristol, David at Aberdeen, Poppy and Ronnie at Barnstaple, Billy at Hereford, Ellie at Didcot, Jo at Cheltenham, Gemma and Charn at Deal, Laura at Falkirk, and the teams at Leeds, Northallerton, Wandsworth, Piccadilly, Trafalgar Square, Trowbridge, Birmingham, Bath, Merry Hill, Sutton Coldfield, Oxford, Lichfield, Derby and Abergavenny. Thanks also to Hazel at Village Books, Dulwich; Abby at Blackwells Westgate; Emma and Adam at the Berwyn Bookshop, Mold; the team at the Green Dragon Bookshop, Crewkerne; Susan at Pengwern

Books, Shrewsbury; the team at Book Case, Chiswick; Emma at Book-Ish, Crickhowell; and the team at Mr B's in Bath. I've also had a great time talking about my writing at bookshop events and literary festivals across the country. So I'm obliged to those who invited me and who put so much effort into bringing readers and writers together, particularly Gail and Jonty Fuller from Mere Literary Festival; Anna, Natalie, Julian and Damian at Lichfield Literature Festival; Alan and Vicki at the Bow Street Police Museum; Penelope and Georgina at Wolverhampton Literature Festival; and Joanna and Claire at Sevenoaks Literary Festival.

My research for *The Walnut Tree* would have been considerably more difficult without the help of library and archive staff up and down the country. Thanks to the staff at the National Archives, the British Library, Ludlow Library, Wirksworth Library, Wolverhampton Archives and Shrewsbury Library. I'm especially grateful to Alison of Clitheroe Library, who helped me find the original publications relating to Emily Jackson's abduction. Thanks to Emma and Edel of the Law Society Library for arranging my access and tracking down books. I spent a fabulous month working on the book in the Peak District during the autumn of 2022, and Coworking Corner in Matlock was a great place to churn some words out.

Thanks to my wonderful agent Euan Thorneycroft for his support and advice on the project throughout. At Mudlark and HarperCollins, I'm grateful to my editor Joel Simons for bringing his expertise to the book and for being a joy to work with again. Thanks also to Sarah Hammond for overseeing the production of the finished book, Ameena Ghori-Khan for her work on the project, Neil Dowden for his careful copy-editing, Fionnuala Barrett for producing the audiobook, Ellie Game for the cover design and to Isabel Prodger and Jessica Cselko for taking care of the publicity and marketing campaigns.

Finally, thanks to the usual suspects for being sounding boards and their regular enquiries of 'How's the book going?' – Mum and Dad; Charlotte and Andrew; Julie and Steve; Bec, Glenn, Aoife and Fin; Nans Freda, Nancy and Mabel; Craig and Fran; Catherine and Steve; and Tia and Raj.

And to James, for everything, always.

PICTURE CREDITS

Page 1: Diper Historic/Alamy Stock Photo

Page 2, top: © British Library Board. All Rights Reserved/ Bridgeman Images

Page 2, bottom: Courtesy of the author

Page 3, top left: © National Portrait Gallery, London

Page 3, top right: World History Archive/Alamy Stock Photo

Page 3, bottom: © Illustrated London News Ltd/Mary Evans

Page 4, bottom: The National Archives, ref. TS11/115/326 (33)

Page 5, top left: Courtesy of the author

Page 5, top right: Photo credit: Bridgeman Images

Page 5, bottom: The History Collection/Alamy Stock Photo

Page 6, top left: Trinity Mirror/Mirrorpix/Alamy Stock Photo

Page 6, top right: PA Photos/TopFoto

Page 6, bottom: Courtesy of the author

Page 7: © British Library Board. All Rights Reserved/Bridgeman Images

Page 8, top left: History and Art Collection/Alamy Stock Photo

Page 8, bottom: Courtesy of the author

INDEX